ISLAMIC FUNDAMENTALISM AND JIHAD

ISLAMIC FUNDAMENTALISM AND JIHAD

S M Arif

MD Publications Pvt Ltd
New Delhi
www.mdppl.com

Published by :

MD Publications Pvt Ltd
"MD House", 11, Darya Ganj,
New Delhi - 110 002
Phone : +91-11-41563325 (Customer Service)
+91-11-41562846 (Editorial)
E-mail (orders): order@mdppl.com
Website: www.mdppl.com

ISBN: 978-81-7533-250-8

Published and Printed by Mr. Pranav Gupta on behalf of **MD Publications Pvt Ltd** at Times Press, Delhi.

PREFACE

Islam is one of the world's largest and fastest-growing religions. Yet its most basic tenets remain mysterious to many non-Muslims. Islamic fundamentalism is a term used to describe religious ideologies seen as advocating a return to the "fundamentals" of Islam: the Quran and the Sunnah. Definitions of the term vary. It is deemed problematic by those who suggest that Islamic belief requires all Muslims to be fundamentalists and by others as a term used by outsiders to describe perceived trends within Islam.

Jihad means "striving or struggling in the way of God" is a central concept in Islam. Historically, the "greater" jihad refers to the struggle each person has within him or herself to do what is right. Because of human pride, selfishness and sinfulness, people of faith must constantly wrestle with themselves and strive to do what is right and good. The "lesser" jihad involves the outward defense of Islam. Muslims should be prepared to defend Islam, including military defense, when the community of faith is under attack. While the vast majority of Muslims clearly reject the violent extremism manifest on Sept. 11, some religiously inspired and politically motivated individuals and groups attempt to justify their behavior in the context of a holy war or struggle in defense of Islam.

Like all other major religions, Muslims interpret and practice their religion in very different ways. There are scrupulously observant Muslims and others who are more lax in their observance, and there are several major theological disputes that have led to the division of Islam into its Sunni,

Shi'a, Druze, and Sufi sects. Islam is like any other religion, a religion that searches for peace and social order. The Quran emphasizes on the Oneness of God and this is one of the very ideals in the Quran that seems to have placed it among the world's most popular and higher religions. But the Quran might come as a shock to most people as it seems to be the most belligerent of all religious texts that glorifies war and polygamy.

Islam is the most vulnerable of all religions; it has too many weaknesses and can easily be misrepresented and become the manual of fanatics, anti-socials and criminals, albeit in a perverted form. Considering a historical sketch, many wars have been caused by Islamic fanatics and fundamentalists. Intolerance maybe one of the basic tenets that some people seem to learn from the Quran but Quran has also called upon tolerance for all other religious texts. It is unfortunate for the Prophet, that his teachings are abused and that the flaws in the Quran seem to have simply eclipsed all the higher ideals that he tried to establish. Today the Prophet is primarily recognized for his flaws and Islam is considered a religion that promotes and spreads hatred.

I am very grateful to Mr Pranav Gupta, Director of MD Publications Pvt Ltd, New Delhi, for his kind cooperation and support for this book.

S M Arif

Contents

1

Fundamentals of Islam

Every religion of the world has been named either after its founder or after the community or nation in which it was born. For instance, Christianity takes its name from its prophet Jesus Christ; Buddhism from its founder, Gautama Buddha; Zoroastrianism from its founder Zoroaster; and Judaism, the religion of the Jews, from the name of the tribe Judah (of the country of Judea) where it originated. The same is true of all other religions except Islam, which enjoys the unique distinction of having no such association with any particular person or people or country. Nor is it the product of any human mind. It is a universal religion and its objective is to create and cultivate in man the quality and attitude of Islam.

Islam, in fact, is an attributive title. Anyone who possesses this attribute, whatever race, community, country or group he belongs to, is a Muslim. According to the Qur'an (the Holy Book of the Muslims), among every people and in all ages there have been good and righteous people who possessed this attribute - and all of them were and are Muslims.

Islam is an Arabic word and connotes submission, surrender and obedience. As a religion, Islam stands for complete submission and obedience to Allah.

Everyone can see that we live in an orderly universe, where everything is assigned a place in a grand scheme. The moon, the stars and all the heavenly bodies are knit together in a magnificent system. They follow unalterable laws and make not even the slightest deviation from their ordained courses. Similarly, everything in the world, from the minute whirling electron to the mighty nebulae, invariably follows its own laws. Matter, energy and life - all obey their laws and grow and change live and die in accordance with those laws. Even in the human world the laws of nature are paramount. Man's birth, growth and life are all regulated by a set of biological laws. He derives sustenance from nature in accordance with an unalterable law. All the organs of his body, from the smallest tissues to the heart and the brain, are governed by the laws prescribed for them. In short, ours is a law-governed universe and everything in it is following the course that has been ordained for it.

This powerful, all-pervasive law, which governs all that comprises the universe, from the tiniest specks of dust to the magnificent galaxies of the heavens, is the law of God, the Creator and Ruler of the universe. As the whole of creation obeys the law of God, the whole universe therefore, literally follows the religion of Islam - for Islam signifies nothing but obedience and submission to Allah, the Lord of the Universe. The sun, the moon, the earth and all other heavenly bodies are thus 'Muslim'. So are the air, water, heat, stones, trees and animals. Everything in the universe is 'Muslim' for it obeys God by submission to His laws. Even a man who refuses to believe in God, or offers his worship to someone other than Allah, has necessarily to be a `Muslim' as far as his existence is concerned.

For his entire life, from the embryonic stage to the body's dissolution into dust after death, every tissue of his muscles and every limb of his body follow the course prescribed by God's law. His very tongue on account of his ignorance advocates the denial of God or professes multiple deities, is in its very nature 'Muslim'. His head which he wantonly bows to others besides Allah is born 'Muslim'. His heart, which, through his lack of true knowledge, cherishes love and reverence for others, is 'Muslim' by intuition. These are all obedient to the Divine Law, and their functions and movements are governed by the injunctions of that law alone.

Man is so constituted that there are two distinct spheres of his activity. One is the sphere in which he finds himself totally regulated by the Divine Law. Like other creatures, he is completely caught in the grip of the physical laws of nature and is bound to follow them. But there is another sphere of his activity. He has been endowed with reason and intellect. He has the power to think and form judgments to choose and reject, to approve and spurn. He is free to adopt whatever course of life he chooses. He can embrace any faith, and live by any ideology he likes. He may prepare his own code of conduct or accept one formulated by others. Unlike other creatures, he has been given freedom of thought, choice and action. In short, man has been bestowed with free will. Both these aspects co-exist side by side in man's life.

In the first he, like all other creatures, is a born Muslim, invariably obeying the injunctions of God, and is bound to remain one. As far as the second aspect is concerned, he is free to become or not to become a Muslim. It is the way a person exercises this freedom which divides mankind into two groups: believers and non-believers. An individual, who chooses to acknowledge his Creator, accepts Him as his real Master, honestly and scrupulously submits to His laws and injunctions and follows the code. He has achieved completeness in his Islam by consciously deciding to obey God in the domain in which he was endowed with freedom of choice. He is a perfect Muslim: his submission of his entire self to the will of Allah is Islam and nothing but Islam.

He has now consciously submitted to Him Whom he had already been unconsciously obeying. He has now willingly offered obedience to the Master Whom he already owed obedience to involuntarily. His knowledge is now real for he has acknowledged the Being Who endowed him with the power to learn and to know. Now his reason and judgment are set on an even keel - for he has rightly decided to obey the Being Who bestowed upon him the faculty of thinking and judging. His tongue is also truthful for it expresses its belief in the Lord who gave it the faculty of speech. Now the whole of his existence is an embodiment of truth for, in all spheres of life, he voluntarily as well as involuntarily obeys the laws of One God - the Lord of the Universe. Now he is at peace with the whole universe for he worships Him Whom the whole universe worships. Such a man is God's vice-gerent on earth. The whole world is for him and he is for God.

THE NATURE OF DISBELIEF

In contrast to the man described above, there is the man who, although a born Muslim and unconsciously remaining one throughout his life, does not exercise his faculties of reason, intellect and intuition to recognize his Lord and Creator and misuses his freedom of choice by choosing to deny Him. Such a man becomes an unbeliever - in the language of Islam a *Kafir*.

Kufr literally means 'to cover' or 'to conceal'. The man who denies God is called *Kafir* (concealer) because he conceals by his disbelief what is inherent in his nature and embalmed in his own soul - for his nature is instinctively imbued with 'Islam'. His whole body functions in obedience to that instinct. Each and every particle of existence - living of lifeless – functions in accordance with `Islam' and is fulfillling the duty that has been assigned to it. But the vision of this man has been blurred, his intellect has been befogged, and he is unable to see the obvious. His own nature has become concealed from his eyes and he thinks and acts in utter disregard of it. Reality becomes estranged from him and he gropes in the dark. Such is the nature of *Kufr*.

Kufr is a form of ignorance, or, rather, it is ignorance. What ignorance can be greater than to be ignorant of God, the Creator, and the Lord of the Universe? A man observes the vast panorama of nature, the superb mechanism that is ceaselessly working, the grand design that is manifest in every aspect of creation - he observes this vast machine, but he does not know anything of its Maker and Director. He knows what a wonderful organism his body is but is unable to comprehend the Force that brought it into existence; the Engineer Who designed and produced it, the Creator Who made the unique living being out of lifeless stuff: carbon, calcium, sodium and the like. He witnesses a superb plan in the universe - but fails to see the Planner behind it. He sees great beauty and harmony in its working - but not the Creator. He observes a wonderful design in nature - but not the Designer! How can a man, who has so blinded himself to reality, approach true knowledge? How can one who has made the wrong beginning reach the right destination? He will fail to find the key to Reality. The Right Path will remain concealed for him and whatever his endeavours in science and arts, he will never be able to attain truth and wisdom. He will be groping in the darkness of ignorance.

Not only that; *Kufr* is a tyranny, the worst of all tyrannies. And what is 'tyranny'? It is an unjust use of force or power. It is when you compel a thing to act unjustly or against its true nature, its real will and its inherent attitude.

We have seen that all that is in the universe is obedient to God, the Creator. To obey, to live in accordance with His Will and His Law or (to put it more precisely) to be a Muslim is ingrained in the nature of things. God has given man power over these things, but it is incumbent that they should be used for the fulfillment of His Will and not otherwise. Anyone who disobeys God and resorts to Kufr perpetrates the greatest injustice, for he uses his powers of body and mind to rebel against the course of nature and becomes an instrument in the drama of disobedience. He bows his head before deities other than God and cherishes in his heart the love, reverence and fear of other powers in utter disregard of the instinctive urge of these organs. He uses his own powers and all those things over which he has authority against the explicit Will of God and thus estab-lishes a reign of tyranny.

Can there be any greater injustice, tyranny and cruelty than that exhibited by this man who exploits and misuses everything under the sun and unscrupulously forces them to a course which affronts nature and justice?

Kufr is not mere tyranny; it is rebellion, ingratitude and infidelity. After all, what is the reality of man? Where do his power and authority come from? Is he himself the creator of his mind, his heart, his soul and other organs of his body - or have they been created by God? Has he himself created the universe and all that is in it - or has it been created by God? Who has harnessed all the powers and energies for the service of man - man or God? If everything has been created by God and God alone, then to whom do they belong? Who is their rightful sovereign? It is God and none else. And if God is the Creator, the Master and the Sovereign, then who would be a greater rebel than the man who uses God's creation against His injunctions - and who makes his mind think against God, harbors in his heart thoughts against Him, and uses his various faculties against the Sovereign's Will.

If a servant betrays his master you denounce him as faithless. If an officer becomes disloyal to the state you brand him as a traitor and renegade. If a person cheats his benefactor you have no hesitation in condemning him as ungrateful. But such acts cannot begin to compare to the one which the disbeliever commits by his *Kufr*. All that a man has and all that he uses for the benefit of others is a gift of God. The greatest obligation that a man owes on this earth is to his parents. But who has implanted the love of children in the parents' heart? Who endowed the mother with the will and power to nurture, nourish and feed her children? Who inspired the parents with the passion to spend everything in their possession for the well being of their children? A little reflection would reveal that God is the greatest benefactor of man. He is his Creator, Lord, Nourisher, Sustainer, as well as King and Sovereign. So what can be greater betrayal, ingratitude, rebellion and treason than *Kufr*, through which a man denies and disobeys his real Lord and Sovereign?

Do not think that by committing *Kufr* man does or can do the least harm to Almighty God. Insignificant speck on the face of a tiny ball in this limitless universe that man is, what harm can he do to the Lord of the Universe Whose dominions are so infinitely vast that we have not yet been able to explore their boundaries even with the help of the most powerful telescope; Whose power is so great that myriads of heavenly bodies, like the Earth, the Moon, the Sun and the stars are, at His bidding, whirling like tiny balls; Whose wealth is so boundless that He is the sole Master of the whole universe; and Who provides for all and needs none to provide for Him? Man's revolt against Him can do Him no harm; on the other hand, by his disobedience, man treads the path of ruin and disgrace.

The inevitable consequence of this revolt and denial of reality is a failure in the ultimate ideals of life. Such a rebel will never find the thread of real knowledge and vision; for knowledge that fails to reveal its own Creator can reveal no truth. Such a man's intellect and reason always run astray; for reason which errs about its own Creator cannot illumine the paths of life.

Such a man will meet with failures in all the affairs of his life. His morality, his civic and social life, his struggle for livelihood and his family life, in short, his entire existence, will be unsatisfactory. He will spread confusion and disorder. He will, without the least compunction, shed blood, violate other men's rights and generally act destructively. His perverted thoughts and ambitions, his blurred vision and distorted scale of values, and his evil activities will make life bitter for him and for all around him.

Such a man destroys the calm and pose of life on earth. And in the life hereafter he will be held guilty for the crimes he committed against his nature. Every organ of his body - his brain, eyes, nose, hands and feet - will complain against the injustice and cruelty he had subjected them to. Every tissue of his being will denounce him before God Who, as the fountain of justice, will punish him as he deserves. This is the inglorious consequence of *Kufr*. It leads to the blind alleys of utter failure, both here and hereafter.

THE BLESSINGS OF ISLAM

These are the evils and disadvantages of *Kufr*. Let us now look at some of the blessings of Islam.We find in the world around us and in the small kingdom of your own self innumerable manifestations of God's divine power. This grand universe, which ceaselessly works with matchless order and in accordance with unalterable laws, is in itself a witness to the fact that it's Designer, Creator and Governor is an Omnipotent, All-Powerful Being with infinite power, knowledge and resources, a Being of perfect wisdom, whom nothing in the universe dares disobey. It is in the very nature of man, as it is with every other thing in this universe to obey Him.

Besides endowing man with the capacity to acquire knowledge, the faculty to think and reflect, and the ability to distinguish right from wrong, God has granted him a certain amount of freedom of will and action. In this freedom lies man's real trial; his knowledge, his wisdom, his power of discrimination and his freedom of will and action are all being tried and tested. Man has not been obliged to adopt any particular course, for by compulsion the very object of the trial would have been defeated. If in an examination you are compelled to write a certain answer to a question, the examination will be of no use. Your merit can be properly judged only if you are allowed to answer the questions freely, according to your own knowledge and understanding. If your answer is correct you will succeed; if it is wrong you will fail, and your failure will bar the way to further progress.

The situation which man faces is similar. God has given him freedom of will and action so that he may choose whatever attitude in life he likes and considers proper for himself - Islam or *Kufr*.

By the correct use of his knowledge and intellect a man recognizes his Creator, reposes belief in Him, and, in spite of being under no compulsion to do so, chooses the path of obedience to Him. He understands both his own nature and the laws and realities of nature itself; despite the power of freedom to adopt any course, he adopts the way of obedience and loyalty to God, the Creator. He is successful in his trial because he has used his intellect and all other faculties properly. He uses his eyes to see the reality, his ears to listen to the truth and his mind to form right opinions. He puts all his heart and soul into following the right way he has so chosen. He chooses Truth, sees the reality, and willingly and joyfully submits to his Lord and Master. He is intelligent, truthful and dutiful, for he has chosen light over darkness. Thus he has proved by his conduct that he is not only a seeker after Truth but is its knower and worshipper as well. Such a man is on the right path, and is destined to succeed in this world and in the world to come.

Such a man will always choose the right path in every field of knowledge and action. The man who knows God with all His attributes knows the beginning as well as the ultimate end of reality. He can never be led astray, for his first step is on the right path, and he is sure of the direction and destination of his journey in life. He will reflect on the secrets of the universe, and will try to fathom the mysteries of nature, but he will not lose his way in mazes of doubt and skepticism. His path being illumined with Divine Vision, his every step will be in the right direction. In science he will endeavor to learn the laws of nature and uncover the hidden treasures of the earth for the betterment of humanity. He will try his level best to explore all avenues of knowledge and power and to harness all that exists on earth and in the heavens in the interests of mankind.

At every stage of his inquiry his God-consciousness will save him from making evil and destructive uses of science and the scientific method. He will never think of himself as the master of all these objects, boasting to be the conqueror of nature, arrogating to himself godly and sovereign powers and nourishing the ambition of subverting the world, subduing the human race and establishing his supremacy over all and sundry by fair means or foul. Such an attitude of revolt and defiance can never be entertained by a Muslim scientist - only a *Kafir* scientist can fall prey to such illusions and by submitting to them expose the entire human race to the danger of total destruction and annihilation.

A Muslim scientist, on the other hand, will behave in an altogether different way. The deeper his insight into the world of science, the stronger will be his faith in God. His head will bow down before Him in gratitude. His feelings will be that as his Master has blessed him with greater power and knowledge so he must exert himself for his own good and for the good of humanity. Instead of arrogance there will be humility. Instead of power-drunkenness there will be a strong realization of the need to serve humanity. His freedom will not be unbridled. He will be guided by the tenets of morality and Divine Revelation. Thus science will in his hands, instead of becoming an instrument of destruction, become an agency for human welfare and moral regeneration. And this is the way in which he will express his gratitude to his Master for the gifts and blessings He has bestowed on man.

Similarly, in history, economics, politics, law and other branches of arts and science, a Muslim will nowhere lag behind a *Kafir* in the fields of inquiry and struggle, but their angles of view and consequently their modus operandi will be widely different. A Muslim will study every branch of knowledge in its true perspective. He will strive to arrive at the right conclusions.

In history he will draw correct lessons from the past experiences of man, and will uncover the true causes of the rise and fall of civilizations. He will try to benefit from all that was good and right in the past and will scrupulously avoid all that led to the decline and fall of nations. In politics his sole objective will be to strive for the establishment of policies where peace, justice, fraternity and goodness reign, where man is a brother of man and respects his humanity, where no exploitation or slavery is rampant, where the rights of the individual are upheld, and where the powers of the state are considered as a sacred trust from God and are used for the common welfare of all. In the field of law, the endeavor of a Muslim will be to make it the true embodiment of justice and the real protector of the rights of all - particularly of the weak. He will see that everybody gets his due share and no injustice or oppression is inflicted on anyone. He will respect the law, make others respect it, and will see that it is administered equitably.

The life of a Muslim will always be filled with godliness, piety, righteousness and truthfulness. He will live in the belief that God alone is the Master of all, that whatever he and other men possess has been given by God, that the powers he wields are only a trust from God, that the freedom he has been endowed with is not to be used indiscriminately, and that it is in his own interest to use it in accordance with God's Will. He will constantly keep in view that one day he will have to return to the Lord and submit an account of his entire life. The sense of accountability will always remain implanted in his mind and he will never behave irresponsibly.

Think of the moral excellence of the man who lives with this mental attitude - his will be a life of purity and piety and love and altruism. He will be a blessing unto mankind. His thinking will not be polluted with evil thoughts and perverted ambitions. He will abstain from seeing evil, hearing evil, and doing evil. He will guard his tongue and will never utter a word of lie. He will earn his living through just and fair means and will prefer hunger to a food acquired unfairly through exploitation or injustice. He will never be a party to any form of oppression of violation of human life and honor. He will never yield to evil, whatever the cost of defiance. He will be an embodiment of goodness and nobility and will defend right and truth even at the cost of his life. Such a man will be a power to be reckoned with. He is bound to succeed.

He will be highly honored and respected. How can humiliation ever visit a person who is not prepared to bow his head before anyone except God the Almighty, the Sove-reign of the universe? No one can be more powerful than he - for he fears none but God and seeks blessings from none but Him. What power can make him deviate from the right path? What wealth can buy his faith? What force can shape his conscience? What power can compel him to behave as he does not want to?

He will be the wealthiest. No one in the world can be richer or more independent than he - for he will live a life of austerity and contentment. He will be neither a sensualist, nor indulgent, nor greedy. He will be contented with whatever he earns fairly and honestly and however much ill-gotten wealth is heaped before him he will not even look at it. He will have peace and contentment of heart - and what can be a greater wealth than this?

He will be the most revered, popular and beloved. No one can be more lovable than he - for he lives a life of charity and benevolence. He will be just to everyone, discharge his duties honestly, and work for the good of others. People's hearts will be naturally drawn towards him.

No one can be more trustworthy than he - for he will not betray his trust, nor will he stray from righteousness: he will be true to his word, and straightforward and honest in his dealings. He will be fair and just in all his affairs, for he is sure that God is ever-present, ever-vigilant. Words fail to describe the credit and goodwill which such a man commands. Can there be anyone who will not trust him? Such is the life and Character of a Muslim.

If you understand the true character of a Muslim, you will be convinced that he cannot live in humiliation, abasement or subjugation. He is bound to prevail and no power on earth can overwhelm him and for Islam inculcates in him the qualities which cannot be driven out.

And after living a respectable and honorable life on this earth, he return to his Creator Who will shower on him the choicest of His blessings - for he will have discharged his duty ably, fulfilled his mission successfully and emerged from his trial triumphantly. He is successful in life in this world and in the hereafter will live in eternal peace, joy and bliss.

This is Islam, the natural religion of man, the religion which is not associated with any person, people, period or place. It is the way of nature, the religion of man. In every age, in every country and among every people, all God-knowing and truth-loving men have believed and lived this very religion. They were all Muslims, irrespective of whether they called that way Islam. Whatever its name was, it signified Islam and nothing but Islam.

The name "Allah" is a word that is heard quite often these days whether it is on the television or passed along in conversation. But most non-Muslims have no idea who Allah is.

Some mistakenly believe that Allah is a deity that Muslims worship similar to the way in which Buddhists worship Buddha.

Others think that Allah is a man or a prophet. Just the name "Allah" is so shrouded in mystery because most people never take the time to unravel the meaning.

Rather they believe what they see portrayed in the heavily biased media and allow their fears to take hold of their chests instead of seeking out the truth for themselves.

The meaning of Allah is so simple. Allah is the Arabic form of the word "The One True God". Muslims worship the exact same God that Jews and Christians do.

However, Muslims prefer to call God by His proper name Allah and refrain from using the word "god" itself since it can be attributed to so many other things. For example, in proper English the feminine form of "god" is "goddess" and let's looks at Greek Mythology where the Greeks worshipped many "gods".

Muslims believe that Allah is the One and Only God without partners and that the name "Allah" is unique to the sole Creator of this World and everything in it. To liken Allah to another supposed god in any way shape or form is to commit the one unforgivable sin of shirk, or ascribing partners to Allah.

Muslims believe in submitting their entire will to Allah through acts of worship, obedience and good deeds.

Islam is the only religion on Earth that remained purely monotheistic. Each time a Muslim prays to Allah, he has a meeting with the Lord of this World without an intercessor or mediator.

Muslims believe in submitting their entire will to Allah through acts of worship, obedience and good deeds. Muslims believe that Allah is ever-present watching over His Creation and is always close to them.

Allah says in the Quran what means,

[And indeed We have created man, and We know what his own self whispers to him. And We are nearer to him than his jugular vein (by Our Knowledge).]

The Quran reveals that there are Beautiful Names of Allah, which is how Muslims get to know the Creator. Muslims are forbidden to ponder upon Allah's appearance or to attribute Him to anything in this World as some faiths liken Allah to man. Islam rejects this entirely. We can know about Allah from His beautiful names of which Prophet Muhammad said:

"Verily, there are ninety-nine names of God, one hundred minus one. He who enumerates (and believes in them) them would get into Paradise."

Some of the names are:

1. Al-Wadud — the Loving
2. Al-Khaliq — the Creator
3. Al-Ahad — the One
4. Al-Aziz — the Mighty and Strong

Allah gave mankind one final chance to be mindful of Him and to obey Him. According to Islam, the message of the Quran and the Sunnah of the Prophet Muhammad is the very same one that was given to the Jews and Christians.

However, meanings were lost in translation and the books revealed to past generations were corrupted and distorted by the hands of humans.

Allah gave mankind one final chance to be mindful of Him and to obey Him. And that chance came in the form of an unlettered man from the deserts of Arabia named Muhammad and through him Allah revealed His final revelation.

The Quran is the last book that Allah gave to humans and it is preserved which means Allah will safeguard it from corruption. Over the past 14 centuries, not a single letter has been changed or altered. No more books or Prophets will come to this world. And it is up to humans as to whether they believe in this final message or turn their backs on it as scores have done before and continue to do every day.

The best way for humans to understand Allah as the Creator is to open their eyes and see His design. Who else but Allah could create a flower as perfect as the rose? Or cover Earth with so much vegetation and foliage that scientists today are still unearthing new species?

Allah is the Most Kind and the Most Merciful. All that Allah has asked for humans to do is to be pious, worship Him alone and be kind to our fellow man. In return, humans are the veritable owners of the Earth to rule it as they see fit as Allah continuously showers His innumerable blessings upon humanity as well as punishments for those who disobey and wreak havoc on the Earth.

Islam is not a new religion or something that a few simply chose one day to follow. Islam is a continuation of the previous messages that were revealed to past Prophets.

Prophet Muhammad seals the line of prophets who came to this world both, to warn humans and give glad tidings of Allah's mercy. It is only through Allah's love and mercy for mankind that He bothered to send prophets so that we may know Him... the One and Only God.

FREEDOM, MYTH AND ARTISTIC INNOVATION

When Islam dawned, it enunciated the principle of freedom. Commander of the Faithful, Umar Ibn Al-Khattab declared his famous saying: "When, on earth, have you enslaved people while their mothers delivered them free human beings!" The fourth caliph, Ali Ibn Abi Talib, advised some people: "Never be somebody else, since Allah has created you as a free man from the beginning."

The original principle is that all people are free, in accordance with the fact that Allah creates them in freedom and that they are born free. They are entitled to be free and not be slaves. When Islam proclaimed freedom as a principle, it was during an epoch when most people were virtually enslaved intellectually, politically, socially, religiously, and economically, etc.

Running counter to all those forms of human bondage, Islam came to announce all possible forms of freedom: freedom of belief, freedom of thought, freedom of speech and freedom of criticism. Those categories have always been the foremost kind of freedom usually sought by people.

FREEDOM OF BELIEF

Despite Islam being a religion itself, Islam has set forth religious freedom. It has never allowed coercion in converting to Islam or any specific religion. Many texts can be cited here. Verses in the Quran from the Makkan period show Allah, the Almighty, as saying: "And had your Lord willed, those on earth would have believed, all of them together. So, will you (O Mohammed) then compel mankind, until they become believers?"

During the period in Madina, we have this Quranic revelation: "There is no compulsion in religion. Verily, the Right Path has become distinct from the wrong path." (Surat Al-Baqarah: verse 256). The significance in this revelation, in particular, shows how far Islam has gone to sanctify freedom and how it holds it in high esteem.

It had been an observed custom among the tribes of Aws and Khazraj during the pre-Islamic epoch of ignorance and misguided ness that whenever a woman failed to conceive she made a sacred vow that if ever she had a baby, she will make him a Jew. That explains why, throughout time, there was a presence of Jews in those two "Arab" tribes in the Arabian Peninsula.

When Islam appeared and some of the Aws and Khazraj tribes embraced it with utmost conviction and satisfaction as Allah's gift to them, some parents wanted to restore their children, already given to Judaism due to their vows, to their own religion, Islam. They were keen on ridding them of that alien religion, Judaism. What was Islam's position? Despite the abnormal circumstances in which the people's children were made Jews, and despite the state of war between Muslims and Jews at that time, Islam did not allow anyone to compel another to leave his religion and convert to another one, even if it was Islam.

This was at a time when the Byzantine Empire used to say: "Either become Christian or be killed." Islam announced its magnificent principle: "No compulsion in religion". Such a glorious declaration by Islam also coincided with a strange situation in Persia where reformers of religion were being accused of the most heinous charges.

It should be noted that Islam's principle of freedom has not appeared as an upshot of a social evolution or following a revolution that clamoured for it. Nor has it emerged on account of society reaching a certain degree of maturity. Rather, it has been something far more elevated than any existing society at that time: something descending from Heaven to raise and upgrade people on Earth.

Islam means to promote, advance and refine mankind by means of such tenet: freedom of belief and religion. But with all that kept in mind, we must notice that this principle, which is adopted and encouraged by Islam, is not without conditions or constraints.

The main condition is that religion should not be a toy in the hands of people like the Jews who said: "Believe in the morning in that which is revealed to the believers (Muslims), and rejects it at the end of the day, so that they may turn back." (Surat Al-Imran: verse 72) They used to say, "Believe in the morning, and say in the evening we abandoned Muhammad's religion because we found in it such and such". They encouraged one another to pretend to believe in Islam for a day or a week, and then speak about it in a slanderous manner.

That is why Allah, Exalted be He, has willed Islam never to become a plaything, so that whoever embraces it upon free conviction and complete awareness must adhere to it, or else they will make themselves prone to punishment for apostasy. So the first freedom then is that of religion and belief.

FREEDOM OF THOUGHT

The second one is freedom of thought and meditation. Ever since its onset, Islam has called upon people to contemplate the whole universe. The Quran says: "Say (to them O Muhammad): 'I exhort you on one (thing) only: that you stand up for Allah's sake in pairs and singly...and reflect (within yourselves the life history of the Prophet)..." (Surat Saba': verse 46) "Say: 'Behold all that is in the heavens and the earth..." (Surat Yunus: verse

101). "Have they not travelled through the land, and have they hearts wherewith to understand and ears wherewith to hear? Verily, it is not the eyes that grow blind, but it is the hearts which are in the breasts that grow blind" (Surat Al-Hajj: verse 46)

Islam censors those who follow suspicions and illusions, saying: "... and verily, guess is no substitute for the truth." (Surat Al-Najm: verse 28)

It has also denounced those who pursue their own prejudices or blindly imitate fathers and superiors. It has lambasted those who would say on the Day of Resurrection: "Verily, we obeyed our chiefs and our great ones, and they misled us from the (Right) Way." (Surat Al-Ahzab: verse 67)

Another verse says: "Nay! They say: 'we found our fathers following a certain way and religion, and we guide ourselves by their footsteps!" (Surat Al-Zukhruf: verse 22) Allah considers such people like cattle who are astray from the Straight Path.

Another significant position of Islam is its rejection of old liners and diehards. It has called for free thinking, reasoning and contemplation at all times. It says in the Quran: "Say (O Muhammad) 'Produce your proof if you are truthful."(Surat Al-Baqarah: verse 111)

Islam has always relied on intellectual evidence to prove the Islamic belief, and that is why Muslim scholars have stated: "direct intellectual reasoning is the grounds for authentic relation of religious tenets." This applies to issues like Allah's existence and the prophet hood of Muhammad, which are all proved by means of intellect in the first place.

It is reason that says he is a genuine messenger as all evidence corroborates his truthfulness, besides the miracles that confirm his authentic messenger ship. In the case of a false prophet, it is reason that tells us he is a liar and an impostor since he has not produced evidence or any miracles to support his claim. This indicates Islam's essential respect of the mind and thought.

This also explains how Islam encompassed scientific and scholastic freedom that emerged as a result of intellectual freedom. We have found 'ulama' (Muslim scholars) differ, oppose each other, and refute each other's views, neither feeling unease or guilt on account of that.

A prominent example is of one book satisfying two divergent schools of thought, called Al-Kashshaf by Imam Al-Zamakhshari. Even though the author was a Mu'tazilite, the Sunnites considered making use of it and deemed it a very reliable source. A typical response was that some Sunni 'ulama', such as Ibn Al-Munir, wrote annotations on it by attempting to reply to some points or expose some weaknesses. The same thing was done by a great Sunni Imam, Ibn-Hajar, who wrote another treatise entitled "Al-Kafi Al-Shafi" in which he traced the hadiths in Al-Zamakhshari's book to check their degree of authenticity.

Hence, the Muslim 'ulama' have seen no problem in having discussions and debates, rebutting each other's opinions, and benefiting from each other's studies. This is performed in a true atmosphere of freedom and mutual respect, with no fanaticism or rancor and all that lends proof to freedom of thought and learning in the Muslim world.

FREEDOM OF EXPRESSION AND CRITICISM

When it comes to freedom of expression and criticism, Islam not only adopts it among its principles, but calls for more than just 'freedom', making it an obligation to say, express, and criticize whatever relates to the interest of the community, general morals and public ethics. Within Islam, it is a religious duty to speak the truth, not fear anyone and act for the sake of Allah, and enjoin what is right and forbid what is wrong. It is incumbent on you to call for the good, to encourage the good people, and reproach the wrongdoers. This turns a right into a duty on you when there is nobody else to do it, or when your silence will lead to general damage. In such case, you ought to shoulder your responsibility and speak the truth, heeding nothing in the way and fearing no mishap that might befall you as a result.

"Enjoin (people) for Al-Ma'ruf – (Islamic Monotheism and all that is good), and forbid (people) from Al-Munkar (i.e.

disbelief in the Oneness of Allah, polytheism of all kinds and all that is evil and bad), and bear with patience whatever befalls you. Verily! These are some of the important commandments ordered by Allah with no exemption." (Surat Luqman: verse 17).

This is the extent of Islam, since Islam rejects muzzling people so that they may only speak on permission and believe on command. One sees this in the story of Pharaoh when he asked his magicians indignantly: 'Believe you in him (Moses) before I give you permission?'" (Surat Taha: verse 71) Such behavior and mentality is outrageous as he prevented people from holding a particular belief except on his agreement, and gagged everyone unless they had permission from high authorities!

Contrary to this, Islam has come to allow people to think freely, and even 'orders' them to do so. It permits people to believe in what they think is right. It makes it incumbent on them not to hold any belief they do not think is the right one. It obliges everyone believing in a certain creed to protect his or her creed, even with arms. It orders Muslims to defend the freedom of belief, and avert the outbreak of fitnah (internal strife) so that all and every kind of worship is for Allah alone. So, if such a situation arises, resorting to the use of arms will only be to protect freedom and preclude persecution so that there will be no coercion by anyone, as far as religion or creed is concerned.

The first Quranic verse on the lawfulness of fighting and Jihad in Islam, Allah, Glorified and Exalted be He, says: "Permission to fight is given to those (i.e. believers against disbelievers), who are fighting them, (and) because they (believers) have been wronged..." (Surat Al-Hajj: verse 39). In the verse that follows Allah says: "... For had it not been that Allah checks one set of people by means of another, monasteries, churches, synagogues, and mosques, wherein the Name of Allah is mentioned much would surely have been pulled down..." (Surat Al-Hajj: verse 40)

If it had not been for Allah giving humanity those

believing Muslims who defended religious freedom and all other public freedoms - even with their Swords - then no one would have been able to worship Allah on earth. No church, synagogue, mosque or any other kind of temple where the Name of Allah is mentioned would have remained.

This is Islam that has brought forth those liberties. But it must be known that Islam distinguishes between freedom of rights and freedom of disbelief, sinfulness and moral depravity. By no means does it refer to the kind of freedom that some people claim today, calling it "personal or private freedom".

This is in fact a misrepresentation of things when they describe it in this manner. What they mean is that you are free to commit fornication or adultery, drink alcohol, and indulge in all possible crimes and sins, but when it comes to other things relating to the real interests of society, freedom is categorically denied. Their freedom means you are not allowed to express your beliefs on opinions freely; you cannot criticize; you cannot state the obvious.

On the other hand, you have "personal" freedom, which means that you are free to corrupt yourself, your morals, your ethics, your conscience, your worship, and your family. If this is what they mean by "freedom", then of course Islam does not approve of it at all, because it is a freedom of sinning and not of exercising lawful rights.

The freedom Islam adopts is the freedom of thought, science and learning, opinion, criticism and free expression, as well as freedom of belief and religion. It is those kinds of freedom that represent the foundation for life. Equally important for people's daily activities is the freedom of having a contract; dealing in money and taking appropriate action provided it doesn't harm anyone; and owning anything under lawful conditions and restrictions without any kind of illegality.

There is a golden rule in Islam: there should neither be harm to the self, nor harm to others. So, any kind of freedom that leads to harm ought to be prevented and restricted, as your own freedom ends where others' freedom begins. For instance, you are free to pass or drive in the street, but on the condition that you adhere to traffic laws. It will then be preposterous for you to run over passersby, crash into other cars or break traffic rules, under the pretext of freedom. Such restrictions such as stopping at a red light or driving on the correct side of the road are purely in the interest of the public.

By the same token, every religion and every system must involve such checks and controls; Islam is no excep-tion. But what Islam has brought, however, has never reached any other civilization. It is the best way of life for humanity.

FAITH AND OBEDIENCE

Islam means obedience to God. And it is common sense that this obedience cannot be complete unless man knows certain basic facts of life and places firm faith in them. What are those facts? And what are the essentials which a man must know to fashion his life in accordance with the Divine Way? This we propose to discuss in the present chapter.

First of all, one should have an unshakable belief in the existence of God; without this, obedience to Him is clearly impossible.

Then, one must know the attributes of God. It is the knowledge of the attributes of God which enables man to cultivate the noblest of human qualities and to fashion his life in virtue and godliness. If a man does not know that there is One and only One God who is the Creator, the Ruler and the Sustainer of the Universe and there is none else to share with Him even a shred of Divine power and authority, he may fall prey to false gods, and offer his homage to them in search of favours.

But if he knows the divine attribute of *tawhid* (Oneness of God), there is no possibility of this. Similarly, if a man knows that God is Omnipresent and Omniscient and sees, hears and knows everything that we do in public or private - including our unexpressed thoughts! - then how can he afford to be disobedient to God? He will feel that he is under eternal vigil and will, therefore, behave accordingly. But he who is not aware of these attributes of God may be led, because of his ignorance, into disobedience. It is the same with all the other attributes of God.

The fact is that the qualities and attributes which a man must possess, if he wants to pursue the way of Islam, can be cultivated and developed only out of profound knowledge of the attributes of God. It is the knowledge of God's attributes which purifies a man's mind and soul, his beliefs, morals and actions. And a mere cursory acquaintance with or just an academic knowledge of these attributes is not sufficient - there must be an unflinching conviction firmly rooted in the mind and heart of man so that he may remain immune from insidious doubts and perversions.

Moreover, one must know in detail the way of living by following which one can seek the pleasure of God. Unless a man knows the likes and dislikes of God, how can he choose the one and reject the other? If a man has no knowledge of the Divine Law, how can he follow it? Thus knowledge of the Divine Law and the Revealed Code of Life is essential.

But here, again, mere knowledge is not enough. Man must have full confidence and conviction that it is the Divine Law and that his salvation lies in following this code alone. For knowledge without this conviction will fail to spur man to the Right Path and he may be lost in the blind alley of disobedience.

Finally, man must also know the consequences both of belief and obedience and of disbelief and disobedience. He must know what blessings will be showered upon him if he chooses God's way and leads a life of purity, virtue and obedience. And he must also know what consequences follow if he adopts the way of disobedience and revolt. Thus, knowledge of life after death is absolutely essential for this purpose. Man must have an unwavering belief in the fact that death does not mean the end of life, that there will be resurrection and he will be brought to the highest court of justice, to be presided over by God

Himself; that on the Day of Judgement complete justice will prevail; and that good deeds will be rewarded and misdeeds punished. Everybody will get his due; there will be no escape. This is bound to happen. A sense of accountability is essential for fully-fledged obedience to the Law of God.

A man who has no knowledge of the world to come many considers obedience and disobedience quite immaterial. He may think that the obedient and the disobe-dient will both meet a similar end: after death, both will be reduced to mere dust. With this attitude of mind, how can he be expected to submit to all the inconveniences and troubles that are inextricably associated with the life of active obedience, and avoid committing those sins which do not apparently bring him any moral or material loss in this world? With this mental attitude a man cannot acknowledge and submit to God's Law.

Nor can a man, who lacks firm belief in the life hereafter and in the Divine Court of Judgment, remain steadfast in the turbulent waters of life with its temptation to sin, crime and evil; for doubt and hesitancy rob a man of his will to action. You can remain consistent in your behavior only if you are firm in your beliefs. You can whole-heartedly follow a course only if you are sure of the benefits that will accrue to you by following it and of the losses that will engulf you if you disobey it. Thus, a profound knowledge of the cons-quences of belief and disbelief and of the life after death is crucial.

These are the essential facts which one must know if one wants to live the life of obedience, that is, Islam.

FAITH-WHAT DOES IT MEAN?

Faith is what we have described in the foregoing discussion as 'Knowledge and Belief'. The Arabic word Iman, which we have rendered in English as faith, literally means 'to know', 'to believe' and 'to be convinced beyond the least shadow of doubt'. Faith, thus, is firm belief arising out of knowledge and conviction. And the man who knows and reposes unshakable belief in the Unity of God, in His Attributes, in His Law and the Revealed Guidance, and in the Divine Code of Reward and Punishment is called *Mu'min* (faithful). This faith invariably leads man to a life of obedience and submission to the Will of God. And one who lives this life of submission is known as *Muslim*.

It is therefore clear that without faith (*Iman*) no man can be a true Muslim. It is the indispensable essential; rather, the very starting point, without which no beginning can be made. The relation of Islam to *Iman* is the same as of a tree to its seed. As a tree cannot sprout forth without its seed, in the same way it is not possible for a man who has no belief to start with, to become a 'Muslim'. On the other hand, just as it can happen that, in spite of sowing the seed, the tree may, for many reasons, not grow, or if it does grow, its develop-ment may be impaired or retarded, in the same way, a man may have faith, but due to a number of weaknesses, he may not become a true and staunch Muslim.

From the viewpoint of Islam and *Iman*, men may be classified into four categories:

1. Those who have firm faith a faith that makes them whole-heartedly submit to God. They follow the way of God and devote themselves heart and soul to seeking His pleasure by doing all that He likes and by avoiding all that He dislikes. In their devotion they are even more fervent than is the common man in pursuit of wealth and glory. Such men are true Muslims.
2. Those who do have faith, who believe in God, His Law and the Day of Judgment, but whose faith is not deep and strong enough to make them totally submit to God. They are far below the rank of true Muslims, deserve punishment for their defaults and misdeeds, but are still Muslims. They are wrongdoers but not rebels. They acknowledge the Sovereign and His Law and, although they are violating the Law, they have not revolted against the Sovereign. They admit His supremacy and their own guilt. Thus they are guilty and deserve punishment, but Muslims they remain.

3. Those that do not possess faith at all. These people refuse to acknowledge the sovereignty of God and are rebels. Even if their conduct is not bad and even if they are not spreading corruption and violence, they remain rebels and their apparent good deeds are of little value. Such men are like outlaws. Sometimes outlaws may act in accordance with the laws of the land, but this does not make them loyal and obedient citizens; in the same way the apparent good deeds of those who revolt against God cannot compensate for the gravity of the real wrongs, revolt and disobedience.
4. Those who neither possess faith nor do good deeds. They spread disorder in the world and perpetrate all kinds of violence and oppression. They are the woof the people; for they are both rebels and wrongdoers and criminals.

The above classification of mankind shows that the real success and salvation of man depends of faith (*Iman*). The life of obedience (*Islam*) takes its birth from the seed of *Iman*. This Islam of a person may be flawless or defective. But without *Iman* there can be no Islam. Where there is no *lman* there is no Islam. Where there is no Islam there is *Kufr*. Its form and nature may vary, but it remains *kufr* and nothing but *kufr*.

HOW TO ACQUIRE KNOWLEDGE OF GOD?

Now the question arises of how to acquire knowledge of and belief in God, His Attributes, His Law and the Day of Judgement?

We have already referred to the countless manifestation of God around us and in our own selves, which bear witness to the fact that there is One and only One Creator and Governor of this Universe and it is He Who controls and directs it. These manifestations reflect the divine attributes of the Creator: His great wisdom, His all-embracing knowledge, His omnipotence, His mercy, His all-sustaining power - in short His attributes can be traced everywhere in His works. But man's intellect and capacity for knowledge have erred in observing and understanding them. Some men have argued that there are two gods, others have professed belief in a trinity, and still others have succumbed to polytheism. Some have worshipped nature and others divided the Creator into the gods of rain, air, fire, life, death and so on.

Similarly, men have put forward many erroneous not-ions about life after death; for instance, that man is reduced to dust after death and will not rise to life again; or that man is subject to a process of continuous regeneration in this world and is punished or rewarded in future cycles of life.

Even greater difficulty arises when we come to the question of a code of living. To formulate a complete and balanced code that conforms to God's pleasure merely using human reason is an extremely difficult task. Even if a man is equipped with the highest faculties of reason and intellect and possesses matchless wisdom and experience, the chances of his formulating the correct views on existence are slight. And even if, after a lifetime of reflection, he does in fact succeed he will still lack the confidence that he has really discovered the truth and adopted the right path.

The fullest and fairest test of man's wisdom, reason and knowledge might have been to have left him to his own resources without any external guidance. But this would have meant that only those with the determination and ability to find the path of truth would find salvation. God, therefore, spared His human creatures such a hard test. Through His Grace and Benevolence He raised for mankind men from among themselves to whom He imparted the true knowledge of His attributes, revealed to them His Law and the Right Code of Living, gave them the knowledge of the meaning and purpose of life and of life after death and thus showed them the way by which man can achieve success and eternal bliss.

These chosen men are the Messengers of God - His Prophets. God has communicated knowledge and wisdom to them by means of revelation (*wahi*), and the book containing the Divine Communications is called the Book of God, or the Word of God. The test of man's wisdom and intellect therefore lies in this: does he recognize God's Messengers after observing their pure and pious lives and carefully studying their noble and flawless teachings? A man of wisdom and common sense would accept instructions given by the Messengers of truth. If he denies the Messengers of God and their teachings, his denial would signify that he was devoid of the capacity to discover truth and righteousness. He would fail his test. Such a man will never be able to discover the truth about God and His Law and life after death.

FAITH IN THE UNKNOWN

It is an everyday experience that when you do not know a thing, you look for somebody who does know. If you get ill and you cannot treat and cure yourself, you go to a doctor and follow his instructions without question. Why? Because he is properly qualified to give medical advice, possesses experience and has treated and cured a number of patients. Similarly, in matters of law you accept whatever a legal expert says and act accordingly.

In educational matters you trust m your teacher. When you want to go to some place and do not know the way, you ask somebody who knows it, and follow the way he points out. In short, the course that you adopt in your day-to-day life about matters which you do not or cannot know is that you approach someone who does know about them, accept his advice and act accordingly. You make every effort to select the proper person. But from then on you accept his advice unquestioningly. This kind of belief is called "belief in the unknown" (*Iman-bi'l-ghayb*).

Iman-bi'l-ghayb signifies that you get knowledge of what was not known to you from one who knows. You do not know God and His real attributes. You are not aware that His angels are directing the machinery of the whole Universe according to His orders, and that they surround you on all sides. You have not the proper knowledge of the way of life through which you can seek the pleasure of your Creator. And you are in the dark about the life to come. Such knowledge is given to you by the Prophets, who have had direct contact with the Divine Being. They are the persons whose sincerity, integrity, trustworthiness, godliness and absolute purity stand as irrevocable witnesses to the truth of their claim to knowledge. And above all, the wisdom and force of their message makes you admit that they speak the truth and deserve to be believed and followed.

This conviction of yours is *Iman-bi'l-ghayb*. Such a truth-discerning and truth-acknowledging attitude is essential for obedience to God and for acting in accordance with His pleasure; for you have no other medium than God's Mess-engers for the achievement of true knowledge, and without true knowledge you cannot proceed on the path of Islam.

THE PROPHETHOOD

PROPHETHOOD: ITS NATURE AND NECESSITY

God has most graciously provided man with all that he needs in this Universe. Generally every new-born child arrives in the world endowed with eyes to see, ears to hear, a nose to smell and breathe, hands to touch, feet to walk and a mind to think. All those potentialities, powers and faculties that a man needs or can need are most carefully provided and marvelously set in his tiny body. Every minute requirement is foreseen and provided for.

It is the same with the world he lives in. Everything essential for his life is provided: air, light, heat, water and so on. A child on opening his eyes finds his food in his mother's breast. His parents love him instinctively and in their hearts has been implanted an irresistible urge to look after him, to bring him up and to sacrifice their all for his welfare.

Under the sheltering care of His system of sustenance the child grows to maturity and at every stage of his life obtains from nature that entire he needs. All the material conditions of survival and growth are provided for; he finds that the whole Universe is at his service.

Furthermore, man is blessed with all those powers, capacities and faculties -physical, mental and moral- which he requires in his struggle for life. But God has not distributed these gifts equally. This would have made men totally independent of each other and would have excluded mutual care and co-operation. Thus, although mankind as a whole possesses all that is needed, between men capacities are distributed unequally and sparingly.

Some possess physical strength and prowess; others distinguish themselves for their mental talents. Some are born with a greater aptitude for arts, poetry and philosophy, some possess sharpness of tongue, others military acumen, commercial intelligence, mathematical keenness, scientific curiosity, literary observation or philosophical bent. These special aptitudes make a man distinct and enable him to grasp those intricacies which elude the common man. These insights, aptitudes and talents are the gifts of God. They are innate in the nature of those men whom God has destined to be thus distinguished. They cannot be acquired merely by education and training.

Reflection on this disposition of God's gifts also reveals that man's talents have been distributed in a marvelous way. Those capacities which are essential for the general maintenance of human culture have been endowed to most people, while extraordinary talents which are required only to a limited extent are given only to a small number. There are many soldiers, peasants, artisans and workers; but military generals, scholars, statesmen and intellectuals are comparatively few. The general rule seems to be: the higher the capacity and greater the genius, the fewer people who possess them. Super-geniuses, who leave an indelible mark on human history and whose achievements guide humanity for centuries, are fewer still.

Here we are faced with another question: do people just need specialists in the fields of law and politics, science and mathematics, engineering and mechanics, finance and economics and the life? Or do they also need men to show them the right path - the way to God and salvation? There must clearly be someone to tell man the purpose of creation and the meaning of life itself: what man himself is and why he has been created; who has provided him with all the powers and resources and why; what are the proper ends of life and how are they to be achieved; what are the proper values of life and how they can be attained.

Our reason refuses to accept that God, Who has provided man with even the smallest of his requirements, would not provide for this greatest and most vital need. It can never be so. And it is not so. While God has produced men of distinction in arts and science, He has also raised men with deep vision, pure intuition and the highest faculties to know and understand Him. To them, He revealed the way of godliness, piety and righteousness. He gave them the knowledge of the aims of life and values of morality and entrusted them with the duty to communicate Divine Revelation to other human beings. These men are the Prophets and Messengers of God.

The Prophets distinguish themselves in human society by their special aptitudes, natural bents of mind and a pious and meaningful way of life; more or less in the same way as other geniuses in art and science distinguish themselves by their extraordinary capacities and natural aptitudes. The genius in man is its own advertisement and automatically persuades others to recognize and acknowledge it.

Thus, a Prophet's mind grasps problems which defy other minds; he throws light on subjects whom no one else can; he has insights into such subtle and intricate questions that no one else would have even understood after years of deep thought and meditation. Reasons accept whatever he says; the heart feels its truth; and experience of the world testifies to every word that flows from his mouth. If, however, we ourselves try to produce the same or a similar work, we inevitably meet with failure. In all affairs his attitude is that of truthfulness, straightforwardness and nobility. He never does or utters wrong, nor does he commit any evil. He always encourages virtue and righteousness, and practices himself what he preaches to others. Neither his words nor his deeds are prompted by self-interest. He suffers for the good of others, and never makes others suffer for his own good.

When it becomes quite clear that a person is a true Prophet of God, the natural dictate of this realization is that his words should be accepted, his instructions followed and his orders obeyed. It is illogical to accept a man as God's true Prophet and yet not to believe in what he says and not to follow what he ordains; for your very acceptance of him as God's Prophet means that you have acknowledged that what he says is from God, and that whatever he does is in accordance with God's Will and Pleasure. Disobedience of him is disobedience of God and disobedience of God leads to ruin.

Therefore, the very acceptance of a Prophet makes it incumbent on you to follow his instructions unconditionally. You may not be able fully to grasp the wisdom and usefulness of this or that order, but the very fact that an instruction has emanated from a Prophet is sufficient guarantee of its truth. One's inability to understand it does not mean there is something wrong with it. Rather it is our understanding which is at fault.

Some men admit the integrity and truthfulness of a Prophet, but do not put faith (*Iman*) in him, nor do they follow him in the affairs of their life. Such men are not only *Kafirs*, but imprudent: for not to follow a Prophet after admitting him to be true means that one knowingly follows untruth. And what folly can be greater than that!

Some people declare: "We do not need a Prophet for our guidance and we can ourselves find the way to truth." This, too, is a wrong view. You have probably learnt geometry, and you know that between points there can be only one straight line; all other lines must be crooked or will fail to touch the point in view. The same is the case with the way to truth, which in the language of Islam, is called the Straight Path (*al-Sirat al-Mustaqim*).

This path begins from man and goes straight up to God, and this path can by definition be one and only one; all other paths must be aberrations. This Straight Path has been indicated by the Prophets, and there is and can be no straight path besides that. The man who ignores that path soon finds himself lost in the maze created by his own fancy. What can you think of a person who loses his way and, when a good man shows him the right one, defiantly declares: "I will not take your guidance nor accept the way you have shown to me, but I will myself grope in this unknown region and try to reach the object of my search in my own way?" This, in the presence of the clear guidance of the Prophets, is sheer stupidity. If everybody tried to start from scratch, it would be a gross waste of time and energy. We never do so in the sciences and arts: why here?

If you go a little deeper into the matter, it will become clear that a person who disbelieves in a true Prophet cannot find any way, straight or otherwise, to God. This is because a man who refuses to believe the advice of a truthful man adopts such a perverse attitude that he ceases to understand the difference between truth and falsehood and becomes a victim of his own obstinacy, arrogance, bias and perversity. This refusal may be due to false arrogance, or blind conser-vatism and obstinate adherence to the way of one's forefathers, or to slavery to the lower desires of the self, whose gratification becomes impossible by submission to the teachings of the Prophets.

On the other hand, if a man is sincere and truth-loving, the road to reality opens up to him. He will find in the teachings of the Prophets the very echo of his own soul and discover himself by discovering the Prophets.

Above all, a true Prophet is raised by God Himself. It is He Who has sent him to mankind to convey His message to His people. It is His Command that one should put one's faith in the Prophet and follow him. Thus, one who refuses to believe in God's Messenger refuses to follow God's Commandment and becomes a rebel. There is no denying that one who refuses to acknowledge the authority of the viceroy of a sovereign actually refuses the authority of the sovereign himself. This disobedience turns him into a rebel. God is the Lord of the Universe, the true Sovereign, the King of Kings, and it is the bounden duty of every man to acknowledge the authority of His Messengers and Apostles and to obey them as His accredited Prophets. Anyone who rejects the Prophets of God is a *Kafir,* be he a believer in God or a disbeliever.

BRIEF HISTORY OF PROPHETHOOD

Now let us look at the history of prophethood. let us see how this long chain began, how it gradually unfolded itself and finally culminated in the prophethood of the last of the Prophets, Muhammad (blessings of Allah and peace be upon him).

The human race began from one man: Adam. It was from him that the family of man grew and the human race multiplied. All human beings born in this world have descended from that earliest pair: Adam and Eve. History and religion are agreed on these points. Nor do scientific investigations into the origin of man show that originally different men came into being, simultaneously or at different points of time, in different parts of the world. Most scientists conjecture that one man would have been brought into existence first the entire human race might have descended from that one man.

Adam, the first man on earth, was also the first Prophet of God. He revealed His religion -Islam- to him and told him to convey and communicate it to his descendents: to teach them that Allah is One, the Creator, the Sustainer of the world: that He is the Lord of the Universe and He alone should be worshipped and obeyed; that to Him they would have to return one day and to Him alone they should appeal for help; that they should live righteous lives in accordance with God's pleasure and that if they did so they would be blessed and if they did not they would suffer both here and in the hereafter.

Those of Adam's descendants who were good trod the right path, but those who were bad abandoned their father's teachings. Some began to worship the sun, the moon and the stars; others took to the worship of trees, animals and rivers. Some believed that air, water, fire, health and all the blessings and forces of Nature were each under the control of a different god and that the favour of each one could be won by worship. In this way ignorance gave rise to many forms of polytheism and idolatry, and scores of religious were formulated. This was the age when Adam's progeny had spread over the globe, and formed different races and nations. Every nation had created a different religion for itself, each with rituals of its own. God - the one Lord and Creator of mankind and the universe - was forgotten. Every kind of evil custom grew; many evils began to be considered right and many right things were either ignored or condemned as wrong.

At this stage God began to raise Prophets among every people. Each one reminded his people of the lesson they had forgotten. They put an end to idol-worship and the practice of associating other deities with God (*shirk*), did away with all customs of ignorance, taught them the right way of living in accordance with God's pleasure, and gave them laws to be followed and enforced in society. God's true Prophets were raised in every land and among every people. They all possessed one and the same religion - the religion of Islam.

No doubt the methods of teaching and the legal codes of different Prophets varied in accordance with the needs and the stage of culture of the people among whom they were raised. The particular teachings of each Prophet were determined by the kind of evils which he was trying to eradicate. When people were in the primitive stages of society, civilization and intellectual development, their laws and regulations were simple; they were modified and improved as the society evolved and progressed.

Such differences were, however, only superficial. The fundamental teachings of all the religions were the same, i.e. belief in the unity of God, adherence to a life of piety, goodness and peace, and belief in life after death with its just mechanism of reward and punishment.

Man's attitudes towards God's Prophets have been strange. He has ill-treated them and refused to accept their teachings. Some of the prophets were expelled from their lands; some were assassinated; some, faced with indifference, preached the whole of their lives without winning more than a few followers. But despite the harassment, derision and indignity, to which they were perpetually subjected, these Apostles of God did not cease to spread their message. Their patient determination at last succeeded: large groups of people and nations were converted to their creed.

The false tendencies, born of centuries of deviation, ignorance and malpractice, now took another form. Though they accepted their Prophets during their lives and practiced their teachings, after their deaths they introduced their own distorted ideas into their religions. They adopted novel methods of worshipping God; some even took to the worship of their Prophets. They made the Prophets the incarnations of God or the sons of God; some associated their Prophets with God in His Divinity.

In short, man's varied attitudes in this respect were a travesty of his reason and a mockery of himself; he made idols of those very persons whose holy mission was to smash idols.

By intermixing religion, rituals born of ignorance, baseless and false anecdotes and man-made laws, men so changed and perverted the teachings of the Prophets over the centuries that they became lost in a welter of fictions to the extent that it became impossible to distinguish the grain from the chaff. Not content with this, they made up so many stories about their Prophets that real and reliable accounts of their lives became impossible to discern. Despite all the work of the Prophets was not altogether vain. Traces of truth survived. The idea of God and of life after death was assimi-lated in some form or other. A few principles of goodness, truthfulness and morality were accepted throughout the world. The prophets thus prepared the mental attitude of their respective peoples in such as way that a universal religion could be safely introduced - a religion which accords with the nature of man, which embodies that all was good in all other creeds and societies, and which is acceptable to mankind.

As we have said above, in the beginning separate Prophets appeared among different nations or groups of people, and the teaching of each Prophet was meant specially and specially for his people. The reason was that at that stage of history, nations were so cut off from each other geographically that opportunities for mutual intercourse were non-existent. In such circumstances it was very difficult to propagate a common World Faith with an accompanying common system of law.

In addition, the ignorance of the early nations was so great that it had given different forms to their moral aberrations and distortions of Faith. It was, therefore, necessary that different Prophets be raised to preach the Truth to them and win them over to God; to gradually eradicate evils and aberrations; to root out ignorance and teach them the simple, pious and righteous life - God alone knows how many thousands of years were spent in thus educating man, and developing him mentally, morally and spiritually.

With the progress and spread of commerce, industry and the arts, intercourse was established between nations. From China and Japan, as far as the distant lands of Europe and Africa, regular routes were opened both by sea and land. Many people learnt the art of writing; knowledge spread. Ideas began to be communicated from one country to ano-ther and learning and scholarship began to be exchanged. Great conquerors appeared, extended their conquests far and wide, established vast empires, and knit many different nations under one political system. Thus nations came closer and closer to one another, and their differences became less and less.

It became possible under these circumstances that one and the same faith, envisaging a comprehensive and all-embracing way of life, meeting the moral, spiritual, social, cultural, political, economic and other needs of men and embodying both religious and secular elements could be sent by God to the whole of mankind. More than two thousand years ago mankind had reached such a mental awareness that it seemed to be craving for a universal religion.

Buddhism, though it consisted only of a set of moral principles and was not a complete system of life, emerged from India, and spread as far as Japan and Mongolia on one side, and Afghanistan and Bokhara on the other. Its missionaries traveled far and wide in the world. A few centuries later, Christianity appeared. Although the religion taught by Jesus Christ (peace be upon him) was pure Islam, his followers reduced it to a hotchpotch called Christianity, and even this overtly Israelised religion spread to far-off Persia and Asia Minor and to the distant climes of Europe and Africa. From these events it is evident that the conditions of mankind in that age demanded a common religion for the whole human race. Indeed, when people found no complete and true religion in existence they began to develop existing religions, however defective, incomplete and unsatisfying they might have been. At such a crucial stage of human civilization, when the mind of man was itself craving for a world religion, a Prophet was raised in Arabia for the whole world and for all nations. The religion he was given to propagate was again Islam - but now in the form of a complete and fully-fledged system, covering all aspects of the life of man. He was Muhammad, the Prophet of Islam (blessings of Allah and peace be upon him)!

In conclusion we can say about prophethood in the following points:

1. The right course for man is to live in obedience to God, and for such a life of obedience knowledge and faith are absolutely essential; knowledge of God and His attributes, His likes and dislikes, His chosen way and the Day of Judgement; and unflinching faith in this knowledge; this is *Iman*.
2. God has graciously spared man the arduous task of acquiring this knowledge through his personal effort alone. Instead, He has revealed this knowledge to the Prophets He has chosen from amongst men and commanded them to convey the Will of God to other human beings and show them the right path. This has saved man from much great misfortune.
3. The duty of men and women is to recognize a true Prophet of God, to have faith in him and his teachings and to scrupulously obey him and follow in his footsteps. This is the road to salvation.

THE PROPHETHOOD OF MUHAMMAD

If we cast a glance at the world atlas, we find that no other country could have been more suitable than Arabia for the much-needed world religion. It is situated right in the middle of Asia and Africa, and Europe is not far away. At the time of Muhammad's (blessings of Allah and peace be upon him) appearance, central Europe was inhabited by civilized and culturally advanced nations; these people were about the same distance from Arabia as were the people of India.

Look at the history of that era, too, and you will find that no other people were more suited to be endowed with this Prophet than the Arabs. Great nations of the world had long been struggling for world supremacy; as a consequence they had exhausted their resources and vitality. The Arabs were a fresh and virile people. So-called social progress had produced bad habits among the advanced nations, while among the Arabs no such social organization existed, and they were, therefore, free from the inactivity, debasement and decadence arising out of luxury and sensual satiety.

The pagan Arabs of the fifth century had not been affected by the evil influence of the artificial social systems and civilizations of the great nations of the world. They possessed all the good human qualities of a people untouched by the 'social progresses of the time. They were brave, fearless, generous, faithful to their promises, lovers of freedom and politically independent - not subject to the hegemony of any of the imperial powers.

There were also certain undesirable aspects of their life but the reason for this was that for thousands of years either prophet had risen among them or had there appeared a reformer who might have civilized them and purged their moral life of its impurities. Centuries of free and independent desert life had bred and nourished extreme ignorance among them. They had, therefore, become so fixed in their traditions of ignorance that to humanize them was beyond an ordinary man.

At the same time, however, if some person of extraordinary powers were to give them a noble ideal, they would readily rise to act for the achievement of such an ideal. They would be prepared to face the hostility of the entire world in the cause of their mission. It was just such a young, forceful and virile people that were needed to disseminate the teachings of the World Prophet, Muhammad (blessings of Allah and peace be upon him).

Take also the Arabic language. The more you study its literature, the more you will be convinced that there is no other language more suited to express high ideals, to explain the most subtle aspects of Divine knowledge, and to impress the heart of man and mould it into submission to God. Small phrases and brief sentences express a whole world of ideas; they are so powerful that their very sound can move men to tears and ecstasy. They are so sweet that it is as if honey were being poured into one's ears; they are so full of harmony that every fiber of the listener's body is moved by their symphony. It was a rich and powerful language such as this that was needed for the Qur'an, the Great Word of God.

It was, therefore, a manifestation of God's great wisdom that He chose Arabia as the birth-place of the World Prophet.

MUHAMMAD' S PROPHETHOOD: A RATIONAL

If one were to close one's eyes and imagine oneself in the world of 1400 years ago, one would find that it was a world completely different from ours. How few and far between were the opportunities for the exchange of ideas! How limited and undeveloped were the means of comm-unication! How meager was man's knowledge! How narrow his outlook! How enveloped was he in superstition and wild ideas!

Darkness held sway. There was only a faint glimmer of learning, hardly strong enough to light up the horizons of human knowledge. There was neither radio nor telephone, neither television nor the cinema. Railways and cars and airplanes were undreamed of, and printing presses were unknown. Handwritten books or copyists alone supplied what little literary material was to be transmitted from generation to generation. Education was a luxury, meant only for the most fortunate, and educational institutions were very few and far between.

The store of human knowledge was scanty, man's outlook was narrow, and his ideas of men and things were confined to his limited surroundings. Even a scholar of that age lacked in some respects the knowledge possessed by a layman of today, and the most cultured person was less refined than the modern man in the street.

Indeed, humanity was steeped in ignorance and superstition and whatever light of learning there was seemed to be fighting a losing battle against the darkness prevailing all around. People used to spend a whole lifetime acquiring the modest information which is now everybody's heritage. Things which are classed as 'myth' and 'superstition' today were the unquestionable truths of that age. Acts which we now regard as barbarous were then the order of the day. Methods which appear obnoxious to our moral sense today constituted the very soul of morality; incredulity had assumed such proportions and had become so widespread that people refused to consider anything as sublime unless it appeared in the garb of the supernatural, the uncanny and even the impossible. They had developed such inferiority complexes that they could not imagine human beings possessing saintly souls.

ARABIA-THE ABYSS OF DARKNESS

In that benighted era, there was a territory where darkness lay even heavier than elsewhere. The neighboring countries of Persia, Byzantium and Egypt possessed a glimmer of civilization and a faint light of learning. But Arabia stood isolated, cut off by vast tracts of desert.

Arab traders travelling great distances, which took them months, carried their wares to and from these countries, but they had little chance to find out anything about them. In their own country, they did not have a single educational institution or library. No one seemed interested in the cultivation and advancement of knowledge. The few who were literate were not educated enough to understand the existing arts and sciences. Although they did possess a highly developed language capable of expressing the finest shades of human thought in a remarkable manner, a study of the remnants of their literature reveals how limited was their knowledge, how low was their standard of culture and civilization, how saturated were their minds with super-stitions, how barbarous and ferocious were their thoughts and customs, and how decadent were their moral standards.

It was a country without a government. Each tribe considered itself to be an independent sovereign unit. There was no law except the law of the strongest. Loot, arson and murder of innocent and weak people were the order of the day. Life, property and honor were constantly in jeopardy. Tribes were always at daggers drawn with one another. Any trivial incident was enough to spark off a ferocious war. Indeed, Bedouins from one tribe thought they had every right to kill people from other tribes.

Whatever notions they had of morals, culture and civilization were primitive in the extreme. They could hardly discriminate between pure and impure, lawful and unlawful. Their lives were barbaric. They reveled in adultery, gambling and drinking. Looting and murder were part of their everyday existence. They would stand stark naked before each other without any qualms of conscience. Even their women-folk would strip nude at the ceremony of circum-ambulating the *Ka'bah*. They would bury their daughters alive lest anyone should become their son-in-law. They would marry their step-mothers after the death of their fathers. They were ignorant of even the rudiments of everyday life such as proper eating, dressing and washing.

As regards their religious beliefs, they suffered from the same evils which were playing havoc with the rest of the world. They worshipped stones, trees, idols, stars and spirits; in short, everything conceivable except God.

They knew nothing about the teachings of the Prophets of old. They had an idea that Abraham and Ishmael were their fore-fathers, but they knew next to nothing about their religious preachings and about the God Whom they worshipped. The stories of 'Ad and Thamud were to be found in their folklore, but they contained no traces of the teachings of the Prophets Hud and Salih. The Jews and Christians had passed on to them certain legends relating to the Israelite Prophets. They presented a harrowing picture of those noble souls. Their teachings were adulterated with the figments of their own imagination and their lives were tarred black. Some idea of the religious conceptions of those people can still be got today by looking at those Israelite traditions which Muslim commentators of the Qur'an have conveyed to us. The picture presented of the institution of prophethood and of the character of the Israelite Prophets is the very antithesis of all that those noble followers of truth stood for.

THE SAVIOR IS BORN

In such a dark age and in such a benighted country a man is born. His parents die when he is very young and a few years later the sad demise of his grandfather also occurs. Consequently, he is deprived even of that scant training and upbringing which an Arab child of his time could get. In his boyhood he tends flocks of sheep and goats in the company of Bedouin boys. When of age, he takes to commerce. All his associations and all his dealings are with the Arabs alone, whose condition has just been described.

He is completely illiterate and unschooled. He never gets a chance to sit in the company of learned men, for such men were non-existent in Arabia. He does have a few opportunities to go out of his country, but those journeys are confined to Syria and are nothing more than the usual business trips undertaken by Arab trade caravans. If he meets any learned men there, such random meetings are so rare as to play no part in the forming of his personality. Nor can they be the means of the acquisition of that profound and vast knowledge which transformed an unlettered Bedouin into a leader not only of his own country and age but of the whole world and of all ages to come. These journeys cannot have given him those conceptions and principles of religion, ethics, culture and civilization: they were non-existent in the world of those days. And they cannot have created that sublime and perfect human character which was nowhere to be found in those days.

DIAMOND IN A HEAP OF STONES

We may now look at the life and work of this noble man in the context not only of the Arabian society but also of the entire world as it stood in that period.

He is totally different from the people among whom he is born and passes his youth and early manhood and attains finally his full stature. Even his worst enemies never accuse him of telling a lie. He never uses obscene and abusive language. He has a charming personality and winning manners with which he captivates the hearts of those who come into contact with him. In his dealings with people he always follows the principles of justice and fair play. He remains engaged in trade and commerce for years, but he never enters into any dishonest transaction. Those who deal with him in business have full confidence in his integrity. The entire nation calls him *Al-Amin* (the Truthful and the Trustworthy). Even his enemies deposit their valuable belongings with him for safe custody.

He is the embodiment of modesty in the midst of a society which is immodest to the core. Born and bred among a people who regard drunkenness and gambling as virtues, he never touches alcohol and never indulges in gambling. His people are uncouth, uncultured and unclean, but he personifies the highest culture and the most refined aesthetic outlook.

Surrounded on all sides by cruelty, he himself has a heart overflowing with the milk of human kindness. He helps orphans and widows. He is hospitable to travelers. He harms no one; rather, he suffers hardships for others' sakes. Living among those for whom war is bread and butter, he is such a lover of peace that his heart melts for them when they take up arms and cut each other's throats. He stays aloof from the feuds of his tribe, intervening to bring about reconciliation. Brought up in an idolatrous race, he regards nothing in the heavens and the earth worth worshipping except the One True God. He does not bow before any created thing and does not partake of the offerings made to idols, even in his childhood. Instinctively he hates all worship of any creature and being except God.

In brief, the towering and radiant personality of this man, in the midst of such a benighted and dark environment, may be likened to a beacon-light illumining a pitch-dark night or to a diamond shining in a heap of dead stones.

A REVOLUTION COMES

After spending a great part of his life in such a pure and civilized manner there was a revolution in his being. He has had enough of the darkness and ignorance around him. He wants to swim clear of the horrible sea of corruption, immorality, idolatry and disorder which surround him. He finds society out of harmony with his soul. He withdraws alone to the hills, spending days and nights in total seclusion and meditation. He fasts so that his soul and his heart may become still purer and nobler.

He muses and ponders deeply. He is in search of a light to melt away the encompassing darkness. He wants the power to bring about the downfall of the corrupt and disorderly world of his day and lay the foundations of the new and better world.

Suddenly his heart is illuminated with the Divine Light giving him the power he has yearned for. He comes out of the confinement of his cave, goes to the people, and addresses them thus:

"The idols which you worship are a sham. Stop worshipping them from now on. No mortal being, no star, no tree, no stone, no spirit is worthy of human worship. Therefore bow not your heads in worship before them. The entire universe with everything that it contains belongs to God Almighty. He alone is the Creator, the Nourisher, and the Sustainer and, consequently, the real Sovereign before Whom all should bow down and to Whom all should pray and render obedience. Thus worship Him alone and obey only His commands".

"Loot and plunder, murder and rapine, injustice and cruelty

-all the vices in which you indulge - are crimes in the eyes of God. Leave your evil ways. He hates them all. Speak the truth. Be just. Do not kill anyone. Do not rob anyone. Take your lawful share. Give what is due to others in a just manner".

"You are human beings and all human beings are equal in the eyes of God. None is born with the slur of shame on his face; nor has anyone come into the world with the mantle of honor hung around his neck. He alone is high and honored who is God fearing and pious, true in words and deed. Distinctions of birth and race are no criteria of greatness and honor. One who fears God and does good deeds is the noblest of human beings. One who does not love God and is steeped in bad ways is doomed".

"There is an appointed day after your death when you shall have to appear before your Lord. You shall be called to account for all your deeds, good or bad, and you shall not be able then to hide anything. The whole record of your life shall be an open book to him. Your fate shall be determined by your good or bad actions. In the court of the True Judge -the Omniscient God- the question of unfair recommendation and favoritism does not arise. You will not be able to bribe Him. No consideration will be given to your pedigree or parentage. True faith and good deeds alone will stand you in good stead at that time. He who has them shall take his abode in the Heaven of eternal happiness, while he who is devoid of them shall be cast in the fire of Hell."

This is the message with which he comes. The ignorant nation turns against him. Abuse and stones are showered on his august person. Every conceivable torture and cruelty is perpetrated on him; and this continues not for a day or two but uninterruptedly for thirteen long, troubled years. At last he is exiled. But he is not given respite even there. He is tormented in various ways in his place of refuge. The whole of Arabia is incited against him. He is persecuted and hounded continuously for full eight years there. He suffers it all, but does not budge from the stand he has taken. He is resolute, firm and inflexible in his purpose.

WHY ALL THAT ENMITY?

One might ask: how is it that his nation became his sworn enemy? Was there any dispute about gold and silver or other worldly possessions? Was it due to any blood-feud? Did he ask for anything from them? No! The whole enmity was based on the fact that he had asked them to worship the One True God and to lead lives of righteousness, piety and goodness. He had preached against idolatry and the worship of other beings besides God, and had denounced their way of life. He had cut at the roots of priest craft. He had inveighed against all distinctions of high and low between human beings, and had condemned the prejudices of tribe and race as sheer ignorance; and he wanted to engage the whole structure of society which had been handed down to them from time immemorial.

In their turn, his countrymen told him that the principles of his mission were hostile to their ancestral traditions and asked him either to give them up or to bear the worst consequences.

Why did he suffer all those hardships? His nation offered to accept him as their king and to lay all the riches of the land at his feet if only he would stop preaching his religion and spreading his message. But he chose instead to refuse the tempting offers and to suffer for his cause.

Why? What had he to gain, if those people became pious and righteous?

Why was it that he cared nothing for riches and luxury, kingship and glory, and ease and plenty? Was he playing for some higher material gain so that these blessings sank into insignificance in comparison with them? Were those gains so tempting that he could elect to go through fire and Sword and bear tortures of the soul and torments of the body with equanimity for years? One has to ponder these questions deeply to find the answer.

Can anyone imagine a higher example of self-sacrifice, fellow-feeling and humanity than that a man may ruin his own happiness for the good of others, while those very people for whose betterment he is striving should stone him, abuse him, banish him and harass him even in his exile, and that, in spite of all this, he should continue striving for their well-being?

Can anyone who is insincere undergo so much suffering for a false cause? Can anyone who is dishonest exhibit such determination to stick to his guns in the face of dangers and tortures of every description when a whole country rises up in arms against him?

The faith, perseverance and resolution with which he led his movement to ultimate success is eloquent proof of the supreme truth of his cause had there been the slightest doubt and uncertainty in his heart, he could never have been able to brave the storm which continued unabated for twenty-one long years.

This is one side of the revolution wrought in his being. The other is even more wonderful and remarkable

A CHANGED MAN AT FORTY

For forty years he lived as an Arab among Arabs. During that long period he was not known as a statesman, a preacher or an orator. No-one had heard him imparting gems of wisdom and knowledge as he began to do hereafter. He was never seen discoursing on metaphysics, ethics, law, politics, economics and sociology. Let alone being a great general, he was not even known as an ordinary soldier. He had uttered no word about God, the Angels, the Revealed Books, the early Prophets, and the bygone nations, the Day of Judgement, Life after Death, Hell and Heaven.

Although he possessed an excellent character and charming manners, and was highly cultured, there was nothing so striking about him which could make men expect something great and revolutionary from him in the future. He was known among his acquaintances as a sober, calm, gentle, law-abiding citizen of good nature. But when he came out of the cave with his Message he was transformed.

When he began preaching his Message the whole of

Arabia stood in and wonder was bewitched by his wonderful eloquence and oratory. It was so impressive and pursue that his worst enemies were afraid of hearing it, lest it should penetrate deep into their hearts or the very marrow of their beings and convert them from their old religion and culture. It was so unique that the whole legion of Arab poets, preachers and orators of the highest caliber failed to match it in beauty of language and splendor of diction when he threw the challenge to his opponents to produce even a single line like the ones he was reciting.

HIS ALL-EMBRACING MESSAGE

Along with this, he now appeared before his people as a unique philosopher, a wonderful reformer, a renowned molder of culture and civilization, an illustrious politician, a great leader, a judge of the highest eminence and an incomparable general. This unlettered Bedouin, this desert dweller, spoke with learning and wisdom, the like of which none had said before and none could say after him.

He expounded the complex problems of metaphysics and theology. He delivered speeches on the decline and fall of nations and empires, supporting his thesis with historical fact. He reviewed the achievements of the old reformers, passed judgements on the various religions of the world, and gave verdicts on the differences and disputes between nations. He taught ethical canons and principles of culture. He formulated laws of social culture, economic organization, group conduct and international relations whose wisdom even eminent thinkers and scholars can grasp only after life-long research and vast experience of men and things. Their beauties, indeed, unfold themselves progressively as man advances in theoretical knowledge and practical experience.

This silent and peace-loving trade who had never even handled a Sword before turned suddenly into such a brave soldier that he was never known to retreat however fierce the battle. He became such a great general that he conquered the whole of Arabia in nine years, at a time when the weapons of war were primitive and the means of communication very poor. His military acumen and his ability to transmit the skills of war to a motley crowd of Arabs (who had no equipment worth the name) meant that within a few years he had overthrown the two most formidable military powers of the day and become the master of the greater part of the then known world.

This reserved and quiet man who, for forty years, never gave any indication of any political interest or activity, appeared suddenly on the stage of the world as such a great political reformer and statesman that, without the aid of the media, he brought together under one banner, one law, one religion, one culture, one civilization and one form of government the scattered inhabitants of a desert of twelve hundred thousand square miles - a people who were warlike, ignorant, unruly, uncultured and plunged in internecine tribal warfare.

He changed their modes of thought, their customs and their morals. He turned the uncouth into the cultured, the barbarous into the civilized, the evil-doers and bad characters into pious God-fearing and righteous persons. Their unruly and obstinate natures were transformed into models of obedience and submission to law and order. A nation which had not produced a single great man worth the name for centuries gave birth, under his influence and guidance, to thousands of noble souls who went forth to far-off corners of the world to preach and teach the principles of religion, morals and civilization.

He accomplished this feat not through any worldly lure, oppression or cruelty, but by his humanity, his moral personality and his teaching. With his noble and gentle behavior he befriended even his enemies. He captured the hearts of the people with his unbounded sympathy and the milk of human kindness. He ruled justly. He did not deviate from truth and righteousness. He did not oppress even his deadly enemies who were after his life, who had stoned him, who had turned him out of his native place, who had set the whole of Arabia against him - nay, not even those who had chewed the raw liver of his dead uncle in a frenzy of vengeance. He forgave them all when he triumphed over them. He never took revenge on anyone.

Although he became the ruler of his country, he was so selfless and modest that he remained very simple and sparing in his habits. He lived poorly, as before, in his humble mud-cottage. He slept on a mattress, wore coarse clothes, ate either the simplest food of the poor or went without food at all. He used to spend whole nights standing in prayer before his Lord. He came to the rescue of the destitute and the penniless. He felt not the least insult in working like a laborer. Till his last moments there was not the slightest tinge of royal pomp or hauteur of the high and mighty in him. Like any ordinary man he would sit and talk with people and share their joys and sorrows. He would so mingle with the crowd that a stranger would find it difficult to single out the leader of the people and the ruler of the nation from the rest of the company.

He never sought any reward or profit for himself, nor left any property to his heirs. He dedicated his all to his *Millah*. He did not ask his adherents to earmark anything for him or his descendants, so much so that he forbade his progeny to receive the benefit of poor-tax (Zakah).

HIS CONTRIBUTION TO HUMAN THOUGHT

The achievements of this great man do not end here. To arrive at a full appreciation of his worth one has to view them against the background of the history of the world as a whole. This reveals that this unlettered dweller of the desert of Arabia, who was born in the 'dark ages' some 1400 years ago, is the real pioneer of our modern age. He is not only the leader of those who accept his leadership but also of those who do not, even of those who denounce him - the only difference being that the latter are unaware that he is still imperceptibly influencing their thoughts and their actions and is the governing principle of their lives and the guiding spirit of the modern times.

It was he who turned the course of human thought from superstition-mongering, love for the unnatural and the inexplicable, and monasticism towards a rational approach, love for reality, and a pious, balanced worldly life. It was he who in a world which regarded only supernatural happenings as miracles and demanded them for the verification of the truth of a religious mission, urged that rational proof should be the criterion of truth. It was he who opened the eyes of those who had been accustomed to look for the signs of God in natural phenomena.

It was he who, in place of groundless speculation, led human beings to the path of rational understanding and sound reasoning on the basis of observation, experiment and research. It was he who clearly defined the limits and functions of sense perception, reason and intuition. It was he who brought about a rapprochement between spiritual and material values. It was he who harmonized Faith and Knowledge and Action, who, in short, evolved true religiosity on the basis of the scientific spirit.

It was he who eradicated idolatry, man-worship and polytheism in all forms so thoroughly and created such a firm faith in the Unity of God that even those religions which were based entirely on superstition and idolatry were forced to adopt a monotheistic approach.

It was he who changed the basic concepts of ethics and spirituality. Those who believed that asceticism and self-annihilation alone led to moral and spiritual purity - that purity could only be achieved by running away from life, disregarding all the desires of the flesh and subjecting the body to all types of tortures - he showed the path of spiritual evolution, moral emancipation and attainment of salvation through active participation in the affairs of the world around them.

It was he who brought home to man his true worth; those who acknowledged only a God-incarnate or a son of God as their moral preceptor or spiritual guide were told that human beings with no pretensions to Godhead could become vicegerents of God on earth; those who proclaimed and worshipped powerful personages as their gods were made to understand that their false lords were ordinary human beings and nothing more. It was he who stressed the point that no person could claim holiness, authority and over lordship as his birthright and that no-one was born with the stigma of untouchability, slavery or serfdom. It was he and his teaching which inspired thoughts of the unity of mankind, equality of human beings, true democracy and real freedom.

Laws which he gave have penetrated deep into the structures of society, and this process continues up to this day. The basic principles of economics which he taught have ushered in many a movement in world history and hold out the same promise for the future. The law of governance which he formulated brought about many upheavals in political theories and continues to have influence even today. The fundamental principles of law and justice which bear the stamp of his genius have influenced to a remarkable degree the administration of justice in the courts of nations. This unlettered Arab was the first person to formulate a frame-work of international relations and lay down laws of war and peace. No one previously had even the remotest idea that there could be an ethical code of war and that relations between different nations could be regulated on the basis of common humanity.

THE GREATEST REVOLUTIONARY

In the cavalcade of world history the sublime figure of this wonderful person towers so high above all others that they appear to be dwarfs when contrasted with him. None of them possessed a genius capable of making a deep impre-ssion on more than one or two aspects of human life. Some are brilliant theoreticians but are lacking when it comes to practical action. Some are men of action but with little knowledge. Some are renowned as statesmen only, others are masters of strategy. Others again have devoted their energies to ethical and spiritual problems but have ignored economics and politics. In short, one comes across heroes who are expert in one walk of life only.

His is the only example where all the excellences have been blended into one personality. He is a philosopher and a seer as well as a living embodiment of his own teachings. He is a great statesman as well as a military genius. He is a legislator and also a teacher of morals. He is a spiritual luminary as well as a religious guide. His vision penetrates every aspect of life. His orders and commandments cover a vast field from the regulation of international relations down to the habits of everyday life like eating, drinking and personal hygiene. On the foundations of his philosophy he established a civilization and a culture without the slightest trace of a flaw, deficiency or incompleteness. Can anyone point to another example of such a perfect and all-round personality?

Most of the famous personalities of the world are said to be the products of their environment. But his case in unique. His environment seems to have played no part in the making of his personality. At most one might accept in the light of Hegel's philosophy of history or Marx's historical materialism that the time and environment demanded the emergence of a leader who could create a nation and build an empire. But Hegelian or Marxist philosophy cannot explain how such an environment could produce a man whose mission was to teach the highest morals, to purify humanity and to wipe out prejudice and superstition, who looked beyond the artificial compartments of race and nation-state, who laid the foundations of a moral, spiritual, cultural and political superstructure for the good of the whole world, who practically, not theoretically, placed business transactions, civics, politics and international relations on moral grounds and produced such a balanced synthesis between worldly life and spiritual advancement that even to this day it is considered a masterpiece of wisdom and foresight. Can anyone honestly call such a person a product of the all-pervading darkness of Arabia?

He does not only appear to be independent of his environment. When we look at his achievements we are irresistibly drawn to the conclusion that he actually transcends the limitations of time and space. His vision breaks through all temporal and physical barriers, passes beyond centuries and millenniums and encompasses within itself the whole of human history. He is not one of those whom history has cast into oblivion, and he is not praised only because he was a good leader in his own time. He is that unique and incomparable leader of humanity who marches with time, who is modern in every age and in every era.

Those whom people style 'makers of history' are only 'creatures of history'. In fact, in the whole of the history of mankind, he is the unique example of a 'maker of history'. One may scan the lives and circumstances of the great leaders of the world who brought about revolutions and one will find that on such occasions the forces of revolution were gathering momentum for the destined upheaval, were taking their course in certain directions and were only waiting for the right moment. In harnessing these forces the revolutionary leader played the path of an actor for whom the stage and the role is set beforehand. On the other hand, the Prophet is the only person who had to genuinely create a revolution; he had to mould and produce the kind of men he wanted because the spirit of revolution and its necessary conditions were nonexistent.

He made an indelible impression on the hearts of thousands of his disciples by his forceful personality and molded them to his way of thinking. By his iron will be prepared the ground for revolution and directed events into the channels he wanted Can anyone cite another example of a maker of history of such distinction, another revolutionary of such brilliance and splendor?

THE FINAL TESTIMONY

One may wonder how, in the dark ages 1400 years ago in a benighted region of the earth like Arabia, an illiterate Arab trader and herdsman came to possess such light, such knowledge, such power, such capabilities and such finely developed moral virtues?

One may say that there is nothing peculiar about his Message, that it is that product of his own mind. If this is so, then he should have proclaimed himself God. And if he had done so at that time, the peoples of the earth who did not hesitate in calling Krishna and Buddha gods and Jesus the Son of God, and who could without compunction worship such forces of nature as fire, water and air - would have readily acknowledged him as such.

But he argued just the opposite. For he proclaimed: I am a human being like yourselves. I have not brought anything to you of my own accord. It has all been revealed to me by God. Whatever I possess belongs to Him. This message, the like of which the whole of humanity is unable to produce, is the message of God. It is not the product of my own mind. Every word of it has been sent down by Him and all glory to Him Whose Message it is. All the wonderful achievements which stand to my credit in your eyes, all the laws which I have given, all the principles which I have enunciated and taught - none of them is from me. I find myself incompetent to produce such things out of my sheer personal ability and capabilities. I look to Divine Guidance in all matters. Whatever He wills I do, what He directs I proclaim.

Hearken! What a wonderful and inspiring example of honesty, integrity, truth and honor those sentiments are! Liars and hypocrites often try to take all the credit for the deeds of others, even when they can easily be found out. But this great man does not claim any of these achievements for himself even when no-one could contradict him as they were no way of establishing the source of his inspiration.

What more proof of perfect honesty of purpose, uprightness of character and sublimity of soul can there be! Who else can be more truthful than he who received such unique gifts through a secret channel and still pointed out their source? All these factors lead to the irresistible conclusion that such a man was the true Messenger of God.

Such was our Holy Prophet Muhammad (blessings of Allah and peace be upon him). He was a prodigy of extraordinary merits, a paragon of viand goodness, a symbol of truth, a great apostle of God and His Messenger to the entire world. His life and thought, his truthfulness and straightforwardness, his piety and goodness, his character and morals, his ideology and achievements - all stand as unimpeachable proofs of his prophethood. Any human being who studies his life and teachings without bias will testify that he was the true Prophet of God and the Qur'an -the Book he gave to mankind- the true Book of God. No serious seeker after truth can come to any other conclusion.

It must also be clearly understood that now, through Muhammad (blessings of Allah and peace be upon him) alone can we know the straight path of Islam. The Qur'an and the life-example of Muhammad (blessings of Allah and peace be upon him) are the only reliable sources that are available to mankind to learn God's Will in its totality. Muhammad (blessings of Allah and peace be upon him) is the Messenger of God for the whole of mankind and the long chain of Prophets has come to an end with him. He was the last of the Prophets and all the instructions which it was God's Will to impart to mankind through direct revelation were sent by Him through Muhammad (blessings of Allah and peace be upon him) and are enshrined in the Qur'an and the Sunnah. Anyone who seeks to become a sincere Muslim must have faith in God's last Prophet, accept his teachings and follow the way he has pointed out to man. This is the road to success and salvation.

THE FINALITY OF PROPHETHOOD

This brings us to the question of the finality of the prophethood of Muhammad (blessings of Allah and peace be upon him).

We have already discussed the nature of prophethood and this discussion makes it clear that the advent of a prophet is not an everyday occurrence. Nor is the presence in person of the Prophet essential for every land, people and period. The life and teachings of the Prophet is the beacon to guide a people to the right path, and as long as his teachings and his guidance are alive he is, as it were, himself alive.

The real death of a Prophet consists not in his physical demise but in the ending of the influence of his teachings. The earlier Prophets have died because their followers have adulterated their teachings, distorted their instructions, and besmirched their life-examples by attaching fictitious events to them. Not one of the earlier books - Torah, Zabur (Psalms of David), Injil (Gospel of Jesus), for example - exists today in its original text and even the adherents of these books confess that they do not possess the original books. The life-histories of the earlier Prophets have been so mixed up with fiction that an accurate and authentic account of their lives has become impossible. Their lives have become tales and legends and no trustworthy record is available anywhere. It cannot even be said with certainty when and where a certain Prophet was born, how he lived and what code of morality he gave to mankind. Thus the real death of a Prophet consists in the death of his teachings.

By this criterion no-one can deny that Muhammad (blessings of Allah and peace be upon him) and his teachings are alive. His teachings stand uncorrupted and are incorruptible. The Qur'an -the book he gave to mankind- exists in its original text, without a word, syllable or even letter having been changed. The entire account of his life -his sayings, instructions and actions- is preserved with complete accuracy. It is as though it all happened yesterday rather than thirteen centuries ago. The biography of no other human being is as detailed as that of Muhammad, the Prophet of Islam (blessings of Allah and peace be upon him). In every thing affecting our lives we can seek the guidance of Muhammad (blessings of Allah and peace be upon him) and the example of his life. That is why there is no need of any other Prophet after Muhammad, the last Prophet (blessings of Allah and peace be upon him).

Furthermore, there are three conditions which necessi-tate the advent of a new Prophet over and above the need to replace a deceased Prophet. These may be summed up as follows:

1. That the teachings of the earlier Prophets have been distorted or corrupted or they have died and their revival is needed.
2. That the teachings of the Prophet who has passed away were incomplete and it is necessary to amend them, improve on them or add something to them.

3. That the earlier Prophet was raised for a particular nation or territory and a Prophet for another nation, people or country is required.

None of these conditions exist today. The teachings of the last Prophet Muhammad (blessings of Allah and peace be upon him) are alive, have been fully preserved and made immortal. The guidance he has shown unto mankind is complete and flawless, and is enshrined in the Holy Qur'an. All the sources of Islam are fully intact and each and every instruction or action of the Holy Prophet can be ascertained without the least shadow of doubt.

Secondly, God has completed His revealed guidance through the Prophet Muhammad (blessings of Allah and peace be upon him) and Islam is a complete religion for mankind. God has said that, "Today I have perfected your Faith -religion- for you, and have completed My bounty upon you" and a thorough study of Islam as a complete way of life proves the truth of these Qur'anic words. Islam gives guidance for life in this world and in the hereafter and nothing essential for human guidance has been left out. There is no ground for new prophethood on the plea of imperfection.

Lastly, the Message of Muhammad (blessings of Allah and peace be upon him) was not meant for any particular people, place or period. He was raised as the World Prophet - the messenger of truth for the whole of mankind. The Qur'an has commanded Muhammad (blessings of Allah and peace be upon him) to declare: "O mankind, I am God's Messenger to all of you". He has been described as "a blessing for all (the people of) the world" and his approach has been universal and human. That is why after him there remains no need for new prophethood and he has been described by the Qur'an as *Khatam-an-Nabiyyin* (the last of the chain of the true Prophets).

The only source, therefore, for the knowledge of God and His Way is Muhammad (blessings of Allah and peace be upon him). We can know of Islam only through his teachings which are so complete and so comprehensive that they can guide men through all ages to come. The world does not need a new prophet; it needs only such people as have full faith in Muhammad (blessings of Allah and peace be upon him) to become the standard-bearers of his message, propagate it throughout the world, and endeavor to establish the culture which Muhammad (blessings of Allah and peace be upon him) gave to man. The world needs such men of character as can translate his teachings into practice and establish a society which is governed by Divine Law, whose supremacy Muhammad (blessings of Allah and peace be upon him) came to establish.

2

The Articles of Faith

TAWHID: FAITH IN THE UNITY OF GOD

The most fundamental and the most important teaching of Prophet Muhammad (blessings of Allah and peace be upon him) is faith in the unity of God. This is expressed in the primary *Kalimah* of Islam as "There is no deity but Allah" (La ilaha illa allah). This beautiful phrase is the bedrock of Islam, its foundation and its essence. It is the expression of this belief which differentiates a true Muslim from a *kafir* (unbeliever), mushrik (one who associates others with God in His Divinity) or *dahriyah* (an atheist).

The acceptance or denial of this phrase produces a world of difference between man and man. The believers in it become one single community and those who do not believe in it form an opposing group. For the believers there is unhampered progress and success in this world and in the hereafter, while failure and ignominy are the ultimate lot of those who refuse to believe in it.

But the difference between the believers and the unbelievers does not result from the mere chanting of a few words. Obviously, the mere utterance of a phrase or two is not in itself important. The real difference lies in the conscious acceptance of this doctrine and complete adherence to it in practical life. Mere repetition of the word 'food' cannot dull hunger; mere chanting of a medical prescription cannot heal the disease.

In the same way, if the *Kalimah* is repeated without any understanding, it cannot work the revolution which it is meant to bring about. This can occur only if a person grasps the full meaning of the doctrine and accepts and follows it in letter and spirit. We avoid fire because we know that it burns; we keep away from poison because we know that it can kill. Similarly, if the real meanings of *Tawhid* are fully grasped, we avoid, in belief as well as in action, every form of disbelief, atheism and polytheism. This is the natural consequence of belief in the Unity of God.

Our discussion so far can be summarized as follows:

1. Islam consists of submission and obedience to Allah, the Lord of the Universe. Since the only authentic source of knowing Him and His Will and Law is the teachings of the true Prophet, we may define Islam as that religion which stands for complete faith in the teachings of the Prophet and steadfast obedience to his ways of life. Consequently, one who ignores the medium of the Prophet and claims to follow God directly is not a 'Muslim'.
2. In earlier epochs there had been separate Prophets for different nations, and the history of prophethood shows that even in one and the same nation several Prophets appeared one after the other. In that age Islam was the name of that religion which was taught to a nation by its own Prophet or Prophets. Though the nature and substance of Islam was the same in every age and country, the modes of worship, codes of law and other detailed rules and regulations of life varied according to local and particular conditions. It was not, therefore, necessary for any nation to follow another nation's Prophet and responsibility was confined to following the guidance given by its own Prophet.
3. This period of poly-prophetism came to an end with the advent of Muhammad (blessings of Allah and peace be upon him). The teachings of Islam were made complete through him; one basic law was formulated for the whole world and he was made a Prophet for all mankind. His

prophethood was not meant for any particular nation or country or period; his message was for all peoples and for all ages. The earlier codes were abrogated by the advent of Muhammad (blessings of Allah and peace be upon him) who gave the world a complete code of life. This means there will be no new Prophets and no new religious code until the Last Day. Muhammad's (blessings of Allah and peace be upon him) teachings are meant for all the children of Adam, the entire human race.

Now Islam consists in following Muhammad (blessings of Allah and peace be upon him), that is, acknowledging his prophethood, believing in all that he has asked us to believe in, following him in letter and spirit, and submitting to all his commands and injunctions, the most fundamental of which is *La ilaha illallah* "There is no deity but Allah".

This brings us to the question: What has Muhammad (blessings of Allah and peace be upon him) asked us to believe in? What are the articles of Islamic faith? We shall discuss these articles and see how simple. how true, how lovable and how valuable they are and to what high pinnacle they raise the status of Man in this world and the world to come.

THE MEANING OF THE KALIMAH

In Arabic the word ilah means 'one who is worshipped' that is, a being which on account of its greatness and power is considered worthy to be worshipped: to be bowed to in humility and submission. Anything or any being possessing power too great to be comprehended by man is also called ilah. The concept ilah also includes the possession of infinite powers and conveys the sense that others are dependent on ilah and that he is not dependent on any one else. The word ilah carries, too, a sense of concealment and mystery. The word Khuda in Persian, Deva in Hindi and God in English have similar connotations. Other languages also contain words with a similar meaning.

The word *Allah,* on the other hand, is the essential personal name of God. La ilaha illallah literally means "There is no ilah other than the One Great Being known by the name Allah."It means that in the whole of the universe, there is absolutely no being worthy to be worshipped other than Allah, that it is only to Him that heads should bow in submission and adoration, that He is the only Being posse-ssing all powers, that we are all in need of His favour, and that we are all obliged to seek His help. He is concealed from our senses, and our intellect cannot perceive what He is.

From the earliest known history of man as well as from the oldest relics of antiquity that we have been able to obtain, it appears that we have been able to obtain, it appears that in every age man recognized some deity or deities and worshipped them. Even today every nation, from the most primitive to the most advanced, believes in and worships some deity. Having a deity and worshipping him is ingrained in human nature. There is something within man's soul which forces him to do so.

But the question is: what is that thing and why does man feel impelled to do so? The answer to this question can be discovered if we look at the position of man in this huge universe. Neither man nor his nature is omnipotent. He is neither self sufficient nor self-existing; nor is his powers limitless. In fact, he is weak, frail, needy and destitute.

He is dependent on a multitude of forces to maintain his existence, but all of them are not essentially and totally within his powers. Sometimes they come into his possession in a simple and natural way, and at times he finds himself deprived of them. There are many important and valuable things which he endeavours to get, but sometimes he succeeds in getting them, while sometimes he does not, for it is not completely in his own power to obtain them. There are many things injurious to him; accidents destroy his life's work in a single moment; chance brings his hopes to a sudden end; illness, worries and calamities are always threatening him and marring his way to happiness. He attempts to get rid of them, and meets with both success and failure.

There are many things whose greatness and grandeur overawe him: mountains and rivers, gigantic animals are ferocious beasts. He experiences earthquakes, storms and other natural disasters. He observes clouds over his head and sees them becoming thick and dark, with peals of thunder, flashes of lightning and heavy rain. He sees the sun, the moon and the stars in their constant motions. He reflects how great, powerful and grand these bodies are, and, in contrast to them, how frail and insignificant he is!

These vast phenomena, on the one hand, and the consciousness his own frailty, on the other, impresses him with a deep sense of his own weakness, humbleness and helplessness. And it is quite natural that a primitive idea of divinity should coincide with this sense. He thinks of the hands which are wielding these great forces. The sense of their greatness makes him bow in humility. The sense of their powerfulness makes him seek their help. He tries to please them so that they may be beneficent to him, and he fears them and tries to escape their wrath so that he may not be destroyed by them.

In the most primitive state of ignorance, man thinks that the great objects of nature whose grandeur and glory are visible and which appear to be injurious or beneficent to him, hold in themselves the real power and authority, and, therefore, are divine. Thus he worships trees, animals, rivers, mountains, fire, rain, air, heavenly bodies and numerous other objects. This is the worst form of ignorance.

When his ignorance dissipates to some extent and some glimmers of light and knowledge appear on his intellectual horizon, he comes to know that these great and powerful objects are in themselves as helpless and dependent, or rather, they are still more dependent and helpless. The biggest and the strongest animal dies like a tiny germ, and loses all his power, great rivers rise and fall and become dry; the highest mountains are blasted and shattered by man himself; the productiveness of the earth is not under the earth's control - water makes it prosperous and lack of water makes it barren. Even water is not independent. It depends on air which brings the clouds. Air, too, is powerless and its usefulness depends on other causes. The moon, the sun, and the stars are also bound by a powerful law outside whose dictates they cannot make the slightest movement.

After these considerations, man's mind turns to the possibility of some great mysterious power of divine nature which controls the objects he sees and which may be the repository of all authority. These reflections give rise to belief in mysterious powers behind natural phenomena, with innumerable gods governing various parts and aspects of nature such as air, light and water. Material forms or symbols are constructed to represent them and man begins to worship these forms and symbols. This, too, is a form of ignorance, and reality remains hidden to the human eye even at this stage of man's intellectual and cultural pilgrimage.

As man progresses still further in knowledge and learning, and as he reflects more and more deeply on the fundamental problems of existence, he finds an all-powerful law and all-encompassing control in the universe. What a complete regularity is observed in sunrise and sunset, in winds and rains, in the motions of stars and the changes of seasons! With what a wonderful harmony countless different forces are working jointly. And what a highly effective and supremely wise law it is according to which all the various causes in the universe are made to work together at an appointed time to produce an appointed event! Observing this uniformity, regularity and complete obedience to one great law in all fields of Nature, even a polytheist finds himself obliged to believe that there must be a deity greater than all the others, exercising supreme authority. For, if there were separate, independent deities, the whole machinery of the universe would be upset.

He calls this greatest deity by different names, such as *Allah, Permeshwar, God, Khuda-i-Khuda'igan*. But as the darkness of ignorance still persists, he continues worshipping minor deities along with the Supreme One. He imagines that the Divine Kingdom of God may not be different from earthly kingdoms. Just as a ruler has many ministers, trusted associates, governors, and other responsible officers, so the minor deities are like so many responsible officers under the Great God Who cannot be approached without winning the favour of the officers under Him. So they must also be worshipped and appealed to for help, and should in no case be offended. They are taken as agents through whom an approach can be made to the Great God.

The more a man increases his knowledge, the greater becomes his dissatisfaction with the multiplicity of deities. So the number of minor deities begins to decrease. More enlightened men bring each one of them under the searchlight of scrutiny and ultimately find that none of these man-made deities has any divine character; they themselves are creatures like man, though rather more helpless. They are thus eliminated one by one until only one God remains.

But the concept of one God still contains some remnants of the elements of ignorance. Some people imagine that He has a body as men have, and is in a particular place. Some believe that God came down to earth in human form; others think that God, after settling the affairs of the universe, retired and is now resting. Some believe that it is necessary to approach God through the media of saints and spirits, and that nothing can be achieved without their intercession. Some imagine God to have a certain form or image, and they believe it necessary to keep that image before them for the purposes of worship.

Such distorted notions of godhead have persisted and lingered, and many of them are prevalent among different people even today.

Tawhid is the highest conception of godhead, the knowledge of which God has sent mankind in all ages through His Prophets. It was this knowledge with which, in the beginning, Adam was sent down to earth; it was the same knowledge that was revealed to Noah, Abraham, Moses and Jesus (God's blessings be upon them all). It was this knowledge which Muhammad (blessings of Allah and peace be upon him) brought to mankind. It is Knowledge, pure and absolute, without the least shade of ignorance. Man became guilty of shirk, idol-worship and *kufr* only because he turned away from the teachings of the Prophets and depended on his own faulty reasoning, false perceptions or biased interpretations. Tawhid dispels all the clouds of ignorance and illuminates the horizon with the light of reality.

Let us see what significant realities the concept of *Tawhid* - this little phrase: *la ilaha illallah* embraces: what truth it conveys and what beliefs it fosters.

First, we are faced with the question of the universe. We are face to face with a grand, limitless universe. Man's mind cannot discern its beginning or visualize its end. It has been moving along its chartered course from time immemorial and is continuing its journey in the vast vista of the future. Creatures beyond number have appeared in it - and go on appearing every day. It is so bewildering that a thinking mind finds itself wonder-struck. Man is unable to understand and grasp its reality by his unaided vision. He cannot believe that all this has appeared just by chance or accident. The universe is not a fortuitous mass of matter. It is not a jumble of uncoordinated objects. It is not a conglomeration of chaotic and meaningless things. All this cannot be without a Creator, a Designer, a Controller, a Governor.

But who can create and control this majestic universe? Only He can do so Who is Master of all; Who is Infinite and Eternal; Who is All-Powerful, All-Wise, Omnipotent and Omniscient; Who is All-Knowing and All-Seeing. He must have supreme authority over all that exists in the universe. He must possess limitless powers, must be Lord of the universe and all that it contains, must be free from every flaw and weakness and none may have the power to interfere with His work. Only such a Being can be the Creator, the Controller and the Governor of the universe.

Second, it is essential that all these divine attributes and powers must be vested in One Being: it is impossible for two or more personalities having equal powers and attributes to co-exist. They are bound to collide. Therefore, there must be one and only one Supreme Being having control over all others. You cannot think of two governors for the same province or two supreme commanders of the army! Similarly, the distribution of these powers among different deities, so that, for instance, one them is all-knowledge, the other all-grand still another life-giver -and each having an independent domain- is also unthinkable. The universe is an indivisible whole and each one of such deities will be dependent upon others in the execution of his task. Lack of co-ordination is bound to occur. And if this happened the world would fall to pieces. These attributes are also untransferable. It is not possible that a certain attribute might be present in a certain deity at one time and at another time be found in another deity. A divine being who is incapable of remaining alive himself cannot give life to others. The one who cannot protect his own divine power cannot be suited to govern the vast limitless universe.

The more you reflect on the problem, the firmer must your conviction be that all these divine powers and attributes must exist in one and the same Being alone. Thus, polytheism is a form of ignorance that cannot stand rational scrutiny. It is a practical impossibility. The facts of life and nature do not fit in with it. They automatically bring men to Reality that is *Tawhid*, the Unity of God.

Now, keeping in mind this concept of God, look closely at this vast universe. Exert yourself to the utmost and say if you find among all the objects that you see, among all the things that you perceive, among all that you can think, feel or imagine -all that your knowledge can comprehend- anyone possessing these attributes. The sun, the moon, the stars, animals, birds or fishes, matter, money, any man or a group of men - does any of them possess these attributes? Most certainly not! For everything in the universe is created, controlled and regulated, is dependent on others, is mortal and transitory; its slightest movements are controlled by an inexorable law from which there can be no deviation. Their helpless condition proves that the attire of divinity cannot fit their body. They do not possess the slightest trace of divinity and have absolutely nothing to do with it. It is a travesty of truth and a folly of the highest magnitude to attribute divine status to them.

This is the meaning of *La ilaha,* (i.e. there is no god) no human and material object possesses the divine power and authority deserving worship and obedience.

But this is not the end of our quest. We have found that divinity is not vested in any material or human element of the universe, and that none of them possesses even the slightest trace of it. This leads us to the conclusion that there is a Supreme Being, over and above all that our eyes see in the universe, Who possesses Divine attributes, Who is the Will behind all phenomena, the Creator of this grand universe, the Controller of its superb Law, the Governor of its serene rhythm, the Administrator of all its workings: He is Allah, the Lord of the Universe and no one and nothing is associated in His Divinity. This is what *illallah* (but Allah) means.

This knowledge is superior to all other kinds of knowledge and the greater you exert yourself; the deeper will be your conviction that this is the starting point of all knowledge. In every field of inquiry - be it that of physics, chemistry, astronomy, geology, biology, zoology, economics, politics, sociology or the humanities, you will find that the deeper you probe, the clearer become the indications of the truth of *La ilaha illallah.* It is this concept which opens up the doors of inquiry and investigation and illumines the pathways of knowledge with the light of reality. And if you deny or disregard this reality, you will find that at every step you meet disillusionment, for the denial of this primary truth robs everything in the universe of its meaning and significance.

EFFECTS OF TAWHID ON HUMAN LIFE

Now let us study the effects which the belief in *La ilaha illallah* has on the life of a man and see why he should always make a success of life and why one who denies it becomes a failure in life, both here and in the hereafter.

1. A believer in this *Kalimah* can never be narrow in outlook. He believes in a god Who is the Creator of the heavens and the earth, the Master of the East and the West and Sustainer of the entire universe. After this belief he does not regard anything in the world as a stranger to himself. He looks on everything in the universe as belonging to the same Lord he himself belongs to. His sympathy, love and service are not confined to any particular sphere or group. His vision is enlarged, his intellectual horizon widens, and his outlook becomes as

liberal and as boundless as is the Kingdom of God. How can this width of vision and breadth of mind be achieved by an atheist, a polytheist or one who believes in a deity supposed to possess limited and defective powers like a man?

2. This belief produces in man the highest degree of self-respect and self-esteem. The believer knows that Allah alone is the Possessor of all power, and that none besides Him can benefit or harm a person, or provide for his needs, or give and take away life or wield authority or influence. This conviction makes him indifferent to, and independent and fearless of, all powers other than those of God. He never bows his head in homage to any of God's creatures, nor does he stretch out his hand before anyone else. He is not overawed by anybody's greatness. This attitude of mind cannot be produced by any other belief. For it is necessary that those who associate other beings with God, or who deny God, should bow in homage to some creatures, regard them able to benefit or harm them, fear them and place their hopes in them.
3. Along with self-respect this belief also generates in man a sense of modesty and humbleness. It makes him unostentatious and unpretending. A believer never becomes proud, haughty or arrogant. The boisterous pride of power, wealth and worth can have no room in his heart, because he knows that whatever he possesses has been given to him by God, and that God can take away just as He can give. In contrast to this, an unbeliever, when he achieves some worldly merit, becomes proud and conceited because he believes that his merit is due to his own worth. In the same way pride and self-conceit are a necessary outcome and concomitant of *shirk* (association of others with God in His divinity), because a *mushrik* believes that he has a particular relation with the deities which does not exist between them and other people.

4. This belief makes man virtuous and upright. He has the conviction that there is no other means of success and salvation for him except purity of soul and righteousness of behavior. He has perfect faith in God Who is above all needed, is related to none and is absolutely just. This belief creates in him the consciousness that, unless he lives rightly and acts justly, he cannot succeed. No influence or underhand activity can save him from ruin. As against this, the *kafirs* and the *mushriks* always live on false hopes. Some of them believe that God's son has atoned for their sins; some think that they are God's favorites, and will not be punished; others believe that their saints will intercede with God on their behalf; while others make offerings to their deities and believe that by so bribing the deities they acquire a license to do whatever they like. Such false beliefs keep them enmeshed in sin and evil deeds; depending on their deities, they do not bother about their souls and living pure and good lives. As to atheists, they do not believe that there is any Being having power over them, to whom they should be responsible for their good or bad actions; therefore they consider themselves independent to act in whatever way they like. Their own fancies become their gods and they live like slaves of their wishes and desires.
5. The believer never becomes despondent. He has a firm faith in God who is Master of all the treasures of the earth and the heavens, whose grace and bounty have no limit and whose powers are infinite. This faith imparts to his heart extraordinary consolation, fills it with satisfaction and keeps it filled with hope. Although he may meet with rejection from all sides in this world, faith in and dependence on God never let him, and on their strength he goes on struggling. Such profound confidence can result from no other belief than belief in one God. *Mushriks, kafirs* and atheists have small hearts; they depend on limited powers; therefore in times of

trouble they are soon overwhelmed by despair and, frequently, they commit suicide.

6. This belief produces in man a very strong degree of determination, patient perseverance and trust in God. When he makes up his mind and devotes his resources to fulfillling the Divine Commands in order to secure God's pleasure, he is sure that he has the support and backing of the Lord of the universe. This certainty makes him firm and strong like a mountain and no amount of difficulties, impediments and opposition can make him give up his resolution. *Shirk; kufr* and atheism have no such effect.
7. This declaration inspires bravery in man. There are two things which make a man cowardly: (i) fear of death and love of safety, and (ii) the idea that there is someone else besides God who can take away life and that man, by adopting certain devices, can ward off death. Belief in *La ilaha illallah* purges the mind of both these ideas. The first idea goes out of his mind because he knows that his life and his property and everything else really belong to God, and he becomes ready to sacrifice his all for His pleasure. He gets rid of the second idea because he knows that no weapon, no man or animal has the power of taking away his life; God alone has the power to do so. A time has been ordained for him, and all the forces of the world combined cannot take away anyone's life before that time. It is for this reason that no one is braver than the one tempest of adversity and the migh-tiest of armies. Where can the *mushriks, the kafirs* and the atheists get such great determination, force and power from? They hold life the dearest thing in the world; they believe that death is brought about by the enemy and can be warded off by running away from him!
8. The belief in *La ilaha illallah* creates an attitude of peace and contentment, purges the mind of jealousy, envy and greed and keeps away the temptations of resorting to

base and unfair means for achieving success. The believer understands that wealth is in God's hands, and He apportions it out as He likes; that honor, power, reputation and authority -everything- is subjected to His will, and He bestows them as He will; and that man's duty is only to endeavor and to struggle fairly. He knows that success and failure depend on God's grace; if He wills to give, no power in the world can prevent Him from so doing; and if He does not will it, no power can force Him to. On the other hand, the *mushriks, the kafirs* and the atheists consider success and failure as dependent on their own efforts and the help or opposition of earthly powers. Therefore, they always remain slaves to cupidity and envy. They never hesitate to turn to bribery, flattery, conspiracy and other kinds of base and unfair means to achieve their ends. Jealousy and envy of others' success eat them away, and they will stop at nothing to bring about the downfall of a successful rival.

9. The most important effect of *La ilaha illallah* is that it makes man obey and observe God's Law. One who has belief in it is sure that God knows everything hidden or open and is nearer to him than his own jugular vein. if he commits a sin in a secluded corner and in the darkness of night, He knows it He even knows our thoughts and intentions, bad or good. We can hide from everyone, but we cannot hide anything from God; we can evade everyone, but it is impossible to evade God's grip. The firmer a man's belief in this respect, the more observant will he be of God's commands; he will shun what God has forbidden and he will carry out His best even in solitude and in darkness, because he knows that God's 'police' never leaves him alone, and he dreads the Court whose warrant he can never avoid. It is for this reason that the first and the most important conditions for being a Muslim is to have faith in *La ilaha illallah*. 'Muslim', as you have already been told, means one 'obedient to God'

and obedience to God is impossible unless one firmly believes in *La ilaha iilallah.*

In the teachings of Muhammad (blessings of Allah and peace be upon him) faith in One God is the most important and fundamental principle. It is the bedrock of Islam and the mainspring of its power. All other beliefs, commands and laws of Islam stand firm on this foundation. All of them receive strength from this source. Take it away, and there is nothing left of Islam.

BELIEF IN GOD'S ANGELS

The Prophet Muhammad (blessings of Allah and peace be upon him) has further instructed us to have faith in the existence of God's angels. This is the second article of Islamic faith and is very important; because it absolves the concept of *Tawhid* from all impurities and frees it from the danger of every conceivable shadow of *shirk* (polytheism). The polytheists have associated two kind of creatures with God:

1. Those which have material existence and are perceptible to the human eye, such as the sun, moon, stars, fire, water, animals, great men.
2. Those who have no material existence and are not perceptible to the human eye: the unseen beings who are believed to be engaged in the administration of the universe; for instance, one controls the air, another imparts light, another brings rains, and so on and so forth.

The alleged deities of the first kind have material existence and are before man's eye. The falsity of their claim has been fully exposed by the *Kalimah - La ilaha illallah.* This is sufficient to dispose of the idea that they enjoy any share in divinity or deserve any reverence at all. The second kind of things, being immaterial, are hidden from the human eye and are mysterious; the polytheists are more inclined to pin their faith in them. They consider them to be deities, gods and God's children. They make their images and render offerings to them. In order to purify belief in the Unity of God, and to clear it from the admixture of this second kind of unseen creatures, this particular article of faith has been expounded.

Muhammad (blessings of Allah and peace be upon him) has informed us that these imperceptible spiritual beings, whom people believe to be deities of gods or God's children, are really His angels. They have no share in God's divinity; they cannot deviate from His commands even by the slightest fraction of an inch. God employs them to administer His Kingdom, and they carry out His orders exactly and accurately. They have no authority to do anything of their own accord; they cannot present to God any scheme conceived by themselves, they are not even authorized to intercede with God for any man.

To worship them and to solicit their help is degrading and debasing for man. For, on the very first day of man's creation, God had made them prostrate themselves before Adam, granted to him greater knowledge than they possessed and bestowed on Adam His own vicegerency on this earth in preference to them. What debasement can, therefore, be greater for man than prostrating himself before those who had prostrated themselves before him!

Muhammad (blessings of Allah and peace be upon him) forbade us to worship angels, and to associate them with God in His divinity. He also informed us that they were the chosen creatures of God, free from sin, from their very nature unable to disobey God, and ever engaged in carrying out His orders. Moreover, he informed us that these angels of God surround us from all sides, are attached to us, and are always in our company. They observe and note all our actions, good or bad. They preserve a complete record of every man's life. After death, when we shall be brought before God, they will present a full report of our life's-work on earth, wherein we shall find everything correctly recorded, not a single movement left out, however insigni-ficant and however carefully concealed it may be.

We have not been informed of the intrinsic nature of the angels. Only some of their virtues or attributes have been mentioned to us, and we have been asked to in their existence.

We have no other means of knowing their nature, their attributes and their qualities. It would therefore, be sheer folly on our part to attribute any form or quality to them of our own accord. We must believe in them exactly as we have been asked to do. To deny their existence is *kufr* for, first, we have no reason for such a denial, and, second, our denial of them would be tantamount to attributing untruth to Muh-ammad (blessings of Allah and peace be upon him). We believe in their existence only because God's true Messenger has informed us of it.

FAITH IN THE BOOKS OF GOD

The third article of faith which Muhammad (blessings of Allah and peace be upon him) has commanded us to believe is faith in the Books of God; Books which He has sent down to mankind through His Prophets.

God had revealed His Books to His Prophets before Muhammad (blessings of Allah and peace be upon him) and these books were sent down in the same way as He sent down the Qur'an to Muhammad (blessings of Allah and peace be upon him). We have been informed of the names of some of these books: Books of Abraham, the Torah of Moses, *Zabur* (Psalms) of David, and the *Injil* (Gospel) of Jesus Christ. We have not been informed of the names of Books which were given to other Prophets. Therefore with regard to other existing religious books, we are not in a position to say with certainty whether they were originally revealed books or not. But we tacitly believe that whatever Books were sent down by God is all true.

Of the Books we have been told, the Books of Abraham are extinct and not traceable in existing world literature. David's *Zabur*, the Torah and the *Injil* exist with the Jews and the Christians, but the Qur'an informs us that people have changed and added to these books, and God's words have been mixed up with texts of their own making. This corruption and pollution of the Books has been so large and so evident that even the Jews and the Christians themselves admit that they do not possess their original texts, and have only their translations, which have been altered over many centuries and are still being changed. On studying these Books we find many passages and accounts which evidently cannot be from God. God's words and those of man are mixed together in these books, and we have no means of knowing which portions are from God and which from man.

We have been commanded to believe in previously revealed Books only in the sense of admitting that, before the Qur'an, God had also sent down books through His Prophets, that they were all from one and the same God, the same God Who sent the Qur'an and that the sending of the Qur'an as a Divine Book is not a new and strange event, but only confirms, restates and completes those divine instructions which people had mutilated or lost in antiquity.

The Qur'an is the last of the Divine Books sent down by God and there are some very pertinent differences between it and the previous Books. These differences may briefly be stated as follows:

1. The original texts of most of the former Divine Books were lost altogether, and only their translations exist today. The Qur'an, on the other hand, exists exactly as it was revealed to the Prophet; not a word -nay, not a syllable of it- has been changed. It is available in its original text and the Word of God has been preserved for all time.
2. In the former Divine Books man mixed his words with God's, but in the Qur'an we find only the words of God – and in their pristine purity. This is admitted even by the opponents of Islam.
3. In respect of no other sacred Book possessed by different peoples can it be said on the basis of authentic historical evidence that it really belongs to the same Prophet to whom it is attributed. In the case of some of them it is not even known in what age and to which Prophet they were revealed. As for the Qur'an, the evidence that it was revealed to Muhammad (blessings of Allah and

peace be upon him) is so voluminous, so convincing, so strong and so compelling that even the fiercest critics of Islam cannot cast doubt on it. This evidence is so detailed that even the occasion and place of the revelation of many verses and injunctions of the Qur'an can be known with certainty.

4. The former Divine Books were sent down in languages which died long ago. No nation or community now speaks those languages and there are only a few people who claim to understand them. Thus, even if the Books existed today in their original and unadulterated form, it would be virtually impossible in our age to correctly understand and interpret their injunctions and put them into practice in their required form. The language of the Qur'an, on the other hand, is a living language; millions of people speak it, and millions more know and understand it. It is being taught and learnt in nearly every university of the world; every man can learn it, and he who has no time to learn it can find men everywhere who know this language and can explain to him the meaning of the Qur'an.
5. Each one of the existing sacred Books found among different nations of the world has been addressed to a particular people. Each one contains a number of commands which seem to have been meant for a particular period of history and which meet the needs of that age only. They are neither needed today, nor can they now be smoothly and properly put into practice. It is evident from this that these Books were particularly meant for that particular people and not for the world. Furthermore, they were not sent to be followed permanently by even the people they were intended for; they were meant to be acted upon only for a certain period. In contrast to this the Qur'an is addressed to all mankind; not a single injunction of it can be suspected as having been addressed to a particular people. In the same manner, all the commands and injunctions in the Qur'an

can be acted upon at any place and in any age. This proves that the Qur'an is meant for the whole world, and is an eternal code for human life.

6. There is no denying the fact that the previous divine Books also enshrined good and virtue; they also taught the principles of morality and truthfulness and presented the mode of living which was to God's pleasure. But none of them was comprehensive enough to embrace all that is necessary for a virtuous human life. Some of them excelled in one respect, others in some other. It is the Qur'an and the Qur'an alone which enshrined not only all that was good in the former Books but also perfects the way of Allah and presents it in its entirety and outlines that code of life which comprehends all that is necessary for man on this earth.
7. On account of man's interpolations, many things have been inserted in those Books which are against reality, revolting to reason and an affront to every instinct of justice. There are things which are cruel and unjust, and vitiate man's beliefs and actions. Furthermore, things have unfortunately been inserted that are obscene, indecent and highly immoral. The Qur'an is free of all such rubbish. It contains nothing against reason, and nothing that can be proved wrong. None of its injunctions is unjust; nothing in it is misleading. Of indecency and immorality not a trace can be found. From the beginning to the end the Book is full of wisdom and truth. It contains the best of philosophy and the choicest of law for human civilization. It points out the right path and guides man to success and salvation.

It is on account of these special features of the Qur'an that all the peoples of the world have been directed to have faith in it, to give up all other Books and to follow it alone.

The study of the difference between the Qur'an and other divine Books makes one easily understand that the nature of faith in the Qur'an and of belief in the former Books are not similar.

Faith in the earlier divine Books should be limited to the confirmation that they were all from God, were true and were sent down to fulfilll, in their time, the same purpose for which the Qur'an has been sent. On the other hand, belief in the Qur'an should be of the nature that it is purely and God's own words, that it is perfectly true, that every word of it is preserved, that everything therein is right, that it is the bounden duty of man to carry out in his life and every command of it and that whatever be against it must be rejected.

3

Faith in God's Prophets

God's Messengers had been raised among every people, and that they all brought essentially that same religion -Islam- which the Prophet Muhammad (blessings of Allah and peace be upon him) propagated. In this respect all the Messengers of God stand on a par with each other. If a man belies any one of them, he, as it were, belies all, and if a man affirms and believes in one of them, he must and ought to affirm all. The reason is simple. Suppose ten men make one and the same statement; if you admit one of them to be true, you *ipso facto* admit the remaining nine as true, and if you belie any one of them, by implication you belie all of them. It is for this reason that in Islam it is necessary to have implicit faith in all the Prophets of God. One who does not believe in a particular Prophet would be a *Kafir*, though he may profess faith in all the other Prophets.

Tradition has it that the total number of Prophets sent to different peoples at different times is 124,000. If you consider the life of the world since it was first inhabited and the number of different peoples and nations that have been on it, this number will not appear too great. We have to positively believe in those of the Prophets whose names have been mentioned in the Qur'an. Regarding the rest, we are instructed to believe that all the Prophets sent by God for the guidance of mankind were true.

Thus we believe in all the Prophets raised in India, China, Persia, Egypt, Africa, Europe and other countries of the world, but we are not in a position to be definite about a particular person outside the list of Prophets named in the Qur'an, whether or not he was a Prophet, for we have not been told anything definite about him. Nor are we permitted to say anything against the holy men of other religions. It is quite possible that some of them might have been God's Prophets, and their followers corrupted their teachings after their demise, just as the followers of Moses and Jesus (peace be upon them) have done. Therefore, whenever we express any opinion about them, it should be about the tenets and rituals of their religions; as for the founders of those religions, we will remain scrupulously silent, lest we should become guilty of irreverence towards a Prophet.

All the Prophets of God have been deputed by Him to teach the same straight path of 'Islam'. In this sense there is no difference between Muhammad and other Prophets (blessings of Allah and peace be upon them all), and we have been ordered to believe in all of them alike. But in spite of this equality, there are the following three differences between them:

1. The Prophets of the past came to certain people for certain periods of time, while Muhammad (blessings of Allah and peace be upon him) has been sent for the whole world and for all time to come.
2. The teachings of those Prophets have either disappeared altogether from the world, or whatever of them remains is intermingled with many erroneous and fictitious statements. For this reason, even if anyone wishes to follow their teachings, he cannot do so. In contrast to this, the teachings of Muhammad (blessings of Allah and peace be upon him), his biography, his discourses, his way of living, his morals, habits and virtues, in short, all the details of his life and work, are preserved. Muhammad (blessings of Allah and peace be upon him), therefore, is the only one of the whole line of Prophets who is a living personality, and in whose footsteps it is possible to follow correctly and confidently.

3. The guidance imparted through the Prophets of the past was not complete. Every Prophet was followed by another who effected alterations and additions in the teachings and injunctions of his predecessors and, in this way, the chain of reform and progress continued. That is why the teachings of the earlier Prophets, after the lapse of time, were lost in oblivion. Obviously there was no need to preserve earlier teachings when amended and improved guidance had taken their place. At last the most perfect code of guidance was imparted to mankind through Muhammad (blessings of Allah and peace be upon him) and all previous codes were automatically abrogated, for it is futile and imprudent to follow an incomplete code when the complete code exists. He who follows Muhammad (blessings of Allah and peace be upon him) follows all the Prophets, for whatever was good and eternally workable in their teachings has been embodied in his teachings. Whoever, therefore, rejects and refuses to follow Muhammad's (blessings of Allah and peace be upon him) teachings, and chooses to follow some other Prophet, only deprives himself of that vast amount of useful and valuable instruction and guidance which is embodied in Muha-mmad's (blessings of Allah and peace be upon him) teachings, which never existed in the books of the earlier Prophets and which was revealed only through the Last of the Prophets.

This is why it is incumbent on each and every human being to have faith in Muhammad (blessings of Allah and peace be upon him) and follow him alone. To become a true Muslim (a follower of the Prophet's way of life) it is necessary to have complete faith in Muhammad (blessings of Allah and peace be upon him) and to affirm that:

a. He is a true Prophet of God;
b. His teachings are absolutely perfect, free from any defect or error; and
c. He is the Last Prophet of God. After him no Prophet will appear among any people till the Day of Judgement,

nor is any such personage going to appear in whom it would be essential for a Muslim to believe.

BELIEF IN LIFE AFTER DEATH

The fifth article of Islamic Faith is belief in life after death. The Prophet Muhammad (blessings of Allah and peace be upon him) has directed us to believe in resurrection after death and in the Day of Judgement. The essential ingredients of this belief, as taught to us by him, are as follows:

That the life of this world and of all that is in it will come to an end on an appointed day. Everything will be annihilated. That day is called *Qiyamah,* i.e. the Last Day.

That all the human beings who have lived in the world since its inception will then be restored to life and will be presented before God Who will sit in judgement on that day. This is called *Hashr* (Resurrection).

The entire record of every man and woman -of all their doings and misdoing- will be presented before God for final judgement.

That one who excels in goodness will be rewarded; one whose evils and wrongs outweigh his good deeds will be punished.

That those who emerge successful in this judgement will go to Paradise and the doors of eternal bliss will be opened to them; those who are condemned and deserve punishment will be sent to Hell - the abode of fire and torture.

THE NEED OF THIS BELIEF

Belief in life after death has always been an integral part of the teachings of the Prophets. Every Prophet asked his followers to believe in it, in the same way as the last of the Prophets Muhammad (blessings of Allah and peace be upon him), has asked us to do. This has always been an essential condition of being a Muslim. All Prophets have categorically declared that one who does not believe in it, or casts doubts on it, is a *Kafir.* This is so because denial of life after death makes all other beliefs meaningless. This denial also destroys the very sanction for a good life and man is driven to a life of ignorance and disbelief. A little reflection makes this quite clear.

In your everyday life, whenever you are asked to do anything, you immediately think: what is the use of doing it and what harm is involved in not doing it? This is in the very nature of man. He instinctively regards a useless action as totally unnecessary. You will never be willing to waste your time and energy in useless and unproductive jobs. Similarly, you will not be very to avoid a thing that is harmless. And the general rule is that the deeper your conviction about the utility of a thing, the fiwill be your response to it; and the more doubtful you are about its efficacy, the more wavering will be your attitude. After all, why does a child put his hand into fire? Because he is not sure that fire burns. Why does he evade study? Because he does not fully grasp the importance and benefits of education and does not believe in what his elders try to impress on his mind.

Now think of the man who does not believe in the Day of Judgement. Will he not consider belief in God and a life in accordance with His code of no consequence? What value will he attach to a life in pursuit of His pleasure? To him either obedience to God is of any advantage, or disobedience to Him of any harm. How, then, can it be possible for him to scrupulously follow the injunctions of God, His Prophet, and His Book? What incentive will there be for him to undergo trials and sacrifices and to avoid worldly pleasures? And if a man does not follow the code of God and lives according to his own likes and dislikes, of what use is his belief in the existence of God, if indeed he has any such belief?

That is not all. If you reflect still deeper, you will come to the conclusion that belief in life after death is the most decisive factor in the life of a man. Its acceptance or rejection determines the very course of his life and behavior.

A man who has in view success or failure in this world alone will be concerned with immediate benefits and ills. He will not be prepared to undertake any good act if he has no hope of gaining thereby some worldly interest, nor will he be keen to avoid any wrong act if it is not injurious to his interests in this world.

But a man who believes in the next world as well and is convinced of the final consequences of his acts will look on all worldly gains and losses as temporary and transitory and will not put his eternal bliss at stake for a passing gain. He will look on things in their wider perspective and always keep the permanent benefit or harm in view. He will do the good, however costly it may be to him in terms of worldly gains, or however injurious it may be to his immediate interests; and he will avoid the wrong, however tempting it may look. He will judge things from the viewpoint of their eternal consequences and not according to his whims and caprices.

Thus there is a radical difference between the beliefs, approaches and lives of the two persons. One's idea of a good act is limited to whether in this brief temporary life it will bring gain in the shape of money, property, public applause and similar other things which give him position, powers, reputation and worldly happiness. Such things become his objectives in life. Fulfillment of his own wishes and self- aggrandizement become the be-all and end-all of his life. And he does not draw beck even from cruel and unjust means to achieve his ends. Similarly, his conception of a wrong act is one which may involve a risk or injury to his interests in this world such as loss of property and life, harming of health, blackening of reputation or some other unpleasant consequence.

In contrast to this man, the believer's concept of good and evil will be quite different. To him all that pleases God is good and all that invokes His displeasure and wrath is evil. A good act, according to him, will remain good even if it brings no benefit to him in this world, or even entails loss of some worldly possession or injury to his personal interests. He will be confident that God will reward him in the eternal life and will be the real success. Similarly, he will not fall prey to evil deeds merely for some worldly gain, for he knows that even if he escapes punishment in his short worldly life, in the end he will be the loser because he will not be able to escape punishment from the court of God. He does not believe in the relativity of morals but sticks to the absolute standards revealed by God and lives according to them irrespective of gain or injury in this world.

Thus it is the belief or disbelief in life after death which makes man adopt different courses in life. For one who does not believe in the Day of Judgement it is absolutely impossible to fashion his life as suggested by Islam.

Islam says "In the way of God give charity (*zakah*) to the poor." His answer is: "No, *zakah* will lessen my wealth; I will, instead, take interest on my money." And in its collection he will not hesitate to take everything belonging to the debtors however poor or hungry they may be. Islam says: "Always speak the truth and shun lying, though you may gain ever so much by lying and lose ever so much by speaking the truth." But his reply will he "Well, what shall I do with a truth which is of no use to me here, and which instead brings loss to me; and why should I avoid lying where it can bring benefit to me without any risk, even that of a bad name?" He visits a lonely place and finds a precious metal lying there; in such a situation Islam says. "This is not your property, do not take it," but he would say: "This is a thing I have come by without any cost or trouble; why should I not have it? There is no one to see me pick this up, no one who might report it to the police or give evidence against me in a court of law, or give me a bad name among the people. Why should I not make use of this valuable?" Someone secretly keeps a deposit with this man, and eventually he dies. Islam says: "Be honest with the property deposited with you and give it over to the heirs of the deceased." He says: "Why? There is no evidence of his property being with me; his children also have no knowledge of it. When I can appropriate it without any difficulty, without any fear of legal claim, or stain on my reputation, why should I not do so?"

In short, at every step in life, Islam will direct him to walk in a certain direction and adopt a certain attitude and course of behavior; but he will go in the opposite direction. For Islam measures and values everything from the viewpoint of its eternal consequence; while such a person always has in view only the immediate and earthly outcome. Now, you can understand why a man cannot be a Muslim without belief in the Day of Judgement. To be a Muslim is a very great thing; the fact is that one cannot even become a good man without this belief, for the denial of the Day of Judgement degrades man from humanity to a place even lower than that of the lowest of animals.

LIFE AFTER DEATH: A RATIONAL VINDICATION

So far we have discussed the need and importance of belief in the Day of Judgement. Now let us consider how far the constituents of the belief are rationally understandable. The fact is that whatever Muhammad (blessings of Allah and peace be upon him) has told us about life after death is clearly borne out by reason. Although our belief in that Day is based on our implicit trust in the Messenger of God, rational reflection not only confirms this belief but also reveals that Muhammad's (blessings of Allah and peace be upon him) teachings in this respect are much more reasonable and understandable than any other viewpoint about life after death.

The following viewpoints are found about life after death:

1. Some people say that there is nothing left of man after death, and that after this life-ending event there is no other life. According to these people, belief in life after death has no reality. They say it is scientifically impossible. This is the view of the atheists who also claim to be scientific in their approach and bring in Western science to support their arguments.
2. Other people maintain that man, in order to bear the consequences of his deeds, is repeatedly regenerated in this world. If he lives a bad life, he will assume in the next generation the shape of some animal, such as a dog or a cat, or some tree or some lower kind of man. If his acts have been good, he will be reborn as a man into a higher class. This viewpoint is found in some eastern religions.

3. There is a third viewpoint which calls for belief in the Day of Judgement, Resurrection, man's presence in the Divine Court, and the meting out of reward and punishment. This is the common belief of all the Prophets.

Now let us consider these viewpoints one by one.

The first group, which arrogates to itself the authority and support of science, alleges that there is no life after death. They say that they have never seen anybody coming back from the dead. After death a man is reduced to dust; therefore, death is the end of life and there is no life after death. But consider this reasoning: is this really a scientific argument? Is the claim really founded on reason? If they have not seen a single case of revival after death, they can only say that *they do not know what will happen after death*. But, instead of remaining within this limit, they declare that *nothing will happen after death*, at the same time alleging that they speak out of knowledge! In fact they merely generalize on igno-rance. Science tells us nothing -negative or positive- in this respect and their assertion that life after death has no existence is totally unfounded. Their claim is not dissimilar to the claim of an ignoramus who has not seen an airplane and on that 'Knowledge' proclaims that airplanes do not exist at all! Because somebody has not seen a thing, it does not mean that that thing does not exist. No man, not even the whole of humanity, if it has not seen a thing, can claim that such a thing does not, or cannot, exist. This claim is out and out unscientific. No reasonable man can give it any weight.

Now look at the beliefs of the second group. According to them, a human being is a human being because in his previous animal form he had done good deeds; and an animal is an animal because previously as a human being he had behaved badly. In other words, to be a man or an animal is the consequence of one's deeds in one's former form. One may well ask "Which of them existed first, man or animal?" If they say man preceded animal, then they will have to accept that he must have been an animal before that, and was given a human form for its good deeds. If they say it was animal they will have to concede that there must have been before that a man who was transformed into an animal for his bad deeds. This leads to a vicious circle;

the advocates of this belief cannot settle on any form for the first creature, for every generation implies a preceding generation so that the succeeding generation may be considered as the consequence of the former. This is simply absurd.

Now consider the third viewpoint. Its first proposition is: that "this world will one day come to an end. God will destroy and annihilate the universe, and in its place will evolve another higher and far superior cosmos."

This statement is undeniably true. No doubt can be cast on it. The more we reflect on the nature of the cosmos, the more clearly it is proved that the existing system is not permanent and everlasting; all the forces working in it are limited in their nature, and will one day be exhausted. That is why the scientists agree that one day the sun will become cold and will give up all its energy, stars will collide with one another and the whole system of the universe will be upset and destroyed. Moreover, if evolution is true in the case of the constituents of this universe, why may it not be true for the whole of it? To think of the universe becoming totally non-existent is more improbable than that it will pass into another evolutionary stage, and another, much-improved order of things will emerge.

The second proposition of this belief is that "man will again be given life". Is it impossible? If so, how did the present life of man become possible? It is evident that God Who created man in this world can do so in the next. Not only is it a possibility, it is also a positive necessity, as will be shown later.

The third proposition is that "the record of all the actions of man in this world is preserved and will be presented on the Day of Resurrection". The proof of the truth of this proposition is provided today by science itself. The sounds which we make produce slight waves in the air and die out. It has been discovered that the sound leaves its impression on its surrounding objects and can be reproduced. Gramophone records are made on this principle. From this it can be understood that the record of every movement of man is being impressed on everything which comes into contact with the waves produced by the movements. This shows that the record of all our deeds is completely preserved and can be reproduced.

The fourth proposition is that "on the Day of Resurre-ction, God will hold His Court and, with just judgement, reward or punish man for his good and bad deeds". What is unreasonable about this? Reason itself demands that God should hold His court and pronounce judgement. We see men doing good deeds and gaining nothing in this world. We see other men doing bad deeds and not suffering for it. Not only this, we see thousands of cases of good acts bringing trouble on the doer, and of bad deeds resulting in the happiness and gratification of the guilty person. When we notice these events happening every day, our reason and sense of justice demand that a time must come when the man who does good must be rewarded and the one who does evil must be punished. If you have a tin of petrol and a match-box, you can set fire to the house of your opponent, and apparently escape every consequence. Does this mean that such an offence has no consequences at all? Certainly not! It means only that its physical outcome has appeared, and the moral outcome is hidden. Do you really think it reasonable that it should never appear? If you say it should, the question is, where? Certainly not in this world, where only the physical consequences of actions manifest themselves fully, and rational and moral consequences do not become apparent.

Results and consequences of this higher category can appear only if there comes into existence another order of things wherein rational and moral laws reign supreme and occupy the governing position and where the physical laws are made subject to them. That is the next world which, as we have said before, is the next evolutionary stage of the universe. It is evolutionary in the sense that it will be governed by moral rather than by physical laws. The rational consequences of man's actions, which are hidden wholly or partly in this world, will then appear. Man's stature will be determined by his rational and moral worth judged in accordance with his conduct in this life of test and trial. There you will not find a worthy man serving under a toll, or a morally superior man in a position inferior to a wretch, as is the case in this world.

The last proposition of this belief is the existence of Paradise and Hell, which is also not impossible. If God can make the sun, the moon, the stars and the earth, why should He not be able to make Paradise and Hell? When He holds His Court, and pronounces just judgements, rewarding the meritorious and punishing the guilty, there must be a place where the meritorious may enjoy their reward -honor, happiness and gratification of all kinds- and another place where the condemned may feel debasement, pain and misery.

After considering all these questions, no reasonable person can escape the conclusion that belief in life after death is highly acceptable to reason and commonsense, and that there is nothing in it which can be said to be unreasonable or impossible. Moreover, when a true Prophet like Muham-mad (blessings of Allah and peace be upon him) has started this to be a fact, and it involves nothing but what is good for us, wisdom lies in believing in it implicitly and not in rejecting it without any sound reasons. S

The above are the five articles of faith which form the foundation for the superstructure of Islam. Their gist is contained in the short sentence known as *Kalimah-tayyibah*. When you declare *La ilaha illallah* (there is no deity but Allah), you give up all false deities, and profess that you are a creature of the One God; and when you add to these words *Muhammad-ur-Rasulullah* (Muhammad is Allah's M) you confirm and admit the Prophethood of Muhammad (bless-ings of Allah and peace be upon him). With the admission of his Prophethood it becomes obligatory that you should believe in the divine nature and attributes of God, in His angels, in method of obeying God and worshipping Him which the Prophet Muhammad (blessings of Allah and peace be upon him) has asked us to follow. That way lays the road to success and salvation.

PRAYER AND WORSHIP

THE SPIRIT OF 'IBADAH OR WORSHIP

'Ibadah is an Arabic word derived from *'Abd* (a slave) and it means submission. Allah is your Master and you are His slave

and whatever a slave does in obedience to and for the pleasure of his Master is *'Ibadah*. The Islamic concept of *'Ibadah* is very wide. If you free your speech from filth, falsehood, malice and abuse and speak the truth and talk goodly things, and do all this only because God has so ordained, they constitute *'Ibadah*, however secular they may appear. If you obey the law of God in letter and spirit in your commercial and economic affairs and abide by it in your dealings with your parents, relatives, friends and all those who come into contact with you, all these activities of yours are also *'Ibadah*. If you help the poor and the destitute, give food to the hungry and serve the afflicted and do all this not for any personal gain but only to seek the pleasure of God, this is all *'Ibadah*. Even your economic activities -the activities you undertake to earn your living and to feed your depen-dants- are *'Ibadah* if you remain honest and truthful in them, and observe the law of God.

In short, all your activities are *'Ibadah* if they are in accordance with the law of God and your ultimate objective is to seek the pleasure of God. Thus, whenever you do well or avoid evil for fear of God, in whatever sphere of life and field of activity, you are discharging your Islamic obligations. This is the true significance of *'Ibadah*, that is, total submis-sion to the pleasure of Allah, the molding into the patterns of Islam one's entire life, leaving out not even the most insignificant part. To help achieve this aim, a set of formal *'Ibadah* (worships) has been drawn up as a course of training. The more assiduously we follow the training, the better equip-ped we are to harmonize ideals and practices. The *'Ibadah* are thus the pillars on which the edifice of Islam rests.

The earlier discussion has made it clear that the Prophet Muhammad (blessings of Allah and peace be upon him) has enjoined us to believe in five articles of faith:

1. Belief in one God Who has absolutely no associate with Him in His divinity;
2. Belief in God's Angels;
3. Belief in God's Books, and in the Holy Qur'an as His Last Book.

4. Belief in God's Prophets, and in Muhammad (blessings of Allah and peace be upon him) as His last and Final Messenger; and
5. Belief in life after death.

These five articles make up the bedrock of Islam. One who believes in them enters the fold of Islam and becomes a member of the Muslim community. But one does not become a complete Muslim by mere vocal profession alone. To become a complete Muslim one has to fully carry out in practice the instructions given by Muhammad (blessings of Allah and peace be upon him) as ordained by God.

For belief in God makes practical obedience to Him incumbent; and it is obedience to God which constitutes the religion of Islam. By this belief you profess that Allah, the one God, alone is your God, and this means that He is your Creator and you are His creature; that He is your Master and you are His slave; that He is your Ruler and you are His subject. Having acknowledged Him as your Master and Ruler, if you refuse to obey Him you become a self-admitted rebel. Along with faith in God, you believe that the Qur'an is God's Book. This means that you have admitted all the contents of the Qur'an to be from God. Thus it becomes your bounden duty to accept and obey whatever is contained in it. Along with that, you have admitted Muhammad (blessings of Allah and peace be upon him) to be God's Messenger, which means that you have admitted that each and every one of his orders and prohibitions are from God. After this admission, obedience to him becomes your duty. You will therefore be a fully-fledged Muslim only when your practice is consistent with your profession.

Now let us see what code of conduct Muhammad (blessings of Allah and peace be upon him) has taught as ordained by God Almighty. The first and foremost things in this respect are the *'Ibadah* - the primary duties which must be observed by each and every person professing to belong to the Muslim community.

Salah

Salah is the most fundamental and the most important of these obligations. *Salah* are the prescribed daily prayers which consist in repeating and refreshing five times a day the belief in which you repose your faith.

You get up early in the morning, cleanse yourself, and present yourself before your Lord for prayer. The various poses that you assume during your prayers are the very embodiment of the spirit of submission; the various recitals remind you of your commitments to your God. You seek His guidance and ask Him again and again to enable you to avoid His Wrath and follow His Chosen Path. You read out from the Book of the Lord and express witness to the truth of the Prophets and also refresh your belief in the Day of Judgement and enliven in your memory the fact that you have to appear before your Lord and give an account of your entire life.

This is how your day starts. After a few hours the muezzin calls you to prayers and you again submit to your God and refresh your covenant with Him. You dissociate yourself from your worldly engagements for a few moments and seek audience before God. This, once again, brings to the fore of your mind your real role in life. After this rededication, you revert to your occupations before presen-ting yourself to the Lord again a few hours later. This again acts as a reminder to you, and you once more refocus your attention on the stipulations of your Faith. When the sun sets and the darkness of the night begins to shroud you, you once more submit yourself to God in prayers so that you may not forget your duties and obligations in the midst of the approaching shadows of the night. After a few hours you again appear before your Lord for your last prayer of the day. Thus before going to bed you once again refresh your faith and prostrate yourself before your God. And this is how you complete your day. The frequency and timings of the prayers never let you lose sight of the object and mission of life in the maze of worldly activities.

It is easy to understand how daily prayers strengthen the foundations of your faith, prepare you for the observance of a life of virtue and obedience to God, and refreshes that belief from which springs courage, sincerity, purposefulness, purity of heart, advancement of the soul and enrichment of morals.

Now see how this is achieved. You perform ablution in the way prescribed by the Holy Prophet (blessings of Allah and peace be upon him). You also say your prayers according to the instructions of the Prophet. Why do you do so? Simply because you believe in the prophethood of Muhammad (blessings of Allah and peace be upon him) and deem it your bounden duty to follow him ungrudgingly.

Why do you not intentionally miscrete the Qur'an? Is it not because you regard the Book as the Word of God and deem it a sin to deviate from even a letter? In prayers you recite many things quietly and if you do not recite them or make any deviation from them there is no one to check you. But you never do so intentionally. Why? Because you believe that God is ever watchful, is listening to all that you recite and is aware of things both open and hidden. What makes you say your prayers at places where there is no one to ask you to offer them or even to see you offering them? Is it not because of your belief that God is always looking at you? What makes you leave some important business and hurry towards the mosque for prayers? What makes you break your sweet sleep in the early hours of the morning, come to the mosque in the heat of noon and leave your evening entertainment for the sake of prayer? Is it anything other than your sense of duty - your realization that you must fulfilll your responsibility to the Lord, come what may? And why are you afraid of any mistake in your prayer? Because your heart is filled with the fear of God and you know that you have to appear before Him on the Day of Judgement and give an account of your entire life.

Now look! Can the better course of moral and spiritual training than prayers? It is this training which makes a man a perfect Muslim. It reminds him of his covenant with God, refreshes his faith in Him and keeps the belief in the Day of

Judgement alive and ever-present before his mind's eye. It makes him follow the Prophet and trains him in the observance of his duties. This is indeed a strict training for matching one's practice to one's ideals.

Obviously, if a man's consciousness of his duties towards his Creator is so acute that he prizes it above all worldly gains and keeps refreshing it through prayers, he will be honest in all his dealings for, otherwise, he will be inviting the displeasure of God which he has all along striven to avoid. He will abide by the law of God in all aspects of his life in the same way as he follows it in the five prayers every day. This man can be relied on in other fields of activity as well, for if the shadows of sin or deceit approach him, he will try to avoid them. If even after such training, a man disobeys the law of God, it can only be because of some intrinsic depravity of his self.

Then, again you must say your prayers in congregation and especially so the Friday prayers. This creates among Muslims a bond of love and mutual understanding. It arouses in them a sense of collective unity and fosters among them national fraternity. Prayers are also a symbol of equality, for the poor and the rich, the low and the high, the rulers and the ruled, the educated and the unlettered, the black and the white; all stand in a row and prostrate themselves before their Lord. Prayers also inculcate a strong sense of discipline and obedience to an elected leader. In short, prayers train people in all those virtues which make possible the development of a rich individual and collective life.

These are a few of the myriad of benefits we can derive from our daily prayers. If we refuse to avail ourselves of them we, and only we, are the losers. Shirking the prayers can only mean one of two things. Either we do not recognize prayers as our duty or we recognize them as our duty and still shirk them. In the first case, our claim to faith is a shame-less lie, for if we refuse to take orders, we no longer acknow-ledge God's Authority. In the second case, if we recognize His Authority and still flout His Commands, we are the most unreliable of the creatures that ever trod the earth. For if we can do this to the highest authority in the universe, what guarantee is there that we shall not do the same in our dealings with fellow human beings? And if double dealing dominates a society, terrible discord will be the certain outcome!

Fasting

What prayers seek to do five times a day, fasting in the month of Ramadan (the ninth month of the lunar year) does once a year. During this period we eat not a grain of food nor drink a drop of water from dawn to dusk, no matter how delicious the dish or how hungry or thirsty we feel. What is it that makes us voluntarily undergo such rigors? It is nothing but faith in God and the fear of Him and the Day of Judgement. Each and every moment during our fast we suppress our passions and desires and proclaim, by so doing, the supremacy of the Law of God. This consciousness of duty and spirit of patience that incessant fasting for a whole month inculcates in us help us strengthen our faith. Rigor and discipline during this month bring us face to face with the realities of life and help us make our life, during the rest of the year, a life of true subservience to His Will.

From yet another point of view fasting has an immense impact on society, for all the Muslims irrespective of their status must fast during the same month. This emphasizes the essential equality of men and thus goes a long way towards creating in them sentiments of love and brotherhood. During Ramadan evil conceals itself while good comes to the fore and the whole atmosphere is filled with piety and purity.

This discipline has been imposed on us for our own advantage. Those who do not fulfilll this primary duty cannot be relied on to discharge their other duties. But the worst are those who during this holy month do not hesitate to eat or drink in public. They show by their conduct that they care nothing for the commands of Allah in Whom they profess their belief as Creator and Sustainer. Not only this, they also show that they are not loyal members of the Muslim community - rather, they have nothing to do with it. Only the worst can be expected of such hypocrites.

Zakah

The third obligation is *Zakah*. Every Muslim whose finances are above a certain specified minimum must pay 2.5 per cent of his cash balance annually to a deserving fellow-being, a new convert to Islam, a traveler or a person with debts. This is the minimum. The more you pay, the greater the reward that Allah will bestow on you.

The money that we pay as *Zakah* is not something Allah needs or receives. He is above any want and desire. He, in His benign Mercy, promises us manifold rewards if we help our brethren. But there is one basic condition for being thus rewarded: when we pay in the name of Allah, we shall neither expect nor demand any worldly gains from the beneficiaries nor aim at becoming known as philanthropists.

Zakah is as basic to Islam as other forms of *'Ibadah*: *Salah* (prayer) and *Sawm* (fasting). Its fundamental importance lies in the fact that it fosters in us the quality of sacrifice and rids us of selfishness. Islam accepts within its fold only those who are ready to give away in God's way some of their hard-earned wealth willingly and without any temporal or personal gain. It has nothing to do with misers. A true Muslim will, when the call comes, sacrifice all his belongings in the way of Allah, for *Zakah* has already trained him to do so.

Muslim society has much to gain from the institution of *Zakah*. It is the bounden duty of every well-to-do Muslim to help his lowly-placed, poor brethren. His wealth is not to be spent solely for his own comfort and luxury -there are rightful claimants on his wealth, and they are the nation's widows and orphans, the poor and the invalid; those who have the ability but lack the means to get useful employment and those who have the talent but not the money to acquire knowledge and become useful members of the community. He who does not recognize the call on his wealth of such members of his own community is indeed cruel. For there could be no greater cruelty than to fill one's own coffers while others die of hunger or suffer the agonies of unemployment.

Islam is a sworn enemy of selfishness, greed and acquisitiveness. Disbelievers, devoid of sentiments of universal love, know only how to preserve wealth and to add to it by lending it out on interest. Islam's teachings are the antithesis of this attitude. Here one shares one's wealth with others and helps them stand on their own feet and become productive members of society.

Hajj or Pilgrimage

Hajj, or the pilgrimage to Makkah, is the fourth basic *'Ibadah*.

Makkah today stands at the site of a small house that the Prophet Abraham (God's blessings be upon him) built for the worship of Allah. Allah rewarded him by calling it His own House and by making it the center towards which all must face when saying prayers. He also made it obligatory on those who can afford it to visit this place at least once in a lifetime. This visit is not merely a courtesy call. This pilgri-mage has its rites and conditions to be fulfillled which inculcate in us piety and goodness. When we undertake the pilgrimage, we are required to suppress our passions, refrain from bloodshed and be pure in word and deed. God promises rewards for our sincerity and submissiveness.

The pilgrimage is, in a way, the biggest of all *'Ibadah*. For unless a man really loves God he would never undertake such a long journey leaving all his near and dear ones behind him. And this pilgrimage is unlike any other journey. Here his thoughts are concentrated on Allah; his very being vibrates with the spirit of intense devotion. When he reaches the holy place, he finds the atmosphere filled with piety and godliness; he visits places which bear with the glory of Islam, and all this leaves an indelible impression on his mind, which he carries to his last breath.

Then there are, as in other *'Ibadah*, many benefits that Muslims can derive from this pilgrimage. Makkah is the center towards which Muslims must converge once a year, meet and discuss topics of common interest, and in general create and refresh in themselves the faith that all Muslims are equal and deserve the love and sympathy of others, irrespective of their geographical or cultural origin. Thus the pilgrimage unites the Muslims of the world into one international fraternity.

DEFENSE OF ISLAM

Although the defense of Islam is not a fundamental tenet its need and importance have been repeatedly emphasized in the Qur'an and the Hadith. It is in essence a test of our sincerity and truthfulness as believers in Islam. If we do not defend one whom we call our friend against intrigues or open assaults from his foes, or are guided in our actions towards him solely by selfishness, we are indeed false friends. Similarly, if we profess belief in Islam, we must jealously guard and uphold the prestige of Islam. The sole guide in our conduct must be the interest of Muslims at large and the service of Islam, in the face of which all our personal considerations must take a back seat.

JIHAD

Jihad is part of this overall defense of Islam. *Jihad* means to struggle to the utmost of one's capacity. A man who exerts himself physical or mentally or spends his wealth in the way of Allah is indeed engaged in Jihad. But in the language of the *Shari'ah* this word is used particularly for a war that is waged solely in the name of Allah against those who practice oppression as enemies of Islam.

This supreme sacrifice of life devolves on all Muslims. If, however, a section of Muslims offer themselves for the Jihad, the community as a whole is absolved of its responsibility. But if none comes forward, everybody is guilty. This concession vanishes for the citizens of an Islamic State when it is attacked by a non-Muslim power. In that case everybody must come forward for the Jihad. If the country attacked has not enough strength to fight back, then it is the religious duty of the neighboring Muslim countries to help her; of even they fail,then the Muslims of the whole world must fight the common enemy. In all such cases, Jihad is as much a primary duty of the Muslims concerned as are the daily prayers or fasting. One who shirks it is a sinner. His very claim to being a Muslim is doubtful. He is a hypocrite whose *'Ibadah* and prayers are a sham, a worthless, however show of devotion.

DIN AND SHARI'AH

DISTINCTION BETWEEN DIN AND SHARI'AH

Prophets who have appeared from time to time propagated Islam, that is a belief in God with all His attri-butes, faith in the Day of Judgement and faith in the Prophets and the Books; they asked people to live a life of obedience and submission to their Lord. This is what constitutes al-Din and it was common to the teachings of all the Prophets.

Apart from this *Din* there is the *Shari'ah,* the detailed code of conduct or the canons comprising ways and modes of worship, standards of morals and life and laws that allow and proscribe, that judge between right and wrong. Such canon law has undergone amendments from time to time and though each Prophet had the same *Din,* he brought with him a different *Shari'ah* to suit the conditions of his own people and time. This process ended with the advent of Muhammad, the last Prophet (blessings of Allah and peace be upon him), who brought with him the final code which was to apply to all mankind for all times to come. *Din* has undergone no change, but the entire previous *Shari'ahs* stand abrogated because of the comprehensive *Shari'ah* that Muhammad (blessings of Allah and peace be upon him) brought with him. This is the climax of the great process of training that was started at the dawn of the human era.

The Sources of Shari'ah

We draw upon two major sources to learn about the Shari'ah of Muhammad (blessings of Allah and peace be upon him), the Qur'an and the Hadith. The Qur'an is a divine revelation - each and every word of it is from Allah. The Hadith is a collection of the instructions issued or the memoirs of the last Prophet's conduct and behavior, as preserved by those who were present in his company or those to whom these were handed down by the first witnesses. These were later sifted and collected by divines and compiled in the form of books among which the collections made by Malik, Bukhari, Muslim, Tirmidhi, Abu Dawud, Nasa'i and Ibn Majah are considered to be the most authentic.

FIQH

Detailed law derived from the Qur'an and the Hadith covering the myriad of problems that arise in the course of man's life have been compiled by some of the leading legislators of the past. The Muslims should forever be grateful to those men of learning and vision who devoted their lives to gaining a mastery of the Qur'an and the Hadith, and who made it easy for every Muslim to fashion his everyday affairs according to the requirements of the *Shari'ah*. It is due to them alone that Muslims all over the world can follow the *Shari'ah* easily even though their attainments in religion are never such that they could themselves give a correct and authentic interpretation of the Qur'an or the Hadith.

Although in the beginning many religious leaders applied themselves to the task, only four major schools of thought remain. They are:

1. *Fiqh Hanafi*: This is the Fiqh compiled by Abu Hanifa Nu'man bin Thabit with the assistance and cooperation of Abu Yusuf Mahammad, Zufar and others, all of whom had high religious attainments to their credit. This is known as the Hanafi School of Fiqh.
2. *Fiqh Maliki*: This Fiqh was derived by Malik bin Anas Asbahi.
3. *Fiqh Shafi'i*: Founded by Muhammad bin Idris al-Shafi'i.
4. *Fiqh Hanbali*: Founded by Ahmad bin Hanbal.

All of these were given their final form within two hundred years of the time of the Prophet. The differences that appear in the four schools are but the natural outcome of the fact that truth is many-sided. When different persons employ themselves in interpreting a given event, they come out with different explanations according to their own lights. What gives these various schools of thought the authenticity that is associated with them is the unimpeachable integrity of their respective founders and the authenticity of the method they adopted. That is why all Muslims, whatever school they may belong to, regard all the four schools of thought as correct and true. Even so one can normally follow only one of them in one's life (there is the group of Ahl-Al-Hadith who believe that those who have the required knowledge and learning should directly approach the Qur'an and the Hadith for guidance and those who are not bestowed with such knowledge and faculties should follow whichever school they like in any particular matter.)

TASAWWUF

Fiqh deals with observable conduct, the fulfillling of a duty to the letter. That concerning itself with the spirit of conduct is known as *Tasawwuf.* For example, when we say our prayers, *Fiqh* will judge us only by the fulfilllment of the outward requirements such as ablution, facing towards the *Ka'bah* and the timing and the number of *Raka'ahs. Tasawwuf* will judge our prayers by our concentration and devotion and by their effect on our morals and manners. An *'Ibadah* devoid of spirit, though correct in procedure, is like a man handsome in appearance but lacking in character and an *'Ibadah* full of spirit but defective in execution is like a man noble in character but deformed in appearance.

The above example makes clear the relation between *Fiqh* and *Tasawwuf.* But it is to the misfortune of the Muslims that as they sank in knowledge and character with the passage of time, they also succumbed to the misguided philosophies of nations which were then dominant, partook of them and patched Islam with their perverted dogmas.

They polluted the pure spring of Islamic *Tasawwuf* with absurdities that could not be justified by any stretch of the imagination on the basis of the Qur'an and the Hadith. Gradually a section of Muslims appeared who thought and proclaimed themselves immune to and above the require-ments of the *Shari'ah*. These people are totally ignorant of Islam, for Islam cannot admit to *Tasawwuf* that takes liberties with the *Shari'ah*. No Sufi has the right to transgress the limits of the *Shari'ah* or treat lightly primary obligations (*Fara'id*) such as daily prayers, fasting, *Zahah* and the *Hajj*. *Tasawwuf*, in the true sense, is an intense love of Allah and Muhammad (blessings of Allah and peace be upon him) and such love requires a strict obedience to their commands as embodied in the Book of God and the Sunnah of His Prophet. Anyone who deviates from the divine commands makes a false claim of his love for Allah and His Apostle.

THE PRINCIPLES OF THE SHARI'AH

Our discussion of the fundamentals of Islam will remain incomplete if we do not cast a glance over the law of Islam, study its basic principles, and try to visualize the type of man and society which Islam wants to produce. In this last chapter we propose to undertake a study of the principles of the *Shari'ah* so that our picture of Islam may become complete and we may be able to appreciate the superiority of the Islamic way of life.

THE SHARI'AH - ITS NATURE AND PURPORT

Man has been endowed with countless powers and faculties and Providence has been very bountiful to him in this respect. He possesses intellect and wisdom, will and volition, faculties of sight, speech, taste, touch and hearing, powers of hand and feet, passions of love, fear, and anger and so on. These faculties have been bestowed on him because they are indispensable to him; His very life and success depend on the proper use of these powers for the fulfilllment of his needs and requirements. These God-given powers are meant for his service and unless they are used in full measure life cannot become worth living.

God has also provided man with all those means and resources to make his natural faculties function and to achieve the fulfilllment of his needs. The human body has been so made that it has become man's greatest instrument in his struggle for the fulfilllment of his life's goal. Then there is the world in which man lives. His environment and surroun-dings contain resources of every description: resources which he uses as a means for the achievement of his ends. Nature and all that belongs to it have been harnessed for him and he can make every conceivable use of them. And there are other men of his kind so that they may cooperate with each other in the construction of a better and prosperous life.

These powers and resources have been conferred so that they may be used for the good of others. They have been created for your good and are not meant to harm and destroy you. The proper use of these powers is that which makes them beneficial to you: and even if there be some harm, it must not exceed the unavoidable minimum. That alone is the proper utilization of these powers. Every other use which results in waste or destruction is wrong, unreasonable and unjustified. For instance, if you do something that causes you harm or injury, that would be a mistake, pure and simple. If your actions harm others and make you a nuisance to them then that would be sheer folly and an utter misuse of God-given powers. If you waste resources, spoil them for nothing or destroy them that too are a gross mistake. Such activities are flagrantly unreasonable, for it is human reason which suggests that destruction and injury must be avoided and the path of gain and profit be pursued. And if any harm be countenanced, it must be only in such cases where it is unavoidable and where it is bound to yield a greater benefit. Any deviation from this is self-evidently wrong.

Keeping this basic consideration in view, when we look at human beings, we find that there are two kinds of people: first those who knowingly misuse their powers and resources and through this misuse waste the resources, injure their own vital interests, and cause harm to other people; and, second, those who are sincere and earnest but err because of ignorance. Those who intentionally misuse their powers are wicked and evil and deserve to feel the full weight of the law. Those who err because of ignorance need proper knowledge and guidance so that they see the Right Path and make the best use of their powers and resources. And the code of behavior -the *Shari'ah*- which God has revealed to man meets this very need.

The *Shari'ah* stipulates the law of God and provides guidance for the regulation of life in the best interest of man. Its objective is to show the best way to man and provide him with the ways and means to fulfilll his needs in the most successful and most beneficial way. The law of God is out and out for your benefit. There is nothing in it which tends to waste your powers, or to suppress your natural needs and desires, or to kill your moral urges and emotions. It does not plead for asceticism. It does not say: abandon the world, give up all ease and comfort of life, leave your homes and wander about on plains and mountains and in jungles without bread or cloth, putting yourself to inconvenience and self-annihilation. This view point has no relevance to the law of Islam; a law that has been formulated by God Who has created this world for the benefit of mankind.

The *Shari'ah* has been revealed by that very God Who has harnessed everything for man. He would hardly want to ruin His creation. He has not given man any power that is useless or unnecessary, nor has He created anything in the heavens and the earth which may not be of service to man. It is His explicit Will that the universe -this grand workshop with its multifarious activities- should go on functioning smoothly and graciously so that man -the prize of creation- should make the best and most productive use of all his powers and resources, of everything that has been harnessed for him on earth and in the high heavens. He should use them in such a way that he and his fellow human beings may reap handsome prizes from them and should never, intentionally or unintentionally, be of any harm to God's creation. The *Shari'ah* is meant to guide the steps of man in this respect. It forbids all that is harmful to man, and allows or ordains all that is useful and beneficial to him.

The fundamental principle of the Law is that man has the right, and in some cases the bounden duty, to fulfilll all his genuine needs and desires and make every conceivable effort to promote his interests and achieve success and happiness -

but (and it is an important 'but') he should do all this in such a way that not only are the interests of other people not jeopardized and no harm is caused to their strivings towards the fulfilllment of their rights and duties, but there should be all possible social cohesion, mutual assistance and cooperation among human beings in the achievement of their objectives. In respect of those things in which good and evil, gain and loss are inextricable mixed up, the tenet of this law is to choose a little harm for the sake of greater benefit and sacrifice a little benefit, so avoiding a greater harm. This is the basic approach of the *Shari'ah.*

Man's knowledge is limited. Every man in every age does not, by himself, know what is good and what is evil, what is beneficial and what is harmful to him. The sources of human knowledge are too limited to provide him with the unalloyed truth. That is why God has spared man the risks of trial and error and revealed to him the Law which is the right and complete code of life for the entire human race.

The merits and the truths of this code are becoming more and more clear to man with the passage of time and of knowledge. Even today some people do not appreciate all the merits of this code, but further progress of knowledge will throw new light on them and bring their superiority into even clearer perspective. The world is willy-nilly drifting towards the Divine Code - many of those people who refused to accept it are now, after centuries of groping and trials and errors, being obliged to adopt some of the provisions of this law. Those who denied the truth of the revelation and pinned their faith on unguided human reason, after committing blunders and courting bitter experience, are adopting in one way or another the injunctions of *Shari'ah.* But after what loss! And even then not in their entirety! On the other hand, there are people who repose faith in God's Prophets, accept their word and adopt the *Shari'ah* with full knowledge and understanding.. They may not be aware of all die merits of a certain instruction, but on the whole they accept a code which is the outcome of true knowledge and which saves them from the evils and blunders of ignorance and of trial and error. Such people are on the right path and are bound to succeed.

THE SHARI'AH - RIGHTS AND OBLIGATIONS

The scheme of life which consists of a set of rights and obligations, and every human being, everyone who accepts this religion, is enjoined to live up to them. Broadly speaking, the law of Islam imposes four kinds of rights and obligations on every man: (i) the rights of God which every man is obliged to fulfilll; (ii) his own rights upon his own self; (iii) the rights of other people over him; and (iv) the rights of those powers and resources which God has placed in his service and has empowered him to use for his benefit.

These rights and obligations constitute the corner stone of Islam and it is the bounden duty of every true Muslim to understand them and obey them carefully. The *Shari'ah* discussed clearly each and every kind of right and deals with it in detail. It also throws light on the ways and means through which the obligations can be discharged - so that all of them may be simultaneously implemented and none of them violated or trampled underfoot.

1. *The Rights of God*: First of all we must study the ground on which Islam bases the relationship of man to his Creator. The primary and foremost right of God is that man should have faith in Him alone. He should acknowledge His authority and associate none with Him. This is epitomized in the *Kalimah*: *La ilaha illallah* (there is no god but Allah).

   The second right of God on us is that man should accept wholeheartedly and follow His guidance (*Hidayah*) - the code He has revealed for man - and should seek His pleasure with both mind and soul. We fulfill the dictates of this right by placing belief in God's Prophet and by accepting his guidance and leadership.

   The third right of God on us is that we should obey Him honestly and unreservedly. We fulfill the needs of this right by following God's Law as contained in the Qur'an and the Sunnah.

The fourth right of God on us is to worship Him. This is rendered by offering prayers and other *'Ibadah* as described earlier.

These rights and obligations precede all other rights and as such they are discharged even at the cost of some sacrifice of other rights and duties. For instance, in offering prayers and keeping fasts man has to sacrifice many of his personal rights. He has to get up early in the morning for his prayers and in so doing sacrifices his sleep and rest. During the day he often puts off important work and gives up his recreation to worship his Creator. In the month of Ramadan (the month of fasts) he experiences hunger and inconvenience solely to please his Lord. By paying *zakah* he loses his wealth and demonstrates that the love of God is above everything else. In the pilgrimage he sacrifices wealth and takes on a difficult journey. And in Jihad he sacrifices money, material and all that he has - even his own life.

Similarly, in the discharge of these obligations one has to sacrifice some of the ordinary rights of others and thus injure one's own interests at large. A servant has to leave his work to worship his Lord. A businessman has to stop his business to undertake the Pilgrimage to Makkah. In Jihad a man takes away life and gives it away solely in the cause of Allah. In the same way in rendering God's rights one has to sacrifice many of those things which man has in his control, like animals, wealth etc. But God has so formulated the *Shari'ah* that harmony and equilibrium are established in the different fields of life and the sacrifice of others' rights is reduced to the barest minimum

This is achieved by the limits prescribed by God. He has allowed us every facility in the fulfillment of the obligation of *Salah*. If you cannot get water for ablution, or you are sick, you can perform *tayammum* (dry ablution). If you are on a journey, you can cut short the *Salah*. If you are ill and cannot stand in the prayer, you can offer it while sitting or lying. The recitation of the prayer is so manageable that they can be shortened or lengthened as one may wish; at times of rest and ease we may recite a long chapter of the Qur'an, at busy time we may recite a few verses only. The instruction is that in the congregational prayers and in those prayers which occur during business hours, the recitation should be short. God is pleased with the optional devotions (*Nawafil*), but He disapproves our denying ourselves sleep and rest and the sacrifice of the rights of our children and of the household. Islam wants us to strike a balance between the various activities of life.

It is similar with fasts. In the whole year there is only one month of obligatory fasting. If you are travelling or ill you can omit it and observe it at some other convenient time of the year. Women are exempted from fasting when they are pregnant and during their menstrual or suckling periods. The fast should end at the appointed time and any delay is disapproved of. Permission is given to eat and drink from sunset to dawn. Optional fasts are highly valued and God is pleased at them, but He does not like you to keep fasts continuously and make yourself too weak to do your ordinary business satisfactorily.

Similarly, look at the case of *zakah;* the minimum rate has been fixed by God and man has been left free to give as much more as he likes in the cause of Allah. If one gives *zakah*, one fulfills one's duty, but if one spends more in charity, one seeks more and more of God's pleasure. But He does not like us to sacrifice all our belongings in charity or to deny ourselves and our relatives those rights and comforts which they should enjoy. He does not want us to impoverish ourselves. We are commanded to be moderate in charity.

Then look at the pilgrimage. It is obligatory only for those who can afford the journey and who are physically fit to bear its hardships. Then, it is obligatory to perform it only once in one's life, in any convenient year. If there is a war or any other situation which threatens life, it can be postponed. Moreover, parental permission has been made an essential condition, so that aged parents may not suffer in one's absence. All these things clearly show what importance God Himself has given to the rights of others vis-à-vis His own rights.

The greatest sacrifice for God is made in Jihad, for in it a man sacrifices not only his own life and property in His cause but destroys those of others also. But, as already stated, one of the Islamic principles is that we should suffer a lesser loss to save ourselves from a greater loss. How can the loss of some lives -even if the number runs into thousands- be compared to the calamity that may befall mankind as a result of the victory of evil over good and of aggressive atheism over the religion of God. That would be a far greater loss and calamity, for as a result of it not only would the religion of God be under dire threat, the world would also become the abode of evil and perversion, and life would be disrupted both from within and without.

In order to escape this greater evil God has, therefore, commanded us to sacrifice our lives and property for His pleasure. But at the same time He has forbidden unnecessary bloodshed, injuring the aged, women, children, the sick and the wounded. His order is to fight only against those who rise to fight. He enjoins us not to cause unnecessary destruction even in the enemy's lands, and to deal fairly and honorably with the defeated. We are instructed to observe the agreements made with the enemy and to stop fighting when they do so or when they stop their aggressive and anti-Islamic activities.

Thus Islam allows only for the minimum essential sacrifice of life, property and other people's rights in the discharging of God's rights. It is eager to establish a balance between the different demands of man and adjust different rights and obligations so that life is enriched with the choicest of merits and achievements.

The Rights of One's Own Self: Next come man's personal rights, that is, the rights of one's own self.

The fact is that man is more cruel and unjust to himself than to any other being. On the face of it this may seem astonishing: how can men unjust to him, particularly when we find that he loves himself most? How can he be his own enemy? It seems unintelligible. But deeper reflection shows that it contains a large grain of truth.

The greatest weakness of man is that when he feels an overpowering desire, instead of resisting it, he succumbs to it, and in its gratification knowingly causes great harm to himself. There is the man who drinks: he cannot stop his craving for it and does it at the cost of money, health, reputation and everything that he has. Another person is so fond of eating that in his eating excesses he damages his health and endangers his life. Another person becomes a slave to his sexual appetites and ruins himself in over-indulgence. Still another becomes enamoured of spiritual elevations: he suppresses his genuine desires, refuses to satisfy the physical needs, controls his appetite, does away with clothes, leaves his home and retires into mountains and jungles. He believes that the world is not meant for him and abhors it in all its forms and manifestations.

These are a few of the instances of man's tendency to go to extremes. One comes across such instances of maladjustment and disequilibrium in one's everyday life and there is no need to multiply them here.

Islam stands for human welfare and its avowed objective is to establish balance in life. That is why the *Shari'ah* clearly declares that your own self also has certain rights upon you. A fundamental principle of it is: "there are rights upon you of your own person."

The *Shari'ah* forbids the use of all those things which are injurious to man's physical, mental or moral existence. It forbids the consumption of blood, intoxicating drugs, and fleshes of the pig, beasts of prey, poisonous and unclean animals; for all these have undesirable effects on the physical, moral, intellectual and spiritual life of man. While forbidding these things, Islam enjoins man to use all clean, healthy and useful things and asks him not to deprive his body of clean food, for man's body, too, has a right on him. The law of Islam forbids nudity and orders man to wear decent and dignified dress. It exhorts him to work for a living and strongly disapproves of him remaining idle and jobless. The spirit of the *Shari'ah* is that man should use for his comfort and welfare the powers God has bestowed on him and the resources that He has spread on the earth and in the heavens.

Islam does not believe in the suppression of sexual desire; it enjoins man to control and regulate it and seek its fulfillment in marriage. It forbids him to resort to self-persecution and total self-denial and permits him, indeed, bids him, to enjoy the rightful comforts and pleasures of life and remain pious and steadfast in the midst of life and its problems.

To seek spiritual elevation, moral purity, nearness to God and salvation in the life to come, it is not necessary to abandon this world. Instead, the trial of man lies in this world and he should remain in its midst and follow the way of Allah in it. The road to success lies in following the Divine law in the midst of life's complexities, not outside it.

Islam forbids suicide and impresses on man that life belongs to God. It is a trust which God has bestowed for a certain period of time so that you may make the best use of it - it is not meant to be harmed or destroyed in a frivolous way.

This is how Islam instills in the mind of man that his own person, his own self, possesses certain rights and it is his obligation to discharge them as best he can, in the ways that have been suggested by the *Shari'ah*. This is how he can be true to his own self.

The Rights of Other Men: On the one hand the *Shari'ah* has enjoined man to fulfill his personal rights and be just to his own self, and on the other, it has asked him to seek their fulfillment in such a way that the rights of other people are not violated. The *Shari'ah* has tried to strike a balance between the rights of man and the rights of society so that no conflict arises and there is cooperation in establishing the law of God.

Islam has strictly forbidden the telling of a lie in any shape or form for lies sully the liar, harm other people and become a source of menace to society. It has totally forbidden theft, bribery, forgery, cheating, the levying of interest and usury, for whatever man gains by these means is obtained by causing loss and injury to others. Back-biting, tale-telling and slander have been forbidden. Gambling, lottery, speculation and all games of chance have been prohibited, for in all of them one person gains at the expense of thousands of losers.

All those forms of exploitative commerce have been prohibited in which one party alone is to be the loser. Monopoly, hoarding, black market trading, holding of land from cultivation and all other forms of individual and social aggrandizement have been prohibited. Murder, blood-spilling and spreading of mischief, disorder and destruction have been made crimes, for no-one has a right to take away the life or property of other people merely for his personal gain or gratification.

Adultery, fornication and unnatural sexual indulgence have been strictly prohibited for they not only vitiate the morality and impair the health of the perpetrator but also spread corruption and immorality in society, cause venereal disease, damage both public health and the morals of the coming generations, upset relations between man and man and split the very fabric of the cultural and social structure of the community. Islam seeks to eliminate, root and branch, such crimes.

All these limitations and restrictions have been imposed by the law of Islam to prevent a man encroaching on the rights of others. Islam does not want a man to become so selfish and self-centered that for the attainment of a few desires of the mind and body he unashamedly assails the rights of others and violates morality. The law of Islam regulates life that the welfare of one and all may be achieved. But for the attainment of human welfare and cultural advancement, negative restrictions alone are not sufficient. In a peaceful and prosperous society people should not only not violate the rights of others and injure their interests but should positively cooperate with each other and establish mutual relations and social institutions that contribute towards the welfare of all and the establishment of an ideal human society. The *Shari'ah* has guided us in this respect as well. We therefore propose to give here a brief summary of those injunctions of Islamic law which throw light on this aspect of life and society.

Family is the first cradle of man. It is here that the primary character-traits of man are set. As such it is not only the cradle of man but also the cradle of civilization. Therefore, let us first consider the injunctions of the *Shari'ah* relating to the family. A family consists of the husband, the wife and their children. The Islamic injunctions about the family are very explicit. They assign to man the responsibility for earning and providing the necessities of life for his wife and children and for protecting them from all the vicissitudes of life. To the woman it assigns the duty of managing the household, training and bringing up children in the best possible way, and providing her husband and children with the greatest possible comfort and contentment. The duty of the children is to respect and obey their parents, and, when they are grown up, to serve them and provide for their needs.

To make the household a well-managed and well-disciplined institution, Islam has adopted the following two measures:

- The husband has been given the position of head of the family. No institution can work smoothly unless it has a chief administrator. You cannot think of a school without a headmaster or a city without an administrator if there is nobody to control an institution, chaos results. If everybody in the family goes his own way, nothing but confusion will prevail. If the husband goes one way and the wife another, the future of the children will be ruined. There must be someone as head of the family so that discipline may be maintained. Given this position to the husband and in this way makes the family a well-disciplined primary unit of civilization and a model for society at large.
- The head of the family has responsibilities. It is his duty to work, and do all those tasks which are performed outside the household. Woman has been freed from all activities outside the household so that she may devote herself fully to duties in the home and in the rearing of her children – the future guardians of the nation. Women have been ordered to remain in their houses and discharge the responsibilities assigned to them. Islam does not want to tax them doubly: to bring up their children and maintain the household, as well as to earn a living and do outdoor jobs would be a clear injustice. Islam, therefore, effects a functional division of labour between the sexes.

But this does not mean that the woman is not allowed to leave the house at all. She is, when necessary. The law has specified the home as her special field of work and has stressed that she should attend to the improvement of home life. Whenever she has to go out, certain formalities should be observed.

It is a general rule that the sphere of the family widens through blood-relations and marriage connections. To bind together the members of the family into a unity, to keep their mutual relations close and healthy, and to make each one of them a source of support, strength and contentment to the other, the law of Islam has formulated certain basic laws and rules which embody the wisdom of the ages. They may be summed up as follows:

1. Marriage between those persons who have naturally and circumstantially the closest association and affiliations with each other has been prohibited. Marriage is forbidden between: mother and son, father and daughter, step-father and step-daughter, step-mother and step-son; brother and sister, foster-brother and foster-sister, paternal uncle and his niece, aunt (father's or mother's sister) and her nephew, maternal uncle and his niece, mother-in-law and her son-in-law, and father-in-law and his daughter-in-law. This prohibition strengthens the bonds of the family and makes relations between these relatives absolutely pure and unalloyed: and they can mix with each other without any restraint and with sincere affection.
2. Beyond the limits of the forbidden marriage relations given above, matrimonial relations can be effected between the members of kindred families, so that such relationship may bind them still closer. Marriage connections between two families which are freely associated with each other, and which therefore know each other's habits, customs and traditions, are generally successful. Therefore the *Shari'ah* has not only permitted them but also encouraged and

preferred relations with kindred families to those of entirely strange families (though this is not forbidden).

3. In a group of kindred families, there usually co-exist the rich and the poor, the prosperous and the destitute. The Islamic principle is that a man's relatives have the greatest right on him. Respect for the tie between relatives is technically called *Silah-al-rahm*. Muslims are enjoined to respect this bond in every possible way. To be disloyal to one's relatives and to be negligent of their rights is a great sin and God has disapproved of it. If a relative becomes poor, or is beset by some trouble, it is the duty of his rich and prosperous relatives to help him. Special regard for the rights of relatives has been enjoined in *Zakah* and other charities.
4. The law of inheritance is so formulated in Islam that property left by the deceased cannot be concentrated in one place. It is distributed in such a way that all near relatives get their share. Son, daughter, wife, husband, father, mother brother and sister are the nearest relatives and they get the next nearest relatives. After the death of a man, therefore, his wealth is distributed amongst his kith and kin and a fatal blow is struck against the capitalistic concentration of wealth. This law of Islam is of unique excellence, and other societies are now taking similar action. But the sad irony is that Muslims themselves are not fully aware of its revolutionary potentialities and some of them, through ignorance, are even avoiding it in practice. In several parts of the Indo-Pakistan subcontinent daughters are being deprived of their share of inheritance; this is a palpable injustice and a flagrant violation of the Qur'an injunctions.

After the family and its connections are the man's relations with his friends, neighbors, dwellers of his own locality, village or city, and persons with whom he comes into constant contact. Islam recognizes these relations and enjoins a Muslim to treat them all honestly, truthfully, equitably and courteously. It bids believers to respect others' feelings, to avoid indecent and abusive language, to help each other, to attend to the sick, to support the destitute, to assist the needy and the crippled, to sympathize with the trouble-stricken, to look after orphans and widows, to feed the hungry, to clothe the unclad and to help the unemployed in seeking employment.

Islam says that if God has bestowed upon you wealth and riches, do not squander it on luxurious frivolities. It has prohibited the use of gold and silver vessels, the wearing of costly silk dresses, and the wasting of money on useless ventures and extravagant luxuries. This injunction of the *Shari'ah* is based on the principle that no man should be allowed to squander on himself wealth that could maintain thousands of human beings. It is cruel and unjust that money which can be used to feed teeming, starving humanity should be frittered away in useless ostentation. Islam does not want to deprive a man of his wealth and belongings. What one has earned or inherited is beyond doubt his own property. Islam recognizes his right and allows him to enjoy it and make the best use of it. It also suggests that if you are wealthy, you should have better dress and good accommodation and a decent living. But Islam insists that the human element should not be lost sight of.

What Islam totally disapproves of is conceited self-centered, which neglects the welfare and well-being of others and gives birth to an exaggerated individualism. It wants society as a whole to prosper, and not merely a few individuals. It instills in the minds of its followers social consciousness and suggests that they live a simple and frugal life, that they avoid excesses and, while fulfilling their own needs, keep in mind the needs and requirements of their kith and kin, their near and distant relatives, their friends and associates, their neighbors and fellow-citizens. This is what Islam wants to achieve.

So far we have discussed the nature of man's relations with his close relatives and friends. Now let us look at the wider perspective and see what kind of community Islam wants to establish. Everyone who embraces Islam not only enters the fold of the religion but also becomes a member of the Islamic community. The *Shari'ah* has formulated certain rules of behavior for this as well. These rules oblige Muslims to help each other, to approve good and forbid evil, and to see that no wrong enters their society. Some of the injunctions of the law of Islam, in this respect, are as follows:

1. To preserve the moral life of the nation and to safeguard the evolution of society on healthy lines, free mingling of the sexes has been prohibited. Islam effects a functional distribution between the sexes and sets different spheres of activity for both of them. Women should in the main devote thems-elves to household duties in their homes and men should attend to their jobs in the socio-economic spheres. Outside the pale of the nearest relations between whom marriage is forbidden, men and women have been asked not to mix freely with each other and if they do have to have contact with each other they should do so with prudence. When women have to go out of their homes, they should wear simple dress and be properly veiled. Only in genuine necessity can unveil, and they must re-cover as soon as possible.

   Along with this, men been asked to keep down their eyes and not to look at women. And if someone accidentally looks upon some woman, he should turn away his eyes. To try to see them in wrong and to try to seek their acquaintance is worse. It is the duty of both men and women to look after their personal morality and purge their souls of all impurities. Marriage is the proper form of sexual relationship and no one should attempt to overstep this limit or even think of any sexual license; the very thought and imagination of man should be purified from such perverse ideas.

2. For the same purpose it has been enjoined that proper dress should always be worn. No man should expose his body from the knees to the navel, nor should a woman expose any part of her body except her face and hands to any person other than her husband, however closely related to her he might be. This is technically called *satr* (cover) and to keep these parts covered is the religious duty of every man and woman. Through this directive Islam aims to cultivate in its followers a deep sense of modesty and purity and to suppress all forms of immodesty and moral deviation.
3. Islam does not approve of pastimes, entertainment and recreations which tend to stimulate sensual passions and vitiate the canons of morality. They are a sheer waste of time, money and energy, and destroy the moral fiber of society. Recreation in itself is certainly a necessity. It acts as a spur to activity and quickens the spirit of life and adventure. It is as important to life as water and air; one particularly requires rest and recreation after hard work. But it must be recreation which refreshes the mind and enlivens the spirit, and must not depress the spirit and deprave the passions. Absurd and wasteful entertainments wherein the people witne-ssed the depraving scenes of crime and immorality are the antithesis of healthy recreation. Although they may be gratifying to the senses, their effect upon the minds and morals is horrifying. They can have no place in an Islamic society and culture.

4. To safeguard the unity and solidarity of the nation and to achieve the welfare and well-being of the Muslim community, believers have been enjoined to avoid mutual hostility, social dissension and sectarianism of all kinds. They have been exhorted to settle their differences and disputes in accordance with the principles laid down in the Qur'an and the Sunnah, and if the parties fail to reach a settle-ment, instead of fighting and quarrelling amongst themselves, they should bury their differences in the name of Allah and leave the decision to Him. In matters of common national welfare they should help each other, obey their leaders, and avoid wasting their energies in bickering over trivial things. Such feuds and schisms are a disgrace to the Muslim community and a potential source of national weakness. They must be shunned at all costs.
5. Islam regards knowledge and science as the common heritage of mankind and Muslims have absolute liberty to learn them and their practical uses from whatever sources they can. But as far as the question of culture and the way of life is concerned, it forbids them to imitate the modes of living of other peoples. The psychology of imitation suggests that it springs from a sense of inferiority and abasement and its net results is the cultivation of a defeatist mentality. Cultural aping of others has disastrous consequences on a nation; it destroys its inner vitality, blurs. its vision, befogs its critical faculties, breeds an inferiority complex and gradually but assuredly saps all the springs of culture and sounds its death-bell.

   This is why the Holy Prophet (blessings of Allah and peace be upon him) has positively and forcefully forbidden Muslims to assume the culture and mode of life of non-Muslims. The strength of a nation does not lie in its dress, etiquette or fine arts;

its power and growth owe themselves to right knowledge, science, discipline, organization and energy for action. If you want to learn from others, take lessons from their will to action and social discipline, avail yourselves of their knowledge and technical accomplishments but do not lean towards those arts and crafts which breed cultural slavery and national inferiority. Muslims have been enjoined to guard against such influence.

Now we come to the relationship of Muslims with non-Muslims. In dealing with them, believers have been instructed not to be intolerant or narrow-minded. They have been commanded not to abuse or speak ill of their religious leaders or saints, nor to say anything insulting about their religion. They have been instructed not to seek disputes with them unnecessarily but to live in peace and amity. If the non-Muslims observe peace and conciliatory attitudes towards Muslims, and do not violate their territories and other rights, they also should keep congenial and friendly relations with them and deal with them fairly and justly.

It is the very dictate of our religion that we possess greater human sympathy and politeness than any other people, and behave in most noble and modest ways. Bad manners, ill-behavior, oppression and narrow-mindedness are against the very spirit of Islam. A Muslim is born in the world to become a living symbol of goodness, nobility and humanity. He should win the hearts of people by his character and example. Then alone he can become a true ambassador of Islam.

4. *The Rights of All Creatures*: Now we come to the last kind of rights. God has honored man with authority over His countless creatures. Everything has been harnessed for him. He has been endowed with the power to subdue them and make them serve his objectives.

This superior position gives man authority over them and he enjoys the right to use them as he likes. But that does not mean that God has given him unbridled liberty. Islam says that all creation has certain rights on man. They are: he should not waste them on fruitless ventures nor should he unnecessarily hurt them or harm them. When he uses them for his service he should cause them the least possible harm, and should employ the best and the least injurious methods of using them.

The law of Islam embodies many injunctions about these rights. For instance, we are allowed to slaughter animals for food but have been forbidden to kill them merely for fun or sport. To slaughter them, the method of *dhabh* (slaughtering) has been fixed, the best possible method of obtaining meat from animals. Other methods are either more painful or spoil the meat and deprive it of some of its useful properties. Similarly, killing an animal by causing continuous pain and injury is considered abominable in Islam. Islam allows the killing of dangerous and venomous animals and of beasts of prey only because it values man's life more than theirs. But here, too, it does not allow their killing by resort to prolonged painful methods.

Regarding the beasts of burden and animals used for riding and transport, Islam distinctly forbids man to keep them hungry, to put intolerable burdens on them and to beat them cruelly. To catch birds and imprison them in cages without any special purpose is considered abominable. Islam does not approve even of the useless cutting of trees and bushes. Man can use their fruits and other produce, but he has not the right to destroy them. Vegetables, after all, possess life. Nor does Islam allow waste among even lifeless things; so much so that it disapproves of the wasteful flow of too much water. Its avowed purpose is to avoid waste in every conceivable form and to make the best use of all resources - living and lifeless.

SHARI'AH - THE UNIVERSAL AND ETERNAL LAW

In the foregoing pages we have given a very brief resume of the law of Islam - the law which Prophet Muhammad (blessings of Allah and peace be upon him) delivered to mankind for all times to come. This law admits of no difference between man and man except in faith and religion. Those religious and social systems and political and cultural ideologies which differentiate between men on grounds of race, country or color can never become universal creeds or world ideologies for the simple reason that belonging ta certain country cannot tear his identity from that place, nor can the whole world condense into one country; the color of a negro, a Chinese and a white man cannot be changed. Such ideologies and social systems must remain confined to one race, country or community. They are bound to be narrow, limited and nationalistic. Islam, on the other hand, is a universal ideology. Any person who declares belief in *La ilaha illallah Muhammad-ur-Rasuluullah* (there is no other god worthy of worship than Allah, and Muhammad is His Prophet) enters the pale of Islam and entitles himself to the same rights as those of other Muslims. Islam makes no discrimination on the basis of race, country, color, language or the like. Its appeal is to the whole of humanity.

Its law is also eternal. It is not based on the customs or traditions of any particular people and is not meant for any particular period of human history. It is based on the same principles of nature on which man has been created. And as that nature remains the same in all periods and under all circumstances, law based on it is applicable to every period and under all circumstances.

4

Introduction to Jihad

The Koran invites Muslims to give their lives in exchange for assurances of paradise. The Hadith (accounts of Mohammed's actions and personal statements) elaborate on the Koran, providing specific injunctions about treaties, pay, booty, prisoners, tactics, and much else. Muslim jurisprudents then wove these precepts into a body of law.

During his years in power, the prophet engaged in an average of nine military campaigns a year, or one every five to six weeks; thus did jihad help define Islam from its very dawn. Conquering and humiliating non-Muslims was a main feature of the prophet's jihad.

During the first several centuries of Islam, "the interpretation of jihad was unabashedly aggressive and expansive." After the conquests subsided, non-Muslims hardly threatened and Sufi notions of jihad as self-improv-ement developed in complement to the martial meaning.

The Crusades, the centuries-long European effort to control the Holy Land, gave jihad a new urgency and prompted what Mr. Cook calls the "classical" theory of jihad. Finding themselves on the defensive led to a hardening of Muslim attitudes.

The Mongol invasions of the 13th century subjugated much of the Muslim world, a catastrophe only partially mitigated by the Mongols' nominal conversion to Islam. Some thinkers, Ibn Taymiya in particular, came to distinguish between true and false Muslims and to give jihad new prominence by judging the validity of a person's faith according to his willingness to wage jihad.

Nineteenth-century "purification jihads" took place in several regions against fellow Muslims. The most radical and consequential of these was the Wahhabis' jihad in Arabia. Drawing on Ibn Taymiya, they condemned most non-Wahhabi Muslims as infidels (kafirs) and waged jihad against them.

European imperialism inspired jihadi resistance efforts, notably in India, the Caucasus, Somalia, Sudan, Algeria, and Morocco, but all in the end failed. This disaster meant new thinking was needed. Islamist new thinking began in Egypt and India in the 1920s, but jihad acquired its contemporary quality of radical offensive warfare only with the Egyptian thinker Sayyid Qutb. Qutb developed Ibn Taymiya's distinction between true and false Muslims to deem non-Islamists to be non-Muslims and then declare jihad on them. The group that assassinated Anwar El-Sadat in 1981 then added the idea of jihad as the path to world domination.

The anti-Soviet war in Afghanistan led to the final step (so far) in this evolution. In Afghanistan, for the first time, jihadis assembled from around the world to fight on behalf of Islam. A Palestinian, Abdullah Azzam, became the theorist of global jihad in the 1980s, giving it an unheard-of central role, judging each Muslim exclusively by his contribution to jihad, and making jihad the salvation of Muslims and Islam. Out of this quickly came suicide terrorism and Mr. Bin Laden.

Mr. Cook's erudite and timely study has many implications, including:

The current understanding of jihad is more extreme than at any prior time in Islamic history. This extremism suggests that the Muslim world is going through a phase, one that must be endured and overcome, comparable to analogously horrid periods in Germany, Russia, and China.

Jihad having evolved steadily until now doubtless will continue to do so in the future.

The excessive form of jihad currently practiced by Al Qaeda and others could, Mr. Cook semi-predicts, lead to its "decisive rejection" by a majority of Muslims. Jihad then could turn into a non-violent concept.

Jihad is a subject that non-Muslims find difficult to understand. In fact, there is nothing particularly outlandish about it. All one has to remember is that holy war is not the opposite of pacifism, but rather of secular war - fighting in pursuit of aims lying outside religion. Whether people are militant or not in its pursuit is another matter.

The normal type of jihad is missionary warfare. That's how you'll find it described in the classical law-books, from about 800 to about 1800. What the Quran has to say on the subject is a different question: the rules it presupposes seem to be a good deal more pacifist than those developed by the jurists and exegetes. But it is the work of the latter which came to form the Sharia - the huge mass of precepts on which the public and private lives of Muslims were based (at least in theory), down to the coming of modernity, which still regulates their devotional lives today, and on which Islamists (or "fundamentalists") would like once more to base the entire arena of public life.

The scholars said that jihad consisted in backing the call to Islam with violence, where necessary. It was "the forcible mission assisted by the unsheathed Sword against wrongheaded people who arrogantly refuse to accept the plain truth after it has become clear": thus a scholar who died in 1085. The idea was that God was the only ruler of the universe. Humans who refused to acknowledge this were in the nature of rebels, who had to be brought to heel. At the very least, they had to submit to God politically, by being brought under Muslim government. But ideally, they would submit to him in religious terms as well, by converting.

Holy warriors worked by making regular incursions into the lands of the infidels order to call them to Islam. Normally, they would do so as part of an official expedition launched by the state, but they might also operate on their own. In any case, if the infidels didn't want to convert, they could just surrender politically (at least if they were Christians and Jews). In that case they were placed under Muslim government, but kept their own religion in return for the payment of poll-tax. But if they refused both religious and political surrender, they should be fought until they were defeated. The terms were in that case set by the conquerors, who might kill the men and enslave the women and children (or so at least if they were pagans); or they might treat them as if they had surrendered voluntarily.

Once an infidel community had been subdued politically, one moved on to the next lot of infidels and did the same to them. This had to go on until the whole earth was God's or the world came to an end, whichever would be the sooner.

Missionary warfare was a duty imposed by God on the Muslim community, not on individuals, and it was discharged primarily by the ruler, who'd typically mount one expedition into infidel territory a year, if he had infidel neighbours. But it was highly meritorious for private individuals to go and fight as well, and there were always volunteers on the borders. If you couldn't go yourself, you could earn merit by donating money or giving gifts to the cause, like people in 19th-century Europe would make donations in support of the missionaries working in distant countries.

The way that ordinary Muslims thought of jihad in the past can be compared to Christians' attitude towards those of their co-religionists who chose to become missionaries. Nowadays the latter are often regarded as interfering busybodies, but formerly they were admired for their willingness to devote their lives to the salvation of benighted natives. That's the attitude that prevailed in jihad: it was an extremely noble enterprise. After all, people risked their own lives for it. It was the height of altruism.

The Christian missionaries did not themselves fight; they merely followed in the wake of soldiers. But a holy warrior was a missionary and a soldier all in one. He was engaged in something that modern observers would call religious imperialism.

That's an institution with very long roots in the Middle East. Ancient near-eastern historians call it warfare at the command of a god, and the star example is the Assyrians. Their god Ashshur endlessly told them to go and conquer. The god of the Israelites was of the same type. "I have given into your hands Sihon the Amorite, king of Heshbon, and his land. Begin to possess it and fight him in battle", he says to Moses in Deuteronomy, where Moses reports that "We took all his cities and utterly destroyed the men, the women and the little ones".

In the same vein a Moabite king says in an inscription that "Kamosh (the deity) spoke to me and said, Go and take Nebo from Israel. So I went and fought it...and took it and killed everybody, 7,000 men, boys, women, girls and slave girls". The Muslim God also told his people to conquer, but with one big difference in classical thought, namely that he wanted the victims to convert.

The Assyrians, the Israelites and the Moabites didn't pretend to be doing anything for the good of the victims. They fought for the greater glory of their own god, and their own community, not to save anyone else. The same seems to have been true of the early Arab conquerors. But in classical Islam, the divine command to go and fight is no longer addressed to an ethnic group, only to believers, whoever they may be; and it is now linked to a religious mission civilisatrice: the believers conquer in order to save souls, not (or not just) to glorify their own community.

It is this fusion of religious and political imperialism that makes classical jihad distinctive, for the two don't usually go together. The great universalist religions were apolitical and spread by peaceful proselytisation: thus Buddhism, Christianity, and Manichaeism, and also Bahai'ism. And universalist conquerors are not usually out to save people's souls: think of Alexander the Great, the Romans, or the Mongols. But in Islam, religious mission and world conquest have married up.

WAS ISLAM SPREAD BY FORCE?

The second question posed at the start of this essay was: is it true that Islam was spread by force?

The answer is, in one sense, yes, but even this needs careful qualification. Warfare did play a major role both in the rise of Islam and its later diffusion. But some places were Islamised without any war at all, notably Malaysia and Indonesia. Above all, even where Islam was spread by jihad, it was not usually done the way people imagine. People usually think of holy warriors as engaging in something like Charlemagne's forced conversion of the Saxons, war for the extirpation of wrong beliefs throughout an entire community. But that model is very rare in Islamic history. The effect of war was usually more indirect.

The scholars said that all infidels had to be brought under Muslim sovereignty, but that Jews and Christians acknowledged the true God and had a revelation from him, so they could be allowed to exist under Muslim protection in return for paying poll-tax. All other infidels were pagans, so how were they to be treated? There is general agreement that the Arabs of Mohammed's Arabia got the choice between Islam and the Sword, and that they did so because they had no religion, as one early scholar put it. (Paganism didn't count as one.) That's the best example there is on the Muslim side of the Charlemagne model, if I may call it that, and it is a juristic schematisation of history rather than rather than historical reporting.

Some jurists insisted that this was how all pagans should be treated: people who did not acknowledge the sole sovereignty of God had no right to exist. Others said that for one reason or another, the Arabs were exceptional: all other pagans could be granted protection in return for paying poll-tax in the same way as the Jews and the Christians. This disagreement was enshrined in Muslim law, and modern Islamists typically go for the first view, equating pagans with modern secularists and atheists (among them is an associate of Yusuf al-Qaradawi, lionised in Europe by some of the very secularists whom his associate would force to convert). In pre-modern practice, tolerance usually prevailed as far as conquered communities were concerned. The only infidels who could not be allowed to exist in either theory or practice were apostates - who have become a highly sensitive issue today.

But if people were allowed to keep their religion under Muslim rule, how could the jurists define jihad as missio-nary warfare? How was it different from other forms of imperialism, such as the Crusades (which were fought for the recovery of the holy land, not the conversion of the Muslims) or secular expansionism?

The answer is that in effect jihad just was ordinary imperialism, but it was undertaken, or at least justified, on the grounds that it would result in conversion, if not straightaway, then sooner or later - and it usually did so too, in a number of ways. For a start, the Muslims routinely took a lot of captives. Male captives were often given the choice between Islam and death, or they might recite the Muslim profession of faith of their own accord to avoid execution. More importantly, captives were usually sold off as slaves, and slaves almost always ended up by converting because most slavery was domestic.

And above all, back in the conquered area, Muslim rulers would move in along with judges and religious scholars to build mosques, apply Islamic law, place restrictions on the building of non-Muslim houses of worship and introduce other discriminatory measures so that the original inhabitants were reduced to tributaries in their own land. They were not necessarily persecuted. The Muslim record of tolerance is generally good. (Obviously, there are plenty of examples of persecution of one kind or another; that religious minorities generally speaking did better under Muslim than under Christian rule under pre-modern conditions nonetheless remains true, however hackneyed the claim has become.) But the non-Muslims would soon have a sense that history was passing them by, that all the action was elsewhere, and this would translate into a feeling that their own beliefs were outmoded. So they would convert too, and that's the method that really mattered.

In sum, jihad typically spread Islam in much the same way that 19th-century European imperialism spread western culture (and/or Christianity): nobody was directly forced to accept western modernity, or Christianity, but by moving in as the politically dominant elite, the imperialists gave their own beliefs and institutions a persuasiveness that made them difficult to resist. Medieval Muslim scholars were well aware of this effect, and unlike their modern successors, they never tried to deny the role of war in the expansion of Islam.

MUSLIMS, MORALITY, AND RELIGIOUS WARFARE

That brings me to the third question: did the pre-modern Muslims never worry about the moral status of religious warfare?

The answer is mostly no, but sometimes yes. The scholars insisted that the warriors had to fight with the right intentions, for God, not for booty. They also debated whether it was right to conduct holy war under a wrongful ruler (the Sunni answer was yes). But if everything was in order on the side of the warriors, the jurists were satisfied that the enterprise was in the best interests of the victims. The conquered peoples were being dragged to Paradise in chains, as a famous saying went. Far from feeling ashamed about their use of war, Muslims often stressed that holy war was something that only they would engage in, meaning that they were willing to do much more for their religion than other people. They were willing to sacrifice their own lives so that others might live, as they put it. To them, it proved that only Islam was a truly universalist religion.

But the conquered peoples, above all the Christians, always held the Muslim use of war to be wrong, and this did eventually affect the Muslims. As early as 634 CE, a Greek tract declared that the so-called prophet must be an impostor because prophets don't come armed with the Sword. Fifty years later a Christian patriarch supposedly told the caliph that Islam was a religion spread by the Sword, meaning that therefore it could not be true. The Christians were to harp on this theme for ever after. In the 10th and 11th centuries, the Muslims began to mention this claim, clearly because they were upset by it.

For example, al-Amiri, an Iranian philosopher who died in 996, takes issue with unidentified people who say that "if Islam were a religion of truth, it would be a religion of mercy, and the one who calls to it would not in that case attack people with the Sword to take their property and capture and enslave their families; rather, he would proselytise with words and guide to it by the force of his explanations". In other words, true religion is spread by peaceful mission; holy war is just a religious cover for rapaciousness, whatever people might say about the purity of their intentions.

It isn't always clear in these texts whether the charges were made by Muslims or non-Muslims, but there were certainly Muslims now who felt the association of warfare and religion to be wrong. A 10th-century religious leader by the name of Ibn Karram, for example, was said by his followers to have been worthier of prophethood than Mohammed, because he lived an ascetic life and did not conduct war. And some Muslims (or ex-Muslims) rejected all established religions, not just Islam, on the grounds that all prophets, not just Mohammed, were tricksters who used religion to start wars and accumulate worldly power. So now the concept of holy war had to be defended.

One of the most interesting defences is by this philosopher al-Amiri. He responded by identifying jihad as defensive warfare. That's what many modern apologetes do, too, sometimes writing off offensive jihad - missionary warfare - as an Orientalist invention. (Orientalism often gets used as a grand trash-can in which modern Muslims dump all the aspects of pre-modern Islam that they have come to dislike.) Modern Muslims will even go so far as to cast the prophet's wars and the Arab conquests as defensive, or pre-emptive, but this was more than al-Amiri could bring himself to do.

When it came to the prophet, he fell back on the altruism argument: Mohammed was not in it for material wealth or power. This is clear from the fact that he suffered for ten years in Mecca before setting up a state in Medina; he conquered people for their own good, not for his own sake, and the Iranians ought to be grateful to the Arabs for having destroyed the Persian empire; not only did the Arabs bring the truth, they also freed them from for the oppressive tyranny and rigid social hierarchy that prevailed in that empire. The Muslims came as liberators on all fronts. Of course, al-Amiri says, Mohammed would have preferred not to use the Sword at all, but since the infidels so stubbornly resisted him, he had no choice.

Al-Amiri's tone here is rather like that of the 19th-century British imperialists who felt resentment against all those uncooperative peoples whose recalcitrance had forced Britain to take them over more or less against its will, as they felt it. They didn't like war either, but what could one do when the natives refused to see the light. One had to fight them for their own sake, and the noble purpose elevated the war to a high moral status. That was al-Amiri's response in a nutshell. But what his opponents argued was precisely that on the contrary, the use of war discredited the alleged purpose and proved the religion it was meant to spread to be false. So the more the Muslims defended jihad by yoking it to the service of religion, the more their non-Muslim opponents reacted by thinking that the religion must be bad. That's how Christians and Muslims have been talking past each other for 1,400 years.

Meanwhile, other people defended jihad by observing that religion had two different functions: it organised collective life, and it also offered individual salvation. At the collective level it was a prescription for socio-political order, with its do's and don'ts, its morality, its law and its war. At this level, coercion was indispensable, and holy war was just one form in which it was practiced. At the individual level it was pure spirituality, and at that level coercion was impossible. The only jihad you could fight here was the so-called greater jihad against your own evil inclinations.

So for example, the scholars will say that a man who has been converted by force becomes a full member of the Muslim community and must live as a Muslim in public, even though he is not a believer in his inner self. He had been coerced at the level of social and political affiliation, but one couldn't force him to believe. In fact, they said, one could never know what was going on in people's inner selves, and it wasn't anyone's business either: it was between the individuals and God alone. But what people did externally affected others and so had to be regulated. Having been forced into the Muslim community, the captive would have to live as a Muslim - the rest was up to him. Eventually, they said, the chances were that he or his children would see the light, become sincere believers of their own accord, and grateful for having been forced.

In this formulation the claim was that jihad was better than secular conquest. Unlike Alexander the Great, Mohammed incorporated people in a polity in which they had the option of being saved, in which they had the ability to see for themselves, in which they could choose to become true believers. But it left inner conviction as something over which the individual had full control.

This argument ought to be easy for modern people to understand, or at least Americans, for they also tend to think that war can be legitimated by a high moral purpose - as long as that purpose hasn't got anything to do with individual faith. The moral purposes they have in mind are wholly secular, not the lower level of religion, and the salvation they talk about is in this world. But they too tend to be eager to rescue other people by enabling them to become more like themselves: richer, freer, and more democratic. What do you do when your fingers are itching to intervene, when you have the power to do it, when you are sure you are right and you are convinced that the victims will be grateful - quite apart from all the advantages that may redound to yourself from intervening? Aren't you allowed to use force? Indeed, aren't you obliged to use it? Is it right to save people against their will? Should you force them to be free? If you say yes to these questions, you are in effect a believer in jihad.

But will the victims be grateful? In the Muslim case, the answer was normally yes. The scholars mention it time and again, as something everyone knew. People fell grateful that they had become Muslims, in whatever manner it had happened, voluntarily or by force. This made it difficult to entertain serious doubts about the legitimacy of jihad. In the last resort, most people liked the result. And this is one of the most striking differences between Muslim and European imperialism, which are otherwise so comparable. The one led to Islamisation, the other to westernisation; the one dragged you to Paradise in chains, the other to secular modernity. But people aren't grateful for having been westernised. In line with this, westerners no longer take any pride in their imperial past. Today, westerners often hold imperialism to have invalidated the very civilisation it spread. They have been persuaded by their own arguments against jihad in a way the Muslims never were. Why this difference? It would call for another lecture.

JIHAD, THEN AND NOW

This leads to the fourth question: what is the relevance of all this to the modern world? The Muslims have not practiced missionary jihad since the decline of the Ottoman Empire, at least not under the sponsorship of states, and to my knowledge there are no serious calls for its return. What the tradition has left is a strong activist streak, a sense that it is right to fight for your convictions. "Look at you, you Christians, with your passivity you have turned religion into something that doesn't exist", as demonstrators against Salman Rushdie said in Paris in March 1989. But to under-stand the fundamentalists we need to go to the other kind of jihad, the one practiced when the Muslims are politically weak.

What happens when Muslim territory falls under infidel sovereignty? Can Muslims stay on and live under non-Muslim rule? Some jurists said yes, others denied it on the grounds that Islamic law could only be applied in full under Muslim sovereignty. If infidels conquered Muslim land, the Muslims had to emigrate, they had to make a hijra to a place where they could practice Islamic law - either an existing Muslim state or a new one set up by themselves - and then they should start holy war in order to reconquer their homeland. Not all scholars subscribed to this view, but it was upheld by many in response to the loss of Muslim territory in Spain and it also inspired anti-colonial movements in British India, French Algeria and elsewhere.

Imagine an even worse scenario: what happens when not a single Islamic state exists any more, when all political power has turned infidel? The answer is the same with greater urgency (and probably less disagreement too). You must immigrate to a place where you can establish a Muslim state and then you must wage holy war to get it going. In both cases, the model is Mohammed: first he lived in pagan Mecca, under infidel sovereignty, then he immigrated to Medina where he established a Muslim polity and started jihad and conquered Mecca, which he cleansed and purified; thereafter his followers began the conquest of the rest of the world, in what eventually turned into missionary warfare.

Jihad for the recovery or actual creation of Muslim sovereignty (as opposed to its expansion): that's the type that is practiced today. Modern fundamentalists (or Islamists) call it defensive jihad, though it is not what the classical Muslims understood by that term. It makes sense to them, partly because they feel on the defensive; partly because everyone recognises the legitimacy of defensive war; and not least, because participation in defensive jihad is an individual obligation, like fasting and prayer, not a communal duty like the missionary type, which you don't have to undertake as long as others are doing it. So calling your jihad defensive is good for mobilisation.

Whatever you call it, the missionary element is greatly reduced in this type of warfare. Of course, you have to convert people to your own beliefs in order to get them together for state formation and conquest, but the emphasis is not so much on saving people as on saving Islam, especially in the more extreme version when no Islamic state is deemed to exist at all. For Islam can't exist without political embodiment, according to this view. There has to be a place on earth where God rules. Without it, collective (and individual?) life ceases to have any moral foundations.

In the past, jihad for the actual creation of Muslim sovereignty was only practiced by heretics, for it was only heretics who would deny that existing states were Islamic. The very first to do so were the Kharijites, who are almost as old as Islam itself. There was also Shi'ites who did. But the Sunnis always accepted their own states as Islamic in some (sometimes minimalist) sense, at least until the 18th century, and most still do, including the Muslim Brother-hood, and Hamas. Their jihad is concentrated on the recovery of Muslim territory, such as Palestine, and the defence of Muslims in places such as Chechnya. They don't attack infidels elsewhere, nor don't they believe in fighting Muslim rulers, or not any more.

But other fundamentalists deem all Muslim states, or even all Muslim people apart from themselves, to be infidels. Al-Qaida is among them. They direct their efforts against America rather than fellow Muslims because America is deemed to be behind everything wrong in the Muslim world - you can't correct the shadow cast by a crooked stick, as Osama bin Laden is said to have put it. But when America, the crooked stick, has been removed, it will be the turn of the Muslim world in general, and by that they mean all countries with a Muslim population, which is in effect the whole earth by now. So as far as al-Qaida is concerned, the old distinction between the abode of Islam and the abode of war has disappeared.

The extreme fundamentalists can't see any difference between living in Egypt, for example, and living under non-Muslim rule, thanks to the all-pervasive influence of the modern state. In the old days the political domain was also worldly and corrupt, but the social domain was still shaped by Islam. Nowadays, however, it is the state that regulates marriage, divorce, inheritance, trade, finance, work, health, childcare, schooling, higher education, and so on, often with attention to what the Sharia says, but freely reshaping it to fit modern, secular aims which originate in the infidel and politically dominant west.

So one way or the other, Muslims are ruled by the west wherever they live, not just politically but also socially and culturally. Wherever they are look, they are being invaded by so-called western values - in the form of giant billboards advertising self-indulgence, semi-pornographic films, liquor, pop music, fat tourists in indecent clothes and funny hats, and politicians lecturing people about the virtues of democracy. Religion does not actually shape the social realm any more, except rhetorically. All that religion shapes in modern Muslim societies is voluntary associations such as Sufi orders, Muslim brotherhoods, and fundamentalist cells, which fall short of being whole societies, let alone states, and which you can set up in non-Muslim countries too. So in effect, as the fundamentalists see it, all Muslims have become Diaspora Muslims.

Some Muslims are happy with this. They want the socio-political order to be secularised; they want religious affiliation to be voluntary. They are the secularists, the people we have no trouble understanding. But to the fundamentalists, or rather to the extremists among them, all Muslims are now living in a new age of ignorance (jahiliyya) such as that which prevailed in pagan Arabia before the rise of Islam. This is why one must get together to reenact Mohammed's career and save Islam.

Establishment religious scholars often compare such fundamentalists to the Kharijites of the early Islamic period, and with good reason. They are amazingly similar. There is the same declaration of other Muslims to be infidels, the same sense of fighting for God rather than for people - God has to rule even if the whole world is going to perish in the attempt -the same utter ruthlessness too. The Kharijites allowed assassinations, indiscriminate slaughter, the killing of men, women and children alike, much like Abu Musab al-Zarqawi. Their missions were often suicidal, too, not in the sense that they'd set out on individual missions bound to result in death, but rather in the sense that tiny numbers would take on huge forces bound to exterminate them, inspired by a quest for martyrdom. They had sold their souls to God, as they put it, and got a good price for them, too, namely Paradise; they went into battle intending to collect the price. And then as today, women would fight along with the men.

There is of course no direct link whatever between the Kharijites and modern fundamentalists. People like Osama bin Laden and Ayman al-Zawahiri don't even seem to know their own tradition all that well. Rather, they have stripped Islam of practically everything that most Muslims consider to be their religion.

What's left is an archetypal monotheist of the confrotational type: a separatist and militant zealot. In the view of such zealots, God's people can't live together with infidels; they must have their own political space. Right and wrong must be embodied in separate communities, and every Muslim must fight to bring this about.

The history of Islam starts with a great separation of God's people from the rest of mankind by force of arms, and Islamic history thereafter is punctuated by regular attempts to restore the separation, to get rid of all the complexity that obscured the simplicity of the original vision. Those who engaged in such attempts tended to come from the more peripheral areas of the Middle East, often from a tribal background, and they were always minorities. The fundamentalists, too, are only a small minority today. But you don't need an awful lot of people of this kind for an awful lot of trouble.

5

Ideology of Jihad

In the linguistic sense, the Arabic word "jihad" means struggling or striving and applies to any effort exerted by anyone. In this sense, a student struggles and strives to get an education and pass course work; an employee strives to fulfill his/her job and maintain good relations with his/her employer; a politician strives to maintain or increase his(1) popularity with his constituents and so on. The term strives or struggle may be used for/by Muslims as well as non-Muslims; for example, Allah, the One and Only True God say in the Qur'an:

"We have enjoined on people kindness to parents; but if they strive (Jahadaka) to make you ascribe partners with Me that of which you have no knowledge, then obey them not..." (The Holy Quran, 29:8; also see 31:15)

In the above two verses of the Quran, it is non-Muslim parents who strive (jahadaka) to convert their Muslim child back to their religion. In the West, "jihad" is generally translated as "holy war," a usage the media has popularized. According to Islamic teachings, it is unholy to instigate or start war; however, some wars are inevitable and justifiable.

If we translate the words "holy war" back into Arabic, we find "harbun muqaddasatu," or for "the holy war," "al-harbu al-muqaddasatu." We challenge any researcher or scholar to find the meaning of "jihad" as holy war in the Qur'an or authentic Hadith collections or in early Islamic literature. Unfortunately, some Muslim writers and translators of the

Qur'an, the Hadith and other Islamic literature translate the term "jihad" as "holy war," due to the influence of centuries-old Western propaganda.

This could be a reflection of the Christian use of the term "Holy War" to refer to the Crusades of a thousand years ago. However, the Arabic words for "war" are "harb" or "qital," which are found in the Qur'an and Hadith.

For Muslims the term Jihad is applied to all forms of striving and has developed some special meanings over time. The sources of this development are the Qur'an (the Word of God revealed to Prophet Muhammad(S) [(S) denotes Sall-Allahu 'alayhi wa sallam, meaning peace and blessings of Allah be upon him]. The Qur'an and the Hadith use the word "jihad" in several different contexts which are given below:

- Recognizing the Creator and Loving Him Most:

It is human nature to love what is seen with the eyes and felt with the senses more than the unseen reality. The Creator of the Universe and the One God is Allah. He is the Unseen Reality which we tend to ignore and not recognize. The Qur'an addresses those who claim to be believers:

"O you who believe! Choose neither your fathers nor your brethren for protectors if they love disbelief over belief; whoever of you takes them for protectors, such are wrong-doers. Say: if your fathers, and your children, and your brethren, and your spouses, and your tribe, and the wealth you have acquired, and business for which you fear shrinkage, and houses you are pleased with are dearer to you than Allah and His Messenger and striving in His way: then wait till Allah brings His command to pass. Allah does not guide disobedient folk." (The Holy Quran 9:23, 24)

It is indeed a struggle to put Allah ahead of our loved ones, our wealth, our worldly ambitions and our own lives. Especially for a non-Muslim who embraces Islam, it may be a tough struggle due to the opposition of his family, peers and society.

- Resisting Pressure of Parents, Peers, and Society:

Once a person has made up his mind to put the Creator of the Universe above all else, he often comes under intense pressures. It is not easy to resist such pressures and strive to maintain dedication and love of Allah over all else. A person who has turned to Islam from another religion may be subjected to pressures designed to turn him back to the religion of the family. We read in the Qur'an:

"So obey not the rejecters of faith, but strive (jahidhum) against them by it (the Qur'an) with a great endeavor." (The Holy Quran, 25:52)

- *S*taying on the Straight Path Ssteadfastl*y*:

Allah says in the Qur'an:

"And strive (Jadihu) for Allah with the endeavor (Jihadihi) which is His right. He has chosen you and has not laid upon you in the deen (religion) any hardship..." (The Holy Quran, 22:78)

"And whosoever strives (Jahada), strives (yujahidu) only for himself, for lo! Allah is altogether independent of the universe." (The Holy Quran, 29:6)

As for those who strive and struggle to live as true Muslims whose lives are made difficult due to persecution by their opponents, they are advised to migrate to a more peaceful and tolerant land and continue with their struggle in the cause of Allah. Allah says in the Qur'an:

"Lo! As for those whom the angels take (in death) while they wronged themselves, (the angels) will ask: 'In what you were engaged?' They will way: 'We were oppressed in the land.' (The angels) will say: 'Was not Allah's earth spacious that you could have migrated therein?'" (The Holy Quran, 4:97)

"Lo! Those who believe and those who emigrate (to escape persecution) and strive (Jahadu) in the way of Allah, these have hope of Allah's mercy..." (The Holy Quran, 2:218)

Allah tests the believers in their faith and their steadfastness:

"Or did you think that you would enter Paradise while yet Allah knows not those of you who really strive (Jahadu), nor knows those (of you) who are steadfast." (The Holy Quran, 3:142)

"And surely we shall try you with something of fear and hunger, and loss of wealth and lives and fruits; but give tidings to the steadfast." (The Holy Quran, 2:155)

We find that the Prophet Muhammad(S) and his clan were boycotted socially and economically for three years to force him to stop his message and compromise with the pagans but he resisted and realized a moral victory.

- Striving for Righteous Deeds:

Allah declares in the Qur'an:

"As for those who strive (Jahadu) in us (the cause of Allah), we surely guide them to our paths, and lo! Allah is with the good doers." (The Holy Quran, 29:69)

When we are faced with two competing interests, it becomes jihad to choose the right one, as the following Hadith exemplifies:

"Aisha, wife of the Prophet(S) asked, 'O Messenger of Allah, we see jihad as the best of deeds, so shouldn't we join it?' He replied, 'but the best of jihad is a perfect Hajj (pilgrimage to Makkah).'" (Sahih Al-Bukhari, No. 2784)

At another occasion, a man asked the Prophet Muhammad(S):

"'Should I join the jihad?' He asked, 'Do you have parents?' The man said, 'Yes!' The Prophet(S) said, 'then strives by serving them!'" (Sahih Al-Bukhari, No. 5972)

Yet another man asked the Messenger of Allah(S):

"'What kind of jihad is better?' He replied, 'A word of truth in front of an oppressive ruler!'" (Sunan Al-Nasa'i, No. 4209)

The Messenger of Allah(S) said:

"...the Mujahid (one who carries out jihad) is he who strives against himself for the sake of Allah, and the Muhajir (one who emigrates) is he who abandons evil deeds and sin." (Sahih Ibn Hibbanm, No. 4862)

- Having courage and Steadfastness to Convey the Message of Islam:

The Qur'an narrates the experiences of a large number of Prophets and good people who suffered a great deal trying to convey the message of Allah to mankind. For examples, see the Qur'an 26:1-190, 36:13-32. In the Qur'an, Allah specifically praises those who strive to convey His message:

"Who is better in speech than one who calls (other people) to Allah, works righteous, and declares that he is from the Muslims." (The Holy Quran, 41:33)

Under adverse conditions it takes great courage to remain a Muslim, declare one to be a Muslim and call others to Islam. We read in the Qur'an:

"The (true) believers are only those who believe in Allah and his messenger and afterward doubt not, but strive with their wealth and their selves for the cause of Allah. Such are the truthful." (The Holy Quran, 49:15)

- Defending Islam and the Community:

Allah declares in the Qur'an:

"To those against whom war is made, permission is given (to defend themselves), because they are wronged - and verily, Allah is Most Powerful to give them victory - (they are) those who have been expelled from their homes in defiance of right - (for no cause) except that they say, 'Our Lord is Allah'..." (The Holy Quran, 22:39-40)

The Qur'an permits fighting to defend the religion of Islam and the Muslims. This permission includes fighting in self-defense and for the protection of family and property. The early Muslims fought many battles against their enemies under the leadership of the Prophet Muhammad(S) or his representatives. For example, when the pagans of Quraysh brought armies against Prophet Muhammad(S), the Muslims fought to defend their faith and community(3). The Qur'an adds:

"Fight in the cause of Allah against those who fight against you, but do not transgress limits. Lo! Allah loves not aggressors....And fight them until persecution is no more, and religion is for Allah. But if they desist, then let there be no hostility except against transgressors." (The Holy Quran, 2:190, 193)

- Helping allied People who May not be Muslim:

In the late period of the Prophet Muhammad's(S) life, the tribe of Banu Khuza'ah became his ally. They were living near Makkah which was under the rule of the pagan Quraysh, Prophet Muhammad's(S) own tribe. The tribe of Banu Bakr, an ally of Quraysh, with the help of some elements of Quraysh, attacked Banu Khuza'ah invoked the treaty and demanded Prophet Muhammad(S) to come to their help and punish Quraysh. The Prophet Muhammad(S) organized a campaign against Quraysh of Makkah which resulted in the conquest of Makkah which occurred without any battle.

- Removing Treacherous People from Power:

Allah orders the Muslims in the Qur'an:

"If you fear treachery from any group, throw back (their treaty) to them, (so as to be) on equal terms. Lo! Allah loves not the treacherous." (The Holy Quran, 8:58)

Prophet Muhammad(S) undertook a number of armed campaigns to remove treacherous people from power and their lodgings. He had entered into pacts with several tribes, however, some of them proved them treacherous. Prophet Muhammad(S) launched armed campaigns against these tribes, defeated and exiled them from Medina and its surroundings.

- Defending through Preemptive Strikes:

Indeed, it is difficult to mobilize people to fight when they see no invaders in their territory; however, those who are charged with responsibility see dangers ahead of time and must provide leadership. The Messenger of Allah, Muhammad(S), had the responsibility to protect his people and the religion he established in Arabia. Whenever he received intelligence reports about enemies gathering near his borders he carried out preemptive strikes, broke their power and dispersed them. Allah ordered Muslims in the Qur'an:

"Fighting is prescribed upon you, and you dislike it. But it may happen that you dislike a thing which is good for you, and it may happen that you love a thing which is bad for you. And Allah knows and you know not." (The Holy Quran, 2:216)

- Gaining Freedom to Inform, Educate and Convey the Message of Islam in an Open and Free Environment:

  Allah declares in the Qur'an:

"They ask you (Muhammad) concerning fighting in the Sacred Month. Say, 'Fighting therein is a grave (offense) but graver is it in the sight of Allah to prevent access to the path of Allah, to deny Him, to prevent access to the Sacred Mosque, and drive out its inhabitants. Persecution is worse than killing. Nor will they cease fighting you until they turn you back from your faith, if they can..."

(The Holy Quran, 2:217)

"And those who, when an oppressive wrong is inflicted on them, (are not cowed but) fight back." (The Holy Quran, 42:39)

To gain this freedom, Prophet Muhammad(S) said:

"Strive (Jahidu) against the disbelievers with your hands and tongues." (Sahih Ibn Hibban, No. 4708)

The life of the Prophet Muhammad(S) was full of striving to gain the freedom to inform and convey the message of Islam. During his stay in Makkah he used non-violent methods and after the establishment of his government in Madinah, by the permission of Allah, he used armed struggle against his enemies whenever he found it inevitable.

- Freeing People from Tyranny:

  Allah admonishes Muslims in the Qur'an:

"And why should you not fight in the cause of Allah and of those who, being weak, are ill-treated (and oppressed)? - Men, women, and children, whose cry is: 'Our Lord! Rescue us from this town, whose people are oppressors; and raise for us from You, one who will protect; and raise for us from You, one who will help.'" (The Holy Quran, 4:75)

The mission of the Prophet Muhammad(S) was to free people from tyranny and exploitation by oppressive systems. Once free, individuals in the society were then free to chose Islam or not. Prophet Muhammad's(S) successors continued in his footsteps and went to help oppressed people. For example, after the repeated call by the oppressed people of Spain to the Muslims for help, Spain was liberated by Muslim forces and the tyrant rulers removed. After the conquest of Syria and Iraq by the Muslims, the Christian population of Hims reportedly said to the Muslims:

"We like your rule and justice far better than the state of oppression and tyranny under which we have been living."

The defeated rulers of Syria were Roman Christians, and Iraq was ruled by Zoarastrian Persians.

WHAT SHOULD MUSLIMS DO WHEN THEY ARE VICTORIOUS?

Muslims should remove tyranny, treachery, bigotry, and ignorance and replace them with justice and equity. We should provide truthful knowledge and free people from the bondage of 'associationism' (Shirk, or multiple gods), prejudice, superstition and mythology. Muslims remove immorality, fear, crime, exploitation and replace them with divine morality, peace and education. The Qur'an declares:

"Lo! Allah commands you that you restore deposits to their owners, and if you judge between mankind that you judge justly. Lo! It is proper that Allah admonishes you. Lo! Allah is ever Hearer, Seer." (The Holy Quran, 4:58)

"O you who believe! Stand out firmly for Allah's witnesses to fair dealing, and let not the hatred of others to you make you swerve to wrong and depart from justice. Be just: that is next to Piety and fear Allah. And Allah is well acquainted with all that you do." (The Holy Quran, 5:8)

"And of those whom we have created there is a nation who guides with the Truth and establishes justice with it." (The Holy Quran, 7:181)

"Lo! Allah enjoins justice and kindness, and giving to kinsfolk, and forbids lewdness and abomination and wickedness. He exhorts you in order that you may take heed." (The Holy Quran, 16:90)

"Those who, if we give them power in the land, establish prescribed prayers (salah) and pay the poor-due (zakah) and enjoin right conduct and forbid evil. And with Allah rests the end (and decision) of (all) affairs." (The Holy Quran, 22:41)

DID ISLAM SPREAD BY FORCE, SWORDS OR GUNS?

The unequivocal and emphatic answer is No! The Qur'an declares:

"Let there be no compulsion (or coercion) in the religion (Islam). The right direction is distinctly clear from error." (The Holy Quran, 2:256)

Here is a good study of the question of the spread of Islam by a Christian missionary, T. W. Arnold:

"...of any organized attempt to force the acceptance of Islam on the non-Muslim population, or of any systematic persecution intended to stamp out the Christian religion, we hear nothing. Had the caliphs chosen to adopt either course of action, they might have swept away Christianity as easily as Ferdinand and Isabella drove Islam out of Spain, or Louis XIV made Protestantism penal in France, or the Jews were kept out of England for 350 years. The Eastern Churches in Asia were entirely cut off from communion with the rest of Christiandom throughout which no one would have been found to lift a finger on their behalf, as heretical communions So that the very survival of these Churches to the present day is a strong proof of the generally tolerant attitude of Mohammedan [sic] governments towards them".

Islam does not teach, nor do Muslims desire, conversion of any people for fear, greed, marriage or any other form of coercion.

In conclusion, jihad in Islam is striving in the way of Allah by pen, tongue, hand, media and, if inevitable, with arms. However, jihad in Islam does not include striving for individual or national power, dominance, glory, wealth, prestige or pride.

TYPES OF JIHAD

First, we would like to state that Islam does not call for violence; rather it abhors all forms of violence and terrorism, whether against Muslims or non-Muslims. Islam, moreover, calls for peace, cooperation, and maintaining justice, and provides for the happiness and welfare of humanity as a whole. This fact is declared in the Qur'an when Allah says: "Allah commands justice, the doing of good, and liberality to kith and kin, and He forbids all shameful deeds, and injustice and rebellion: He instructs you, that ye may receive admonition." (An-Nahl: 90)

Islam makes it obligatory upon Muslims to stand by the oppressed regardless of their race, color, religion or affiliation and say NO to the oppressor and ask him to respond to the voice of reason and justice.

Jihad is not restricted to fighting aggressive forces. Rather, there are various kinds that most of people are not aware of. For example, striving against the evil desires of the soul is a kind of jihad that every Muslim should carry out.

For more elaboration on the point, we cite the following fatwa issued by Sheikh M. S. Al-Munajjid, a prominent Saudi Islamic lecturer and author:

"First, jihad is of various kinds, some of which are obligatory upon everyone who is accountable, and some are obligatory upon the community as a whole, i.e., if some people undertake them then the rest are relieved of the obliga-tion. And some kinds of jihad are mustahabb (recom-mended).

Jihad an-nafs (jihad against one's self) and jihad ash-Shaytan (jihad against Satan) are obligatory upon everyone who is accountable. Jihad against the munafiqin (hypocrites), kuffar (disbelievers) and leaders of oppression and innovation is obligatory upon the community as a whole. Physical jihad (i.e., fighting) against the kuffar may become an individual obligation upon everyone who is able to do it in certain circumstances, which will be described below.

Ibn al-Qayyim (may Allah have mercy on him) said: Once this is understood, then jihad is of four kinds: jihad an-nafs (jihad against one's self), jihad ash-Shaytan (jihad against Satan), jihad against the kuffar and jihad against the hypocrites.

1. Jihad an-nafs (jihad against one's self) is of four kinds:
    a. Striving to learn the teachings of Islam without which one cannot attain success and happiness in this world or in the Hereafter. If this is missing, then one is doomed to misery in this world and in the Hereafter.
    b. Striving to make one act in accordance with what one has learned. Simply knowing without acting, even though it may not cause any harm, is not going to bring any benefit.
    c. Striving to call others to Islam, teaching those who do not know about it. Otherwise one will be one of those who conceal the guidance and teaching that Allah has revealed, and it will not benefit him or save him from the punishment of Allah.
    d. Striving to bear patiently the difficulties involved in calling people to Allah and the insults of people, bearing all that for the sake of Allah.

If a person achieves all these four levels, then he will be one of the rabbaniyyin (learned men of religion who practice what they know and also preach to others. The salaf (righteous predecessors) were agreed that the scholar does not deserve to be called a rabbani unless he knows the truth, acts in accordance with it, and teaches it to others. Whoever teaches, acts in accordance with his knowledge, and has knowledge will be called great in the kingdom of heaven.

2. Jihad ash-Shaytan (jihad against Satan) is of two types:
    a. Warding off the doubts that Satan stirs up to undermine faith.

b. Striving against Satan to ward off the corrupt desires that he provokes.

The first jihad is followed by certainty of faith, and the second is followed by patience. Allah says: "And We made from among them [Children of Israel], leaders, giving guidance under Our Command, when they were patient and used to believe with certainty in Our Ayat (proofs, evidences, verses, lessons, signs, revelations, etc.)" (As-Sajdah: 24)

Allah tells us that leadership in religion is attained through patience and certainty of faith. Patience wards off desires and certainty wards off doubts.

3. Jihad against the munafiqin (hypocrites) and kuffar (disbelievers) is of four kinds: with the heart, the tongue, one's wealth and oneself. Jihad against the disbelievers is more along the lines of physical fighting, whereas jihad against the hypocrites is more along the lines of using words and ideas.
4. Jihad against the leaders of oppression and innovation is of three kinds: jihad with one's hand (i.e., physical jihad, fighting) if one is able. If that is not possible, then it should be with one's tongue (i.e., by speaking out). If that is not possible, then it should be with one's heart (i.e., by hating the evil and feeling that it is wrong).

These are the thirteen types of jihad, and "Whoever dies without having fought or having resolved to fight has died following one of the branches of hypocrisy." (Zad al-Ma`ad, 3/9-11)

Sheikh 'Abd al-'Aziz ibn Baz (may Allah have mercy on him) said:

Jihad is of various kinds, with one's self, one's wealth, by making du'a', by teaching and guiding, by helping to do good in any way. The greatest form of jihad is jihad with one's self (i.e., going oneself and fighting), followed by jihad with one's wealth, jihad by speaking out and guiding others. Da'wah is also part of jihad. But going out oneself to fight in jihad is the highest form. (Fatawa ash-Sheikh Ibn Baz, 7/334, 335)

Second, the idea of waging physical jihad against the disbelievers went through a number of stages, depending on the state in which the Muslim Ummah was. Ibn al-Qayyim (may Allah have mercy on him) said:

The first thing which his Lord revealed to him [Prophet Muhammad (peace and blessings be upon him)] was to read in the name of his Lord who had created. That was the beginning of his Prophethood, when Allah commanded him to recite to himself but He did not yet command him to convey that. Then He revealed the words:

'O you (Muhammad) enveloped in garments! Arise and warn!' (Al-Muddaththir: 1-2)

So he became a Prophet with the word 'Iqra' (Read!) and he became a Messenger with the words, 'O you (Muhammad) enveloped in garments...' Then Allah commanded him to warn his closest kinsmen, then to warn his people, then to warn the Arabs around them, then to warn all the Arabs, then to warn all of mankind. He continued to call them for over ten years from the beginning of his Prophethood, without fighting or imposing the jizyah; he was commanded to refrain, to be patient and to be forbearing.

Then permission was given to him to migrate, and permission was given to him to fight.

Then he was commanded to fight those who fought him, and to refrain from fighting those who left him alone and did not fight him.

Then Allah commanded him to fight the disbelievers so that the religion would all be for Allah.

After jihad was enjoined upon him, the disbelievers then fell into three categories: those with whom there was a truce or peace treaty; those with whom he was at war; and those who lived under the rule and protection of the Islamic state. (Zad al-Ma'ad, 3/159)

Third the ruling on physical jihad against the disbelievers is that this is an obligation on the community as a whole (fard kafayah).

Ibn Qudamah said: "Jihad is an obligation upon the community; if some people undertake it, the rest are relieved of the obligation."

What fard kafayah means is that if it is not undertaken by enough people, then all the people are guilty of sin, but if enough people undertake it, the rest will be relieved of blame. Initially the command is addressed to all of them, as in the case of an individual obligation (fard 'ayn), but then in the case of fard kafayah the obligation is dropped if enough of the people undertake to do it, unlike the case with fard 'ayn where the obligation is not dropped if someone else does it. Jihad is a fard kafayah according to the majority of scholars." (Al-Mughni, 9/163)

Sheikh 'Abd al-`Aziz ibn Baz said: "We have previously explained on more than one occasion that jihad is fard kafayah, not fard 'ayn. All Muslims are enjoined to support their brothers with their selves (i.e., physically, by joining them), or with money, weapons, da`wah and advice. If enough of them go out (to fight) then the rest are freed from sin; but none of them do that then all of them are sinners.

The Muslims in Saudi Arabia, Africa, North Africa and elsewhere are obliged to do their utmost, and if there is a Jihad in one country, the surrounding countries should hasten to help them, the closest then the next closest. If one or two states, or three or more, manage to fulfill the obligation, then the rest are freed of responsibility. They deserve to be supported, and it is obligatory to help them against their enemies because they are oppressed. Allah has enjoined jihad upon all Muslims, and they must fight against the enemies of Allah until their brothers are victorious. If they fail to do that, then they are sinners; but if sufficient people undertake to do that, then the rest are absolved of sin." (Fatawa ash-Shaykh Ibn Baz, 7/335)

Fourth: Physical jihad against the disbelievers becomes obligatory in four cases, which are:

1. When the Muslim is present in a jihad situation.
2. When the enemy has come and attacked a Muslim land
3. When the ruler mobilizes the people, they must respond.

4. When a person is needed and no one else can do the task except him.

Sheikh Ibn 'Uthaymin said:

Jihad is obligatory and becomes fard 'ayn if a person is present where fighting is going on. This is the first of the situations in which jihad becomes an individual obligation, because Allah says: "O you who believe! When you meet those who disbelieve, in a battlefield, never turn your backs to them. And whoever turns his back to them on such a day – unless it be a stratagem of war, or to retreat to a troop (of his own), – he indeed has drawn upon himself wrath from Allah. And his abode is Hell, and worst indeed is that destination!" (Al-Anfal: 16)

The Prophet (peace and blessings be upon him) said that running away on the day when the army is advancing is one of the sins that doom a person to Hell. He said: "Avoid the seven sins that doom a person to Hell..." among which he mentioned running away on the day when the army is advancing. But Allah has made exceptions in two cases:

1. When it is a military maneuver, in the sense that he is leaving to bring reinforcements.
2. When he is going to join another group, when he has been told that there is a group of Muslims elsewhere who are about to be defeated, so he goes to join them in order to strengthen their numbers. This is subject to the condition that there is no risk to the group he is in; if there is a risk to the group that he is in, then it is not permissible for him to go to the other group. In this case (jihad) is an individual obligation upon him (fard 'ayn) and it is not permissible for him to leave.

The second situation (in which jihad becomes an individual obligation) is when a city is besieged by the enemy. Then he has to fight to defend the city because there is no alternative but to defend it. For if the enemy is going to prevent people from leaving the city or entering it, and prevent provisions from reaching it, and other things which are well known, and then in this case the people of the city are obliged to fight in order to defend their city.

The third situation is when the leader tells the people to mobilize. The Muslim ruler is the highest authority in the state, but he need not necessarily be the leader of all the Muslims, because there has been no leader of all the Muslims (caliph or khalifah) for a long time. The Prophet (peace and blessings be upon him) said: "Listen and obey, even if you are ruled by an Abyssinian slave." So if a man becomes a leader, then his word is to be heeded and his commands are to obey. (Ash-Sharh al-Mumti`, 8/10-12)."

ON THE MULTI-LAYERED CONCEPT OF JIHAD

Jihad has come to acquire a one-dimensional meaning today - one which goes against the basic precepts of Islam. Islam preaches peace, and jihad through war is only a means of achieving this; the greater jihad is the non-violent one, fought within oneself or for social justice.

Jihad is projected as an integral part of Islam - as an obligatory duty of all Muslims to fight against infidels. To say the least, this is a highly improper representation of the concept of jihad in Islam. The multi-layered concept of jihad has been projected as a one-dimensional concept - to fight with the Sword against all infidels. What happened on September 11 has further harmed the prospects of a correct understanding of the concept.

The first step towards such understanding is to situate the concept of jihad in its historical context. One is often historically determined, without an understanding of how one is historically situated.

Qur'anic pronouncements are multi-layered and multi-dimensional - some of these dimensions are historical, some social, other ethical. To understand the Qur'anic verses in a one-dimensional manner is to do great injustice to them, and also misapply them - either because of a wrong understanding of the verses, or on account of some selfish motive.

To understand the Qur'an better, it is important to understand the pre-Islamic Arab society. Violence and inter-tribal wars were rampant. Reconciliation and conflict resolution through negotiations was virtually unknown. Though the pre-Islamic Arab society was not exactly immoral, it did have tribal traditions and customs that ignored certain ethical aspects. Peace, though appreciated, was not always practiced. As there was no rule of law in pre-Islamic society, things were settled through inter-tribal wars or tribal customs and traditions. This resulted in a great deal of bloodshed.

This prevailing historical situation was not acceptable to Islam, but some of its elements did persist in Muslim behaviour. Also, we have to bear in mind that it was not a modern democratic society, but a tribal society with its own outlook and intellectual understanding. We cannot apply modern norms to the tribal society, nor should we perpetuate its practices in modern times. Islam, while constrained to retain some of it, rejected most of these practices, and provided for transcendent norms and ethical standards. What some Muslims do (and many non-Muslims too) is ignore the historicity of some Qur'anic and Hadith pronouncements, and place them in an a historical context, thus causing great deal of misunderstanding about the Islamic ethics of jihad.

A careful study of the Qur'an and Hadith makes it clear that the concept of jihad is far above mere violence and war. Unfortunately, Islamic history was fraught with wars for several reasons (certainly not for religious reasons), hence the one-dimensional concept of jihad. The Sufis, who kept themselves aloof from power-struggles and attempts by rulers at territorial expansions, realised the dangers of misapplying the concept of jihad. They thought it necessary to emphasise the other social and moral aspects of jihad. It is for this reason that they described jihad bi al-sayf (i.e. war with Sword) as jihad-e-asghar (i.e. small war), and jihad to control one's greed and selfish desires as jihad-e-akbar i.e. great jihad. This was important because Muslim leaders and their cohorts were ignoring the moral precepts and ethical constraints imposed by Qur'anic pronouncements to fulfill their greed for power and territory.

The Sufis had based the concept of the great jihad on the basis of Qur'anic pronouncements, and had not formulated a precept of their own. Jihad, as is well known to any student of the Arabic language, means to make utmost efforts. One must look at the authentic Qur'anic dictionary Mufradat al-Qur'an by Imam Raghib Asfahani.

Imam Raghib first discusses the meaning of the root word jahd, which means working hard or making utmost efforts, and juhud, which means one's utmost capacity. The two together would mean making utmost efforts to one's best capacity. Then he goes on to say that jihad wa al-mujahidah means to spend one's utmost capacity in defending oneself in the face of an enemy. Then he divides jihad in three categories: 1) to fight against enemies, i.e. unbelievers; 2) against shaitan (Satan) and 3) against one's own self, i.e. one's own greed and selfishness.

Imam Raghib also maintains that the Qur'anic verse 22:78 ("And strive hard for Allah with due striving. He has chosen you and has not laid any hardship in religion.") comprises all these three categories. The Qur'an also says, "And strives hard in Allah's way with your wealth and your lives. This is better for you, if you know." (9:41). One also finds in the Qur'an, "Those who believed and migrated (from their homes), and strove hard in Allah's way with their wealth and their lives, and are much higher in rank with Allah. And it is these that shall triumph." (9:20)

It will be seen that all these verses in the Qur'an do not use the word jihad in the sense of war, but in the sense of striving with wealth and one's own life. Muslims were a persecuted lot in Mecca, and many of them faced severe persecution, and strove hard in the way of Allah with their own lives, and those who were wealthy, spent all their wealth for that cause. Thus, it was all about suffering and striving. This is real jihad. Nowhere in the Qur'an is jihad used either in the sense of war, or for seeking revenge. Seeking revenge amounts to using concept of jihad for selfish ends, even if the revenge or retaliation is for one's group or community.

In Hadith literature, we find a Hadith, which prohibits Muslims from seeking revenge. Thus in Sahih al-Bukhari, we find the Hadith of Miqdad ibn Amr al-Kindi. Amr al-Kindi asked the holy Prophet (peace be upon him), "Suppose I met one of the infidels and we fought. He struck one of my hands with his Sword, cut it off and then took refuge in a tree and said, 'I surrender to Allah'. Could I kill him, O Messenger of Allah, after he had said this?" Allah's Messenger (PBUH) said, "You should not kill him." Al-Miqdad said, "O Allah's Messenger, but he had cut off my hands, and then he had uttered those words." Allah's Messenger (PBUH) replied, "You should not kill him, and you would be in his position where he had been before uttering these words." Thus it will be seen that in matters of war also, Islam teaches higher morality, the essence of which is not to seek revenge or retaliate. This is what I call the transcendent morality.

In matters of jihad, Imam Raghib quotes an interesting Hadith, which says, "Fight your desires as you fight your enemies." The Sufi concept of jihad-i-akbar i.e. the great jihad is to fight ones own vain desires has been based on this Hadith. According to the Qur'an, man's life is a constant struggle in the way of Allah, be it through Sword or through one's hands or one's tongue. Thus there is a Hadith which says, "Strive against unbelievers with your hands and your words."

Thus this constant jihad, constant struggle in the way of Allah implies multi-layered efforts. The believers have been charged, by the Qur'an, with the important mission of spreading good and fighting evil (amr bi'l ma'ruf wa nahi 'an al-munkar). In this mission, a believer has to engage himself continuously, controlling his own desires, spreading justice, equality and compassion with wisdom ('adl - justice, ihsan - benevolence, rahmah- compassion and hikmah - wisdom are concepts of goodness in the Qur'an which are repeatedly stressed).

As it is duty of believers to engage in spreading what is good, it is also their duty to engage in containing what is evil. Thus, a believer has to constantly strive to fight against oppression, injustice, iniquity and cruelty. All these result in spreading evil on earth. The world, as we all know, is full of injustices and oppression, and it will be a lifetime mission of a believer to contain them. This is real jihad.

A fight is not always with weapons. It could equally be through moral and intellectual means - through persuasion, wisdom, spreading the good word, and setting good examples. It is for this reason that the Prophet has said that the ink of a writer's pen is more sacred than the blood of a martyr. The word written with ink is lasts longer than a martyr's blood. The Qur'an says, "And fights in the way of Allah against those who fight against you but be not aggressive. Surely Allah loves not the aggressors." (2:190) One has to strictly observe these conditions in jihad.

The noted Urdu poet Iqbal has beautifully described the meaning of jihad in day-to-day life in one of his couplets as follows:

Yaqin muhkam 'amal payham muhabbat fatihi 'alam Jihad-e- zindagani mein yeh hain mardon ki shamshiren

(For a man with strong inner conviction, constant efforts and universe-winning love are the real weapons in the jihad of life.)

The meaning of jihad is not complete without the Qur'anic injunction for believers (men as well as women) to enforce good, and contain evil, and this is the lifelong mission of all the believers. To achieve this objective, believers have to use their persuasive skills, wisdom and goodliness. One cannot enforce good with Sword. Goodness prevails only with goodness. What the Qur'an calls maw'izah hasanah (i.e. exhortation with goodness) and hikmah (wisdom) is more lasting than enforcing something forcibly.

The Prophet (PBUH) always tried all possibilities of negotiated settlement, and resorted to war in self-defence only if all efforts to find a negotiated settlement failed. The best example of this is what is known in the history of Islam as sulh-i-Hudaibiyah. He even accepted terms, which were not apparently favourable to Muslims to avoid human slaughter and in the interest of peace. The terms of peace appeared to be even humiliating to his senior companions.

We find mention of this in Sahih al-Bukhari. Abu Wa'il narrated, "We were in Siffin and Sahl ibn Hunayf stood up and said, 'O people! Blame yourselves! We were with the Prophet (PBUH) on the day of Hudaybiyyah, and if we had been called to fight, we should have fought.' But Umar ibn al-Khattab came and said, 'O Allah's Messenger! Aren't we in the right and our opponents in the wrong?' Allah's Messenger said, 'Yes'. Umar said, 'Then why should we accept hard terms in matters concerning our religion? Shall we return before Allah judges between us and them?' Allah's Messenger (PBUH) said, 'O ibn al-Khattab! I am the Messenger of Allah and Allah will never degrade me.'"

Sulh-Hudaibiyuyah is of fundamental significance in the interest of peace. Peace is the real objective, and war only a necessary evil in certain unavoidable situations. Also, it is a wrong assumption that it is duty of the Muslims to fight against all non-believers or *kafirs*. The Qur'an itself mentions treaties with unbelievers, and according to the Qur'an and Hadith, it is the duty of all Muslims to honour all treaties and alliances with non-believers. All such alliances must be respected by the Muslims as long as they are honoured by non-Muslims.

Thus we find again in Sahih al-Bukhari, "The pagans were of two kinds as regards their relationship with the Prophet (PBUH) and the believers. Some of them were those with whom the Prophet was at war, and used to fight against, and they used to fight him; the others were those with whom the Prophet (PBUH) made a treaty, and neither did the Prophet fight them, nor did they fight him.

Those who work for social justice are as good as *mujahideen* i.e. warriors in the way of Allah. Thus we find in Sahih al-Bukhari: The Prophet (PBU) said, "The one who looks after and works for a widow and for a poor person is like a warrior fighting for Allah's cause, or like a person who fasts during the day and prays all the night."

Thus any one striving for social justice and working to ameliorate the plight of the poor is like a warrior in the way of Allah. Thus, those who spend their own money or collect from others and spend for the poor in the way Allah is no less than a mujahid. According to the Qur'an, zakat money is to be spent on poor, widows, needy, paying off the debt of indebted and for liberation of slaves. These are all weaker sections of society. It is thus a great merit to help these poorer and weaker sections and to work for them is as meritorious as waging jihad in the way of Allah. One should wage war against poverty in all possible ways - by increasing production, by ringing about redistribution of economic resources and by not allowing wealth to be circulated only among the rich. (59:7)

Even when first permission was given to fight in the Qur'anic verse 4:77, it was basically to defend the rights of weak from among the old men, women and children. In some extreme situations, it might mean fighting a war, but it could be a fight in various other ways, particularly in a democratic and modern society. It could be through democratic movements or parliamentary debates also. In those days, when the holy Qur'an was being revealed, such possibilities did not exist. Today, we will have to creatively re-interpret such Qur'anic provisions as above.

The 'Ulama and jurists in early Islam had divided the world in darul harb and darul Islam. The countries where Muslims could not enjoy the freedom of their faith, and were persecuted were declared by the Muslim jurists as darul harb. And it was thought necessary for Muslims to wage war (jihad) in such countries. However, it is important to note that the Hanafi jurists had also created a third category of darul aman i.e. those countries where Muslims, though in minority yet, could enjoy freedom of religion and were not persecuted because of their religious beliefs. India was always considered as darul aman by Islamic jurists, as Muslims here were not persecuted for their religious beliefs. India was always a pluralist society.

But in today's conditions when, democracy prevails, even if Muslims are persecuted in any country or any place, democratic remedies will have priority over waging war. Terrorism which involves shedding the blood of innocent people, and can never is elevated to the category of jihad in any sense of the Qur'anic term.

Also, a few individuals cannot get together and decide to wage jihad. The decision to wage jihad can be taken only by a properly constituted Islamic government ensuring that there is no other way left but to declare jihad. This can be done after due deliberation, and examining all possible consequences, including loss of human lives. In the modern democratic world such decisions can be arrived at only by a duly-elected government. And as far as the Qur'anic injunction on jihad is concerned, it should not in any case involve a selfish motive like grabbing the territory of others or consolidating any group's rule, but should be strictly for higher goals, like justice and fighting persecution.

It should also be noted that peace is far more funda-mental to Islam than war. War at best could be an instrument of establishing peace in some exceptional circumstances, or for defending against aggression. It is unfortunate that some youth come together, and decides that there is no way out but to use violence, and call it jihad. These youth ultimately shed a great deal of innocent blood, without achieving the ultimate objective. Such extremist violence results in more in-group fighting. Such extremist violence is not jihad.

In a modern world, real jihad is to use democracy and democratic institutions to realise the noble goals for which the Prophet of Islam (PBUH) struggled all his life.

The name 'Jihad' was meant to be light-hearted, but it also reflected his commitment to the traditional under-standing of jihad in the Koran, which is best translated as a struggle or striving. It is an inner, spiritual struggle to triumph over evil, to live in submission to God and service to humanity.

Jihad is a very broad concept that includes theories of just war. But the Koran is very clear that Muslims are only to wage defensive wars," he said. "The more important meaning of jihad is the struggle to be good.

The Arabic term for holy war would be al-harb muh-adassa, but "there is no holy war in the Koran. There is no combination of words that means holy war," he said.

Verses such as Koran 9:20-22 are among those that have led suicide bombers to believe they will inherit Paradise:

Those who believe, and who have forsaken the domain of evil and have striven [jihad] hard in God's cause with their possessions and their lives have the highest rank in the sight of God; and it is they, they who shall triumph in the end! Their Sustainer gives those glad tidings of the grace that flows from Him, and of His goodly acceptance, and of the gardens which await them, full of lasting bliss, therein to abide beyond the count of time. Verily, with God is a mighty reward!

The terrorists have ripped such verses out of context and failed to understand their true meaning, McAuliffe said. Passages on fighting refer to a particular war, when enemies of Islam tried to destroy the Prophet Muhammad and his followers. They do not give blanket permission to condemn or kill those who hold political or religious views other than your own, he said.

Take not life, which Allah hath made sacred, except by way of justice and law: Thus doth he command you, that ye may learn wisdom. Koran 6:151

Ihsan Bagby, a Muslim who teaches international relations at Shaw University in Raleigh, N.C., doesn't know how suicide bombers shut out the many verses that extol peace, mercy, restraint and forgiveness. He suspects they convince themselves that military jihad has always had "collateral damage" and that, if American policy sustains injustice, they can target any American interest.

"Of course, such logic is irrational and immoral," Bagby said.

American Muslims have long urged the media not to refer to terrorists as "Islamic" but as "Islamists," meaning those who attempt to impose Islam by force. Few Muslims consider such tactics Islamic.

On the Web, McAuliffe challenges extremists. Their distorted theology "is not so much a matter of which passages of the Koran they read, but which they ignore," he said.

Few extremists would commit violence, he said. They are extreme because they "don't take the book as a whole. They don't grasp its ethos, or see the balance between the different passages."

The Koran is believed by Muslims to have been dictated by the Angel Gabriel to Muhammad in the early 7 th century A.D. Lesser writings, called hadith, are used to interpret the Koran. Hadith include the sayings and biography of Muhammad.

Hadith makes clear that war is only for defense, that innocent civilians must not be targeted, and that fire must not be used to kill, McAuliffe said. In it, Muhammad declares battle the "lesser jihad" and spiritual purification the "greater jihad."

Extremists ignore the historical and social context of hadith, and those few who condone terrorism claim that hadith's restraints on violence are not true sayings of Muhammad, he said.

"We don't have any kind of an official body that interprets the Koran in light of hadith. People look to certain scholars or certain charismatic leaders or groups, and get interpretation from them. But there is no Vatican that can say, 'This is the official teaching.' "

At the center of the quarrel between mainstream Muslims and extremists is how to know when a person or a nation has become an "oppressor" or an enemy of Islam.

In the traditional debate over how to respond to an unjust ruler, "One side maintained that you have to fight back. The other side, which is really the standard Sunni Muslim approach, is that you can't fight anyone unless they prevent you from practicing your religion," he said.

But arguing with extremists is exhausting. Until Sept. 11, if some hothead lectured fellow Muslims about America the Infidel, "People just kind of rolled their eyes," McAuliffe said.

Extremists "don't let up. They are bullies. They seem to have an infinite amount of time and energy and they do not listen. They will not entertain the possibility that they might be incorrect. It's like talking to a wall."

Now, "The good people need to bring as much energy and passions to the confrontation as the evil people do."

Most of those he chats with online share that conviction, he said.

"There is almost a feeling of helplessness that these guys have – and I hate to use this word – hijacked the Islamic message," McAuliffe said.

We ordained for the Children of Israel that if anyone slew a person – unless it is for murder or for spreading mischief in the land – it would be as if he slew the whole people: And if anyone saved a life, it would be as if he saved the life of the whole people.

While extremists have monopolized media attention, respected Muslim groups and leaders have countered extremist theology, said John O. Voll, associate director of the Center for Muslim-Christian Understanding at Georgetown University in Washington, D.C., and co-author of "Islam and Democracy."

He cited Minaret magazine, published by the Islamic Center of Southern California, which circulates nationwide.

"The moderate view is mainstream Islam and always has been," Voll said. "Claiming that someone is an unbeliever and therefore has to be attacked has long been recognized as a heretical approach."

Voll compares the usage of jihad to that of crusade, which was a military term in 1099 when European Christian armies took back Jerusalem from Muslim Turks who had conquered the Holy Land. Now, however, it usually means an evangelistic meeting or a moral crusade against drugs or violence.

Medieval crusaders who slaughtered Muslim civilians, Jews and Orthodox Christians doubtless believed they had sanction from God. But their actions so poisoned the view of Western Christianity in Eastern Europe and Asia that, nearly 1,000 years later, Billy Graham dropped the word "crusade" from his overseas missions.

The consensus of mainstream Islam is that each individual has a duty to apply his or her full intellect to under-standing the Koran.

"You don't just blindly sit down and believe what some teacher has told you," Voll said, "That relatively blind copying of what others have said is the theological foundation of people like Osama bin Laden and it is different from most of the fundamentalists."

McAuliffe worries that a shortage of qualified religion teachers leaves American Muslims vulnerable to simplistic interpretations of many issues. Most teachers are intelligent and devout, but their education often is in medicine or engineering, rather than religion, history, literature and anthropology, he said.

He was struck that the suicide bombers of Sept. 11 were educated men – but educated in technology rather than religion.

"What is very scary is that these were not poor, desperate people whose desire to lash out could at least be understood. You can find these educated people in the extremist groups, but they tend to be trained in the natural sciences."

Children of Abraham, it's time to make a stand/ against the injustice and evil in our lands/ Believers come together and join your voice as one/ We don't care what country you are from/ Jew, Christian, Muslim, it's time that we grew up/ Accept each others' differences and leave the rest to God/ Compete in piety, worship and good deeds/ Give up your hatred, your guns and your greed.

6

Levels of Jihad

The eminent Muslim scholar, Sheikh Muhammad 'Ali Al-Hanooti, member of the North American Fiqh Council, states:

"Jihad in the Qur'an is a term that signifies striving and endeavoring. The root of that word in Arabic is Jahd, which means spending energy and potential for a certain cause. It covers up practically four areas in the Islamic cause:

1. Teaching people the message of Islam: Any plans or steps of making Da'wah is a kind of Jihad. Allah, Most High, says: "O Prophet! Strive against the disbelievers and the hypocrites! Be harsh with them. Their ultimate abode is hell, a hapless journey's end." (At-Tawbah: 73)

   We know that addressing the hypocrites in this verse never means combating, but means Da'wah because a hypocrite is still a Muslim and a Muslim cannot combat another Muslim.
2. Disciplining one's soul: Any disciplinary work for improving one's faith and behavior is Jihad. Refraining from wrongdoing and following stannic ways is Jihad.
3. Spending money in the cause of Islam: Jihad with money is mentioned in many verses of the Glorious Qur'an. Sometimes, it comes before Jihad with the soul. This type of Jihad is strategic in any plan for working in the cause of Islam.
4. Combating the enemy: The Qur'an uses another term for

combating. In Arabic, the term is Qital. So Qital in the Qur'an (combating) is the fourth implementation of Jihad.

JIHAD IN ISLAM

We would like first to clarify the true concept of Jihad and its wider dimensions by citing the following words of Sheikh 'Atiyyah Saqr, former Head of Al-Azhar Fatwa Committee, in which he states:

"Jihad is one of the most misunderstood and abused aspects of Islam. There are some Muslims who exploit and misuse this concept for their own political objectives. There are many non-Muslims who misunderstand it. There are some other non-Muslims who misinterpret it to discredit Islam and Muslims.

That is why the word 'Jihad' has been misused due to misunderstanding its true meaning. The word 'Jihad' is derived from the Arabic word jahd which means fatigue or from the word juhd which means effort. A mujahid is the one who strives in the Cause of Allah and exerts efforts which makes him feel fatigued. Jihad means exerting effort to achieve a desired thing or 'to prevent an undesired one. In other words, it is an effort that aims at bringing about benefit or preventing harm.

Jihad can be observed through any means and in any field whether material or moral and among the types of Jihad are struggling against one's desires, Satan, poverty, illiteracy, and disease, and fighting all evil forces in the world.

There are many religious texts that refer to these types of Jihad. One of the forms of Jihad is defending life, property or honor. Those who die while engaging in Jihad are considered to be martyrs, as confirmed by Prophetic Hadiths. Jihad is also done to avert aggression on home countries and on all that is held sacred, or in order to face those who try to hinder the march of the call of truth."

Thus, Jihad is never a tool of waging war against the innocents. It is never a means of flexing the muscles or bullying the weak and oppressed. Jihad in Islam is something unique that is established to defend the divine message from being eliminated or hindered by its enemies.

Focusing on the question in point, the prominent Al-Azhar scholar Sheikh 'Abdul-Majeed Subh states the following:

"I would like to tell you, dear son or dear daughter, who may share in the same belief or have his or her own, that understanding defensive Jihad as initiating fighting without a religiously acceptable reason is a total misunderstanding of the tenets of faith and the clear Qur'anic verses. In the Qur'an, defensive Jihad is under condition of repelling aggression, whereas preemptive Jihad is done only when the Muslim Ummah seriously expects treason or an attack against its territories from an enemy.

Referring to this, Allah Almighty says: "Fight in the cause of Allah those who fight you, but do not do aggression, for Allah loves not the aggressors. Fight in the way of Allah against those who fight against you, but begin not hostilities. Lo! Allah loveth not aggressors. And slay them wherever ye find them, and drive them out of the places whence they drove you out, for persecution is worse than slaughter. And fight not with them at the Inviolable Place of Worship until they first attack you there, but if they attack you (there) then slay them. Such is the reward of disbelievers. But if they desist, then lo! Allah is Forgiving, Merciful. And fight them until persecution is no more, and religion is for Allah. But if they desist, then let there be no hostility except against wrongdoers."

Contemplating over the meanings and shades of the aforementioned verses that are best misused and misinterpreted by many non-Muslims, I can deduce the following:

1. The apparently preemptive Jihad in the first verse "Fight..." is not an open call for all those who differ in creed. Rather, it is conditioned by "... those who fight..."
2. The phrase "And slay them wherever ye find them..." in the second verse is conditioned by "...but if they attack you..."
3. The general rule that everyone should pay attention to along the line is that "...Allah loves not the aggressors." And "... But if they desist, then let there be no hostility except against wrongdoers."

After the above explanation, I would like to add that Islam prohibits attacking those who do not fight. As I stated above, the preemptive war in Islam is only permitted when there is treason against Muslims from the enemy with whom they live in peace, or imminent attack against the Muslim territories. In such cases, Muslims are not supposed to stand hand-cuffed and wait to be slaughtered by others, although the war they are supposed to launch is not an aim in itself.

Having said this, I would like to classify war in Islam into three main categories:

1. Defensive War is resorted to when the enemies of Muslims attack the religion, honor, property, territories, etc.
2. Liberating War is done to liberate all those who are oppressed, such as slaves? This form of war was normal in the early days of Islam.
3. Preemptive War is launched only when Muslims know for sure that there is treason against their peaceful treaties with the enemy, when the enemy has a serious plan to attack them.

It is worth stressing at the end that all the three kinds of war that are mentioned above are approved by international law, and they are in effect in modern laws."

THE SWORD OF ISLAM

The first few, who embraced the "new" religion in Makkah in the Arabian Peninsula at the hands of the Prophet, were his wife Khadijah, his servant Zaid and his eleven year old cousin Ali. Among the ones who later joined this faith were the honest merchant, Abu Bakr; the iron man of Arabia, Umar the Great; the shy businessman, Uthman; the Prophet's brave uncle Hamza and a slave of a pagan, Bilal. They simply couldn't resist the Magic Sword of a humble and lonely Prophet? The negligible minority of the believers in this new Faith was soon exiled from Makkah and they arrived in the city called Yathreb which later became known as Madinah. The Muslim emigrants to Madinah brought their Sword with them. The Sword continued to work and its magnetic force continued to "pull" people towards it until the whole of Arabia joined the Faith. Compared to the population of the rest of the world at that time, the Arabs constituted a tiny minority. A fraction of this minority decided to take the Sword beyond the boundaries of the Arabian desert to the mighty Mediterranean, the coast of Malabar and the far away East Indies Islands. People after people continued surrendering to this Sword and joining the Faith.

So sharp was the edge of the Sword! It simply conquered the hearts; bodies yielded automatically. It is the Sword of Truth, whose mere shine eliminates falsehood just like light wipes away darkness.

It continues to pierce the hearts of countless men and women today - in spite of the relentless efforts by persons with vested interests who like darkness to prevail, so that they may rob people of their good things. Read below the impressions of some who were recently conquered by the same Sword. They are from different countries, speak different languages and have different backgrounds. Their present addresses are also given. Perhaps you may like to ask them how it feels to be struck by the Sword of Truth.

COMPREHENDING JIHAD

Throughout Islamic history, jihad has been considered to be the core concept of the Islamic perspective on relations between Islam and the rest of the world. The concept stimulated different interpretations in classical and modern Islamic jurisprudence (fiqh) as well as in Orientalist's writings.

The term "jihad" was used to specify different types of external Islamic relations. The changing circumstances surrounding the Muslim world deeply affected the dominant interpretations, as well as the use of the term to justify political and military actions.

The international and regional context that has prevailed since the attacks of 9/11 has shown the urgent need to revisit the term jihad. Linked to terrorism, the term has surfaced again in analyzing the logic of Islam and its nature as a value system.

The attack against the USA was labeled as an act of global terrorism. For the USA, the involved parties are new transnational forces that threaten globalization and Americanization.

On the other side, the Intifada in Palestine is continuing in the face of escalating Israeli aggression and the collapse of the peace process. The acts of legitimate resistance are clearly a sort of legitimate jihad, meaning self-defense against aggressors. Yet the US, Israel, and their allies consider them acts of violence and terrorism. The Israeli Zionist discourse badly conflates what they call Palestinian-Islamic terrorism with the acts of terrorism committed against the US. The dominant international media are portraying a distorted image of Islam and Muslims with jihad as terrorism at its core.

The Bin Laden statements added to the confusion. He welcomed the attacks and renewed his declaration of jihad against the US and Israel, as the main enemies of Islam and Muslims. Hence those who connect jihad and terrorism, as well as Islam and terrorism, found an additional argument.

This raises the following questions:

Why did the concept invade the current political discourse? How can one contribute to that debate concerning the meaning of jihad and its consequences for the image of Islam and Muslims, as well as their actual situation in the international system?

It is very hard to sum up the different factors - contemporary and historical - that explain how the distorted image of Islam and Muslims and the unjust positions and policies against them reached this degree.

Defining jihad in an apologetic way that stresses only the dimension of individual self-discipline as a meaning of the word rooted in Islamic moral teaching does not solve the problem, nor does it necessarily improve the image of Islam and Muslims. It simply disregards the realistic international affairs conflict management dynamics, ranging between peaceful means and legitimate self-defense up to the emerging Republican unilateral American model of pre-emptive wars.

It would be useful to illustrate how the concept of jihad has had different interpretations and different uses in the history of Muslim thought and politics. My object is to clarify that the dominant Western conception of jihad, though not very new - considering the history of confrontation between East and West - nevertheless reflects how the contemporary Islamic-Western encounter has come to an intensive climax.

It is to be noted that during the dominance of the Islamic Civilization and Islamic power, the concept of jihad revealed positive meaning and was the motive for achieving noble ends and objectives. Unfortunately, during the contemporary period of Islamic decadence, jihad has gained a very bad reputation since it is intermingled in the Western minds with terrorism seen as coming from a backward Muslim World that is considered the main threat to Western Civilization.

In other words, if jihad is a historical concept and process, it could be comprehended in light of it historical memory and its significance and context. This memory reveals the paradoxes of the difference between the doctrine and its application in real life. It also helps explain how the image of Islam and Muslims has been distorted not only by Western misunderstanding but, also, mainly by Muslims themselves.

JIHAD: THREE THEORIES

Literally, jihad means that Muslims should fulfill their duties to promote the cause of Islam. It is not only an outward act, but also an inward one to strengthen one's own self and correct one's own mistakes. Clearly, the exertion of the self in all directions - in every effort and act, personal and collective, internal and external - is the essence of jihad in the Islamic sense. This rule illustrates that jihad does not necessarily involve waging a war.

In other words, jihad is supposed to run through all aspects of a Muslim's life, as it is his duty in the world to do well and prevent harm and evil in every possible way. This can, of course, entail the use of force when peaceful means are not successful, but to equate jihad exclusively with waging war is based on the historical experience of the classical period of Islamic history.

It was understandable for classical Muslim jurists to think of Muslims as a powerful established society able to wage war against the sources of threat. This is the same way any empire built its image and saw its mission. It is not very much different from the current American foreign policy missionary statements that are all over the media. But in our time the jurists and scholars are in a different situation, so they speak differently. Seeking to narrow the Islamic position to a purely defensive and peaceful position, the modernists used a methodology of selectivity and a mild tone that represents the reality of dependency and underdevelopment of Muslims rather than the text and jurisprudence of Islam. On the other hand, some Orientalists, either classical or modern, only highlighted the interpretation of jihad that equated it with offensive destructive war. So they were overly selective in their use of interpretations of some Muslim jurists while neglecting others; hence the Western prevailing use the term of jihad refers only to waging war. This type of jihad was also described in various ways. Sometimes it is equated with holy war - Jihad, not... a "Holy" War! and other times it is called the classical theory or modern theory of jihad.

In Muslim thought and Muslim jurisprudence, interpretations of jihad are related to other terms such as Dar Al-Islam (domain of peace) and Dar Al-Harb (domain of war). These terms' relationships pertain to the classical Islamic vision of the nature of international relations. So, the Islamic schools of thought and international law differed according to the divergence (between traditionalists and modernists) concerning the basis of Muslim external relations with non-Muslims, whether it is war or peace. This divergence could be explained in terms of differences in methodology (applying abrogation rule or not) and in historical experiences (periods of Muslim strength or weakness).

A third trend of interpretation could be traced as a middle course based on the six following points:

1. Jihad is the striving of Muslims to fulfill their every responsibility and to serve the Islamic cause and principles in a manner consistent with the framework of Islam. It is not to be taken to mean warfare alone. Jihad in this sense is the active expression of the Islamic commitment, responsibility, and sense of duty wherever it is required in practical life. So, to interpret jihad only as an offensive or defensive war is to misunderstand the meaning of the word and the philosophy behind it. It is equally wrong to assume that jihad is a holy war in the Western sense.
2. To interpret the basis of Muslim external relations as war or peace is to misunderstand the meaning of Islam. It is based on da'wah (inviting people to Islam), which needs jihad.
3. Jihad as a basic Islamic principle neither excludes the possibility of armed conflict nor imposes peace as the sole alternative in all situations. So, it is necessary to pay attention to the variety of its meanings and applications in any specific situation. Only then will a better under-standing of the motivations and consequences of any specific course of Muslim external relations be possible.

   Therefore the question of when, why, and how to use force or a peaceful orientation should be carefully addressed and answered in light of the Islamic rules of warfare and with taking into consideration the realities of the contemporary world and the challenges that face Muslims.

   In other words, the third trend of interpretation does not drop either war or peace for the absolute sake of the other. It stands for the comprehensive meaning of Islam, i.e., all principles, rules, and values of the message and experiences of Islam are valid whenever they are required in the light of changing circumstances in broad human life and experience. The dynamic use of the different phases of Qur'anic outlook is always needed.

4. Jihad is an intellectual instrument and a key value pertaining to da'wah as the main base of Muslim-non-Muslim relations. Hence, war or peace is considered not as a basis of external relations but as instruments for da'wah through a process of jihad.
5. According to this third trend of interpretation, the classical jurists' thought was criticized as being influenced by the non-acceptance of Islam and adversarial stance towards Islam and the rising Muslim state by major non-Muslim powers. It was also criticized as giving absolute weight to the abrogation methodology, regardless of the total meaning, basic objectives and value system of Islam.

   In other words, this middle trend of thought gives more weight to the integrity of the Islamic value system and to the nature of its constructive message. So, stressing the aggressive nature of jihad (i.e., fighting others just because they are not Muslims and forcing them to convert to Islam) could only be done by applying the rule, instead of being concerned with reviving human consciousness for establishing an egalitarian human society. So, this aggressive attitude was seen as reducing the Islamic mission to a kind of spiritual totalitarianism.
6. This middle trend has also criticized the modern jurists who interpreted jihad in a purely defensive way to the extent that they based Muslim external relations only on peace. They were criticized of totally dropping the role of abrogation and underestimating the negative consequences of the unjust and aggressive Western policies towards the Muslim World.

   Finally, this middle trend of thought presents a broad and realistic understanding. It gives place to the different situations and contexts - weakness or strength - that could surround the Ummah (nation), it makes the jihad movement a necessary one aimed at correcting unjust relationships (military or peaceful), and it does not allow room for accusations or exaggerated claims either against or for Islam. The Muslim objection that adaptation to new circumstances might result in loss of identity is also out of place.

At last, according to this middle trend of thought, the spread of Islam and da'wah has taken several forms. This da'wah is the basis of the Muslim external relations, while both peace and war present extreme states of relations that contradict the nature of the Islamic mission. So, this trend differentiates between jihad and war; it refuses to equate jihad with holy war or to qualify jihad as legal or holy; it argues that the term "jihad" should not be used for a war until this war fulfills the legal conditions for launching it. As long as these conditions are not fulfilled, the launched war should not be called jihad.

Then what are these conditions? Who are responsible for launching jihad (defensive or offensive)? What is the relevance of the different Islamic historical experiences? What sort of these experiences illustrates the defensive or offensive jihad? Does the actual situation of Muslims in the world justify a defensive or offensive war? But what is the difference between a defensive and offensive one? And how can we understand the acts against the United States: do they represent a defensive war or an act of terrorism?

LEVEL TWO: THE SIGNIFICANCE OF HISTORICAL EXPERIENCES

Many prominent Orientalists have been selective in understanding jihad by equating it with offensive, destructive war and by qualifying Muslims as violent and non-tolerant. Other scholars have realized the difference between the various interpretations of jihad.

On the other hand, to serve national interests and power politics, the concept of jihad has been manipulated differently by both Western and Muslim statesmen and politicians.

The history of Muslim-Western relations provides us with various experiences that extend through two different periods in Islamic history. Thus, they illustrate the nature of historical and psychological background that surrounded both the classic Muslim thought (offensive war) and the modern one (defensive war). Social, psychological and historical factors decide what attitude shapes the history of a nation and what school of thought responds to its state of strength or weakness.

Hence, these experiences illustrate that jihad was not pursued only by military means, even during the period of extended Muslim power. At the same time, during the periods of Muslim weakness, the military means of jihad still exist besides the peaceful ones. Both instruments revealed new significance and gave different results.

1. During a period when large Muslim powers were playing a central world role, we can shed light on the following experiences:
    a. The difference between the Umayyad and the first Abbassid caliphs. The Umayyads adopted and successfully executed a grand policy of fatah (conquering). In contrast, the first Abbassid caliphs, although they were not less powerful, gave up the military faith orientation. They depended mainly on peaceful instruments to run external relations, with force used mainly for retaliation and defensive purposes.
    b. The similarity between the Mamluke and Ottoman use of peaceful means to run their power politics. Western historians, as well as Muslim ones who only equated jihad with offensive war, considered the flourishing peaceful relations between Mame-luke sultanates and European kingdoms as a sort of relinquishing jihad. The first Ottoman capitul-

ation to François King of France in the 16th century was also seen as a turning point towards a new era of Muslim foreign relations. According to the third interpretation of jihad (as a means of Da'wah either through war or peacefully), the use of peaceful means in these two experiences should be considered as a sort of jihad. These large Islamic states (Mameluke and Ottoman) based their external relations on jihad and adopted an Islamic frame of reference.

In other words, while a trend of modern Muslim writings interpreted all acts of jihad during the period of power in Muslim history in terms of defense, and many non-Muslim writers explained them as aggression against non-Muslims, it must be noticed, in light of the broad interpretations of jihad, that a realistic analysis of the use the term of jihad should take into consideration the internal and external contexts of Muslim states, whether strong or weak.

2. Through the last two centuries, the period of Muslim decadence, acts of jihad narrowed gradually and took new shapes. The Western attacks on and control of the Muslim world seriously challenged the classical approach of thought as well as the policies of Muslim states. The attacks were fatal because of the condition of both Muslim thought and power. Western attacks revealed and uncovered the decay of Muslims, rather than caused it. It became moot to argue over defensive versus offensive jihad. Total comprehension and understanding of the modern world could not be explained in terms of the classical thought. The new exigencies demanded new Muslim thought and policies.

These developments took the form either of apologetics or of protest and revolt against the Western adversary's presence in the Muslim world.

Each of these two broad types of responses has taken various forms through the period of colonialism and after independence till now. Some of these forms have been proclaimed as jihad. The two types complement each other rather than being alternatives.

First: What about the Colonialist Period?

As a result of realizing Muslim weakness and technolo-gical backwardness and being in direct contact with the control of European thought and power, the apologetic trend appealed to liberalism and over-emphasized peace, freedom and tolerance. This trend was a weapon to reform Muslim nations. This reform was considered the main way to get rid of European occupation that threatened not only the land but all the values of Islam. This was typical of the ruling Ottoman elite and its movements of the nineteenth century and of the reformers who came in contact with the West even since the era of Rifa'ah at-Tahtawi.

The other response to the European domination was military. Aimed at the liberation of the Muslim land, it was organized by people and their traditional leadership, such as Al- Mahdi in Sudan, Al-Mokhtar in Libya, Al-Jaza'iri in Algeria, Isma'il Al-Shahid in India, Osman Dan Foudia in Africa, and so on.

All these liberation movements emphasized jihad more or less in terms of classical conceptions. But such a jihad war was bound to fail because the conditions essential for success were not present. The liberal approach to internal reform of government and society also failed.

During the First World War, jihad was proclaimed by both the Ottoman Sultan against the allied powers and by the Sharif Hussein against the Turkish rulers. They also failed. So, the rest of the Arab world failed to gain the promised independence. At the same time, the Balfour Declaration was issued and the aggressive Zionist project established its bases in Palestine.

These experiences brought disenchantment with Western liberalism, Western institutions and cooperation with the West.

In the inter-war period, the liberation movements were waged under various ideological discourses. Other ideological movements stemming from nationalism or Marxism accompanied the Islamic jihad. The Muslim Brotherhood was the main Islamic movement that adopted a compre-hensive strategy for change. It proclaimed jihad both as military resistance against occupation and as social and spiritual reform.

Second: After the Independence of Muslims States

The use of jihad terminology, as well as jihad doctrine, was restricted and narrowed. The indicators were various and extended, causing confusion and renewed the debate of jihad versus terrorism.

1. The national policies terminology dropped the term jihad in favor of other terms such as national liberation movements, population liberation movements, and the right of self-determination. These terms stemmed from non-Islamic frames of reference. But on the other hand, some leaders used the term jihad in critical situations, mainly during wars with Israel. Otherwise, some wars between Muslims were also called jihad. After the end of the Cold War and the beginning of a comprehensive peace process between Arabs and Israel, national governments in the Muslim world adopted another discourse: the "adaptation to globalization" and to peace. So, jihad's reputation worsened as long as it was considered to be a catalyst force against the negative consequences of globalization, and the catastrophic situations prevailing since the peace process with Israel was begun.
2. Some internal opposition movements that were called jihad proclaimed it against national governments. But their use of force in the name of defending Islam and Muslims against tyranny, corruption, dependency, and peace with Israel was equated with terrorism.
3. The doctrine of jihad was also used by the US and its allies to wage war against Communism in the Islamic

world, especially in Afghanistan. After the end of the Cold War, the acts called jihad against the USA and Israel were escalated towards the end of the 20th century, when the unjust and offensive policies against Muslim peoples reached its peak on various levels. The foreign cultural and civilizational aspects that threaten Muslim people have added more critical challenges to the traditional ones, at the military and economic level.

Finally, in light of the previous analysis of theories and historical experiences, I can present the following remarks concerning the consequences of 11 September:

1. The cultural and civilizational aspects of the event, as well as of the global coalition against terrorism, show the extent to which the Israeli-American alliance has evolved. The Israeli aggression against Palestinian people is escalating intensively. It is a sort of state terrorism. It did not spark American opposition or condemnation. At the same time, policies fighting terrorism are firmly executed with the help of Arab and Muslim countries.

   The term jihad is vanishing gradually, under the terrorism vogue. The war against terrorism has become the nightmare of Muslim governments as well as Muslim people. While the stability of the former has become at stake, the existence and identity of the latter has been dangerously threatened.
2. The distorted image of Islam and Muslims is used to an extreme to justify current international policies conducted against terrorism. Islam and the Muslim world are considered the main source of evil that the US should fight to protect humanity and civilization.

   This is not new. Centuries ago when the Ottoman armies knocked at the gates of Vienna, the Orientalists drew a distorted picture of the Turks, the proclaimers of jihad. The motive was to mobilize European resistance against the great Ottoman sultans. Three centuries ago, the image of Muslims as backward, fanatic, uncivilized people was used again to justify expansionists' targets, called the mission of the white man to spread modernity and the message of civilization.

Now at the beginning of the 21st century, while accusing Muslims of using religion to serve political aims, we can notice that the political discourse of the American administration reveals an alliance between the extreme religious right (Protestants) and the political conservatives. This alliance presents a threat not only to the Muslim world but to the entire world. It adopts a strategy of absolute global American hegemony and is motivated by the theory of conflict of civilizations. The politics emanating from this strategy are unjust, intolerant, violent, arrogant, deeply interfering and extremely oriented to power politics.

These policies stimulated Arab and Muslim resistance. The use of any kind of force against these hegemonic policies is always condemned and equated with terrorism. From now on, since the Muslim people faced strong external and internal oppressions that blocked the capacity for opposition and the needed political and economic change, jihad will be pursued even in a way that will be considered as the hated terrorism. The Bin Laden phenomenon is a typical case. He has acquired the admiration and approval of ordinary Muslim people because he took revenge for them. He found a new way to fight injustice where all ordinary ways had been closed.

So, we have to wonder if the current policies against the so-called terrorism are going to cure the cause of the disease or just cure the symptoms. Domestic and international scenes need to change dramatically in order to forge more justice and tolerance, not only for Westerners but also for Muslims everywhere, in Palestine, Kashmir, Chechnya, Balkans, Philippines, Afghanistan, and in all Muslim countries where Islamists are persecuted and restricted.

In such international circumstances that do not favor Islam and Muslims, Islamic thought faces a big challenge because it is necessary to develop a new vision of jihad (especially regarding when and why to use force and by whom). Any thought that does not respond to the personality and identity of the Islamic Ummah will result in more confusion and could be very harmful to the Muslim Ummah's response to serious challenges that threaten not only its territory and wealth but the very essence of the Ummah, its soul and its identity, i.e., jihad in its fullest and broadest meaning.

THE IMAGE OF JIHAD

In religious teaching, Jihad denotes any struggle against the lower, selfish tendencies of the ego. One dimension of this may be to struggle against one's own selfishness and cowardice in order to defend one's people. One form of this was indicated by the Blessed Prophet when he said: 'the best form of jihad is to speak a true word to a tyrannical ruler'. In doing so one risks one's life, but is serving the weak and the oppressed; the Prophet therefore describes it as a form of jihad.

While non-retaliation against a personal injury is frequently a virtue, Islam believes that human communities have the right to collective self-defense, since non-resistance to aggression would result in a world dominated by tyrants. Under some circumstances, Muslim scholars will allow oppressed peoples to rebel against their oppressors. They might, therefore, classify the American War of Independence as a form of jihad, broadly understood. When Bosnia was faced with ethnic cleansing in 1992, the Muslim authorities there authorized the use of force to defend the country's Muslim minority. The alternative would have been mass murder and mass rape, and therefore jihad was lawful. Furthermore, some Muslim scholars will permit a non-defensive 'idealist' war to establish justice and freedom in a neighboring country. This is analogous, perhaps, to the decision of the United Kingdom to declare war on Germany on September 3, 1939, in response to the German invasion of Poland. There are more recent analogies as well, including very recent instances in which Western powers have used force to overthrow tyrants such as Saddam Hussein.

The poet Rumi explains the ethical principle of jihad as follows:

"Knowledge and wealth and office and rank and fortune are a mischief in the hands of the evil-natured. Therefore the Jihad was made obligatory on true believers for this purpose, namely, that they might take the spear-point from the hand of the madman."

Fundamentally, as understood by orthodox Islamic jurists (as opposed to radical Islamists, who reject the classical position), jihad theory closely resembles some versions of Just War theory as this has been developed in several Christian churches since the time of St. Augustine. For some good debates about the resemblance see John Kelsay and James Turner Johnson (eds.), "Just War and Jihad: Historical and Theoretical Perspectives on War and Peace in Western and Islamic Traditions".

Suicide bombing is an innovated practice that has no basis in Islamic law. Particularly when targeted against innocent non-combatants it is a fundamental violation of Islam understands of justice. 'No soul is guilty of the sins of another'. 'Do not kill yourselves' (Holy Qur'an, chapter 4 verse 29). For more, see my essay 'Bombing without Moonlight' and the more technical Sharia discussion by Shaykh Muhammad Afifi al-Akiti).

ISLAM AND APOSTACY

Is it permissable for a Muslim to convert to another faith? How can laws against apostacy and blasphemy be reconciled with the Koranic injunction of "No compulsion in religion"?

Traditional human communities believe that truth leads to salvation, and error to damnation. It is probable that very many religious people in a variety of denominations still believe this. Historically, religiously-faithful princes have therefore seen it as necessary to use the coercive power of the state to forbid apostasy. One of the most powerful and persistent manifestations of this understanding in history was the

Inquisition, which was definitively abolished in 1834. Protestant countries also respected this drastic principle; in fact, the first converts to Islam in Britain were impaled on stakes. In a Hindu context, 'apostasy' was often classified as violation of caste rules and boundaries, and similarly drastic consequences could follow. After the Mongol sack of Baghdad in 1258, Buddhists who converted to Islam were routinely put to death.

The four canonical schools of Sunni Islamic law, and also most pre-modern Shi'a jurists, recommend similarly drastic penalties, although the judge is enjoined to 'look for ambiguities' in order to avert the death penalty wherever possible.

The Ottoman Caliphate, the supreme representative of Sunni Islam, formally abolished this penalty in the aftermath of the so-called Tanzimat reforms launched in 1839. The Shaykh al-Islam, the supreme head of the religious courts and colleges, ratified this major shift in traditional legal doctrine. It was pointed out that there is no verse in the Qur'an that lays down a punishment for apostasy (although chapter 5 verse 54 and chapter 2 verse 217 predict a punishment in the next world). It was also pointed out that the ambiguities in the hadith (the sayings of the Prophet) suggest that apostasy is only an offense when combined with the crime of treason. These ambiguities led some medieval Muslims, long before the advent of modernisation, to reject the majority view. Prominent among them one may name al-Nakha'i (d.713), al-Thawri (d.772), al-Sarakhsi (d. 1090), al-Baji (d. 1081), and al-Sha'rani (d.1565). The debate triggered by the Ottoman reform was continued when al-Azhar University in Cairo, the supreme religious authority in the Arab world, delivered a formal fatwa (religious edict) in 1958, which confirmed the abolition of the classical law in this area.

Among radical Salafis and Wahhabis who do not accept the verdicts of the Ottoman or the Azhar scholars, it is generally believed that the majority medieval view should still be enforced.

RIGHT OF WOMEN IN ISLAM

How does Islam's view of male-female equality differ

from the western view? This question somewhat essentializes Islam and 'the West'. There is a huge diversity of Muslim opinion here, both ancient and modern; and 'the Western view' really does not exist, since villagers in Venezuela, for instance are Westerners, and so are many ultra-orthodox Jews, and conservative Catholics, and radical Californian feminists; and while the views of all these groups are morally coherent, they are not part of a single 'Western view'. Thankfully, Islam and the West are both diverse. And of course they overlap: many people, including myself, consider themselves to be both Western and Muslim.

Virtually all pre-modern ethical, legal and social systems accepted firm assurances about the respective nature of the two sexes. Women were taken to be nurturers and homemakers, while men were to be earners and warriors. There are clear biological reasons why ancient societies should have favored such a division of labor, and the current sharp debate over the 'different wiring' of the male and female brain may clarify this, although it is unlikely to be resolved soon (see, for instance, Ann and Bill Moir, "Why Men Don't Iron: The Fascinating and Unalterable Differences between Men and Women" and whichever way the scientific debate goes, it is evident that our bodies influence our minds, and even our souls, and we can accept this without assuming that one gender is therefore superior to the other.

Islam is a religion that takes our rooted ness in our bodies seriously. We pray with their bodies as well as with our hearts. Turning the body to face Mecca encourages the soul to do the same. Childbearing must have a deep spiritual impact. So Muslims believe that men and women are spiritually different. However the indispensable practices of the religion, including the daily prayers, the hajj pilgrimage to Mecca, and the fasting month of Ramadan, are incumbent on both sexes. For the ancient world, this was a remarkable circumstance, and Muslims are obliged to see it as a sign that women and men are both spiritual beings, with similar spiritual duties.

Some Christian denominations do not accept the validity

of women priests. Islam, too, does not recognize the validity of services conducted by women (unless there are no men in the congregation). However this does not exclude women from positions of religious leadership. Thousands of medieval Muslim scholars were women. They would teach, preach, and give religious verdicts in the mosque. Many others became saints.

The lively Muslim feminist movement today likes to point out that since Islam does not call God 'Father', and does not believe that God was incarnated in a male body, that Muslims can consider that they are worshipping a gender-neutral deity. This, together with many other factors, ensures the continuing popularity of Islam amongst women. In my own community in the UK, around eighty percent of recent converts have been women. For the U.S. see the remarkable and often moving book by Carol Anyway, "Daughters of Another Path: Experiences of American Women Choosing Islam".

The translation of the Arabic word "Jihad" has been distorted and twisted to such an extent, that it no longer gives meaning to the original term. The word "jihad" means "striving; exerting oneself in any endeavour; going the extra mile; endurance in the face of obstacles." For example, a student who is studying for his exams is performing Jihad, because he is striving to succeed in his/her studies. A business owner who is striving to make a success of his business is performing Jihad. A husband, who is trying to save his marriage, is performing Jihad because he is striving in the face of obstacles to make a success of his marriage. The Prophet Mohamed (Peace Be Upon Him) stated that the highest Jihad is against oneself. By this he meant that the best Jihad is controlling ones own desires, controlling ones emotions of anger, jealousy, hatred and revenge. To do this, is not easy - that is why it is a Jihad. It is a struggle. It means developing a strong will power and disciplining the mind and the body for a more noble cause and effort. It is only through struggle and hardships that character is developed. Jihad means controlling ones lower, animalistic base desires (the 'nafs') and thereby unveiling the true inner spirit of compassion, mercy, love, selflessness and kindness for all humanity. The true test of one's character comes when a victim does not take revenge when in a position of strength. For example, Nelson Mandela was incarcerated for 27 years. When victory came to him, he could have extracted revenge, and few people would have blamed him. However, he showed true character and a strong will - he controlled his desire for revenge - by controlling his desire for revenge, Mandela performed Jihad. The Prophet Mohamed (Peace Be Upon Him) was persecuted and forced to flee from the land of his birth. He came back victorious after 10 years - in that moment of victory, he was the Superpower of Arabia and he could have annihilated all his enemies - yet, not a single drop of blood was shed - he performed Jihad of the highest order, when he forgave his enemies. The Prophet Jesus (Peace Be Upon Him) performed Jihad when he prayed to Allah (SWT) to forgive his enemies "for they know not what they do." The Prophet Jesus (Peace Be Upon Him) did not pray for revenge- he controlled his inner desire ('nafs') for revenge. Mahatma Gandhi performed Jihad when he exercised self control and embarked on peaceful (passive) resistance against the British army.

In addition to the types of Jihad described above, even looking after your parents is a Jihad. When a man was about to join a battle, the Prophet (Peace Be Upon Him) encouraged him to instead look after his ailing parents - that is, it is a better form of Jihad than going for a battle. We all know that sometimes it is difficult to be kind and polite to our parents. But for Muslims, to be kind, merciful and respectful to parents is a duty of the highest form, even more rewarding than being a Martyr in a battle.

A man came to the Prophet (Peace Be Upon Him) asking his permission to take part in Jihad. The Prophet (Peace Be Upon Him) asked him, "Are your parents alive?" He replied in the affirmative. The Prophet (Peace Be Upon Him) said to him, "Then exert yourself in their service.

Furthermore, for women, the best form of Jihad is to perform the Hajj. The Pilgrimage of Hajj is a strenuous and arduous journey filled with hardships and requires much tolerance on the part of the one who embarks on this journey.

Sahih Bukhari Hadith 4.43 Narrated by Aisha (RA), that she said " O Allah's Apostle ! We consider Jihad as the best deed. Should we not fight in Allah's cause? "He (Peace Be Upon Him) said: "The best Jihad (for women) is Hajj Mabrur (ie Hajj which is done according to the Prophet's tradition and is accepted by Allah)."

HOLY WAR

Warfare is one type of Jihad. Warfare is also a form of striving. However, fighting and warfare in Islam is only allowed in extreme and very exceptional circumstances. All avenues of discussion, negotiation and communication must be exhausted before the route of warfare is embarked upon.

The Holy Prophet Mohamed (Peace Be Upon Him) said: " The best fighting (Jihad) in the path of Allah is (to speak) a word of justice to an oppressive ruler." {Sunan of Abu Dawood Hadith 4330, Narrated by Abu Said al-Khudri (RA) }

A Muslim is only permitted to take up arms in two main instances. Firstly, against an oppressive government and secondly in self defence. When any of these two conditions are present, then a Muslim is permitted to take up arms, provided that the decision has been made by a group consensus of leading Ulema's (Scholars and Jurists). In this case, striving in this effort, against an oppressor, is known as Jihad. It does not matter who the oppressor is - all Muslims have a duty to fight all forms of oppression, discrimination and slavery (whether it is social, political or economic). If a Muslim is oppressing a Muslim, then all Muslims must perform Jihad against the Muslim ruler to fight on behalf of the silent masses. If a Jewish government is oppressing its Jewish citizens, then Muslims have a duty to perform Jihad against the oppressor. If a Christian government or a Hindu government or a Communist government or any other oppressive government is oppressing its citizens, then Muslims are duty bound to assist and free the victims of oppression.

In the current news media, a lot of media hype was caused when Afghanistan declared 'Holy War". It should be remembered that Afghanistan is not the aggressor. Afghanistan has declared a Holy War, only in self - defence, in response to America's declaration of war against Afghanistan. There is not a single shred of evidence, that this poorest country in the world (Afghans are dying daily due to hunger, lack of water, lack of medical facilities and lack of proper sanitation), which does not believe in technology (citizens are not even allowed Television), or Usama Bin Ladin, a Bedouin, living in the deserts and caves of Afghanistan, could ever be responsible for this precise, very sophisticated military hit on the Pentagon. By declaring a "holy war', Afghanistan is simply doing what any country in the world would do, that is, declare a state of Emergency (Holy War) to defend its citizens against a possible apocalyptic catastrophe. There is nothing sinister in this approach.

ISLAMIC RULES OF CONDUCT IN WARFARE

Islam places great emphasis on the rules of conduct in any war. War is the last resort, when all other measures fail. Discussion and negotiation win more wars and battles than military conflict- "jaw-jaw" is better than "war-war." In the extreme scenario when war is inevitable, then Muslims are duty bound to abide to the following very strict conditions of warfare which have been commanded by the Prophet Mohamed (Peace Be Upon Him) in various authentic Hadith such as:

Al Muwatta Hadith 21.10.

The Prophet (Peace Be Upon Him) said: "I advise you 10 things: Do not kill women or children or aged, infirm person. Do not cut down fruit bearing trees. Do not destroy an inhabited place. Do not slaughter sheep or camels except for food. Do not burn bees and do not scatter them. Do not steel from the booty and do not be cowardly."

1. The war should be confined to the battle field: soldier against soldier
2. No woman or child, or elderly man, or any civilian not involved in the battle, should be harmed in any way;

thus there is no concept of hostages or terrorist attacks on innocent civilians in Islam

3. The environment, fruit bearing trees, water, houses, animals, birds, insects and livestock or essential supplies cannot be harmed or damaged in any way
4. Torture of prisoners is forbidden. In fact, the Prophet Mohamed (PBUH) encouraged his followers to treat the captives with compassion and kindness. In the event that Muslims had prisoners, the Prophet (Peace Be Upon Him) enjoined on his followers to first feed the prisoners, before he ate.
5. A war must only be waged for the sake of Allah, meaning that the war must not be done for any material gain e.g. capturing land for territory, wealth, oil or gold;

   The Holy Prophet (Peace Be Upon Him) said: "The action dearest to Allah Most High is Love for Allah's sake and hatred for Allah's sake." {Al-Tirmidhi, Hadith 5021 Narrated by Abu Dharr (RA)} Sunan of Abu-Dawood Hadith 2510 narrated by Abu Huraira (RA)

   A man said:" Apostle of Allah, a man wishes to take part in Jihad in Allah's path desiring some worldly advantage? The Prophet (Peace Be Upon Him) said: "He will have no reward."
6. A war cannot be waged on another nation to force them to accept Islam, because Allah clearly commands in the Quran "there is no compulsion in religion". Islam is the fastest growing religion in the world, not because of threats or warfare, but simply through the tools of logic, common sense and reason. Unlike other religions, Islam has not been tainted by human follies of inter-polation, additions and deletions to the original Word of Allah.
7. Before any war is contemplated, irrefutable facts and evidence must be presented. No one can act on hearsay or suspicion. Justice and fair-play are necessary preconditions because human lives are at stake. In Islam, the sanctity and sacredness of all human life is firmly

entrenched in the following guidance: if someone kills an innocent person without cause, it is as if he has killed the whole of humanity. If someone saves a human life, it is as if he has saved the whole of humanity.

8. War must be terminated as soon as the opposite party relents – continuation of the war to extract sadistic revenge is totally forbidden
9. Arrogance is totally forbidden and usurping the rights of the defeated nation by making life difficult for them is not allowed as shown in the following:

   The Prophet (Peace Be Upon Him) said:"Those who occupy much space or encroach on the road will not be credited with Jihad." (Sunan of Abu Dawood, Hadith 2623, narrated by Mu'adh ibn Anas al-Juhani (RA)}

   This is what makes war in Islam a 'holy' war – that is, a war that is conducted with the highest morality, ethics and a code of conduct of behaviour. Muslims are fully aware that all their actions will be judged one day by Allah, the one and Only, Who will judge between all humanity. This is the Day of Accountability where every action of every person will be displayed. No Muslim will dare utter that he is performing an action "for the sake of Allah", when his actions are against the Code of Conduct laid down in the Quran and shown by the Prophet Mohamed (Peace Be Upon Him). Thus the word "holy" simply means that it is a war with ethics, compassion and the highest moral conduct by all combatants.

UNHOLY WAR

In contrast, a war that is conducted by some Western nations is not regarded as "holy" or ethical from an Islamic point of view or any other point of view, as the following few examples illustrate:

1. America used 80 000 tons (80 Million kilograms) of cluster bombs which do not discriminate between civilian and non-civilian targets in Iraq. This is 'unholy"

and not ethical. More than 1 million innocent civilians lost their lives. Buildings, land, dams, electrical power stations, schools and hospitals were totally destroyed thus catapulting this 1st World country back to the primitive Stone Age.

2. More than 5000 children under the age of 5 years are dying every month since 1991 in Iraq because America used depleted Uranium (outlawed internationally) and because of ongoing sanctions on this crippled nation. This is unethical and unholy.
3. The use of Agent Orange by America, on Vietnam, is unholy. Agent Orange is carcinogenic and mutanogenic and has not only affected humans, but has also destroyed the environment for decades
4. The use of a nuclear bomb on Hiroshima is unholy and unethical, since it killed many innocent civilians but in addition, the cancer effects on the population and the destruction of the environment are still being felt today and for generations to come
5. The action of an armed Israeli soldier who shoots a 6 year old Palestinian Child in the head is "unholy" and unethical
6. Destroying the homes of Palestinians with bulldozers or Apache Attack Helicopters, killing and torturing thousands of Palestinians who are fighting for their freedom and their land that was unlawfully usurped from them, is unholy and unethical
7. The ethnic cleansing and slaughter of Muslims in Bosnia is unholy and unethical
8. The kamikaze attack on the World Trade centre where innocent civilians died in the planes and on land is unholy and unethical
9. The hoarding of wealth by a few industrial nations who live in opulent luxury, while millions in Africa, India, Pakistan, South America and other parts of the world are living in abject poverty is regarded as 'unholy' and

'unethical' – Muslims are duty bound to restore the living conditions of all humanity. Poverty is economic oppression

11. The unlawful underwater testing of nuclear weapons is unethical and unholy since it destroys millions of marine life and damages the oceans of the world

There is only One God. The One God does not give conflicting information to different religions. We are all children of Prophet Adam (Peace Be Upon Him). One should not condemn a nation or a religion on the basis of the actions of a few misguided people. An American Citizen is no more and no less important than a non-American Citizen. One should conduct our affairs with justice, compassion, dignity, respect and mutual tolerance for all humanity, black or white, great or small, Muslim or non-Muslim. We are one family. We are one humanity. We need a new world order based on the respect, dignity, compassion and love for all humanity. We pray to Allah (SWT), to grant us Guidance, Forgive us our shortcomings and to Grant the Wisdom of Solomon to all world leaders to make decisions that will uplift all humanity and not selfish decisions to earn political points or flaunt the lands with brutal arrogance. All humanity has to embark on a global Jihad to bring peace to this world. Ameen.

7

The Multilayered Concept of Jihad

Jihad is projected as an integral part of Islam - as an obligatory duty of all Muslims to fight against infidels. To say the least, this is a highly improper representation of the concept of jihad in Islam. The multi-layered concept of jihad has been projected as a one-dimensional concept - to fight with the Sword against all infidels. What happened on September 11 has further harmed the prospects of a correct understanding of the concept.

The first step towards such understanding is to situate the concept of jihad in its historical context. One is often historically determined, without an understanding of how one is historically situated.

Qur'anic pronouncements are multi-layered and multi-dimensional - some of these dimensions are historical, some social, other ethical. To understand the Qur'anic verses in a one-dimensional manner is to do great injustice to them, and also misapply them - either because of a wrong understanding of the verses, or on account of some selfish motive.

To understand the Qur'an better, it is important to understand the pre-Islamic Arab society. Violence and inter-tribal wars were rampant. Reconciliation and conflict resolution through negotiations was virtually unknown. Though the pre-Islamic Arab society was not exactly immoral, it did have tribal traditions and customs that ignored certain ethical aspects. Peace, though appreciated, was not always practiced. As there was no rule of law in pre-Islamic society, things were settled through inter-tribal wars or tribal customs and traditions. This resulted in a great deal of bloodshed.

This prevailing historical situation was not acceptable to Islam, but some of its elements did persist in Muslim behaviour. Also, we have to bear in mind that it was not a modern democratic society, but a tribal society with its own outlook and intellectual understanding. We cannot apply modern norms to the tribal society, nor should we perpetuate its practices in modern times. Islam, while constrained to retain some of it, rejected most of these practices, and provided for transcendent norms and ethical standards. What some Muslims do (and many non-Muslims too) is ignore the historicity of some Qur'anic and Hadith pronouncements, and place them in an ahistorical context, thus causing great deal of misunderstanding about the Islamic ethics of jihad.

A careful study of the Qur'an and Hadith makes it clear that the concept of jihad is far above mere violence and war. Unfortunately, Islamic history was fraught with wars for several reasons (certainly not for religious reasons), hence the one-dimensional concept of jihad. The Sufis, who kept themselves aloof from power-struggles and attempts by rulers at territorial expansions, realised the dangers of misapplying the concept of jihad. They thought it necessary to emphasise the other social and moral aspects of jihad. It is for this reason that they described jihad bi al-sayf (i.e. war with Sword) as jihad-e-asghar (i.e. small war), and jihad to control one's greed and selfish desires as jihad-e-akbar i.e. great jihad. This was important because Muslim leaders and their cohorts were ignoring the moral precepts and ethical constraints imposed by Qur'anic pronouncements to fulfill their greed for power and territory.

The Sufis had based the concept of the great jihad on the basis of Qur'anic pronouncements, and had not formulated a precept of their own. Jihad, as is well known to any student of the Arabic language, means to make utmost efforts. One must look at the authentic Qur'anic dictionary Mufradat al-Qur'an by Imam Raghib Asfahani.

Imam Raghib first discusses the meaning of the root word jahd, which means working hard or making utmost efforts, and juhud, which means one's utmost capacity. The two together would mean making utmost efforts to one's best capacity. Then he goes on to say that jihad wa al-mujahidah means to spend one's utmost capacity in defending oneself in the face of an enemy. Then he divides jihad in three categories: 1) to fight against enemies, i.e. unbelievers; 2) against shaitan (Satan) and 3) against one's own self, i.e. one's own greed and selfishness.

Imam Raghib also maintains that the Qur'anic verse 22:78 ("And strive hard for Allah with due striving. He has chosen you and has not laid any hardship in religion.") comprises all these three categories. The Qur'an also says, "And strives hard in Allah's way with your wealth and your lives. This is better for you, if you know." (9:41). One also finds in the Qur'an, "Those who believed and migrated (from their homes), and strove hard in Allah's way with their wealth and their lives, and are much higher in rank with Allah. And it is these that shall triumph." (9:20)

It will be seen that all these verses in the Qur'an do not use the word jihad in the sense of war, but in the sense of striving with wealth and one's own life. Muslims were a persecuted lot in Mecca, and many of them faced severe persecution, and strove hard in the way of Allah with their own lives, and those who were wealthy, spent all their wealth for that cause. Thus, it was all about suffering and striving. This is real jihad. Nowhere in the Qur'an is jihad used either in the sense of war, or for seeking revenge. Seeking revenge amounts to using concept of jihad for selfish ends, even if the revenge or retaliation is for one's group or community.

In Hadith literature, we find a Hadith, which prohibits Muslims from seeking revenge. Thus in Sahih al-Bukhari, we find the Hadith of Miqdad ibn Amr al-Kindi. Amr al-Kindi asked the holy Prophet (peace be upon him), "Suppose I met one of the infidels and we fought. He struck one of my hands with his Sword, cut it off and then took refuge in a tree and said, 'I surrender to Allah'. Could I kill him, O Messenger of Allah, after he had said this?" Allah's Messenger (PBUH) said, "You should not kill him." Al-Miqdad said, "O Allah's Messenger, but he had cut off my hands, and then he had uttered those words." Allah's Messenger (PBUH) replied, "You should not kill him, and you would be in his position where he had been before uttering these words." Thus it will be seen that in matters of war also, Islam teaches higher morality, the essence of which is not to seek revenge or retaliate. This is what I call the transcendent morality.

In matters of jihad, Imam Raghib quotes an interesting Hadith, which says, "Fight your desires as you fight your enemies." The Sufi concept of jihad-i-akbar i.e. the great jihad is to fight ones own vain desires has been based on this Hadith. According to the Qur'an, man's life is a constant struggle in the way of Allah, be it through Sword or through one's hands or one's tongue. Thus there is a Hadith which says, "Strive against unbelievers with your hands and your words."

Thus this constant jihad, constant struggle in the way of Allah implies multi-layered efforts. The believers have been charged, by the Qur'an, with the important mission of spreading good and fighting evil (amr bi'l ma'ruf wa nahi 'an al-munkar). In this mission, a believer has to engage himself continuously, controlling his own desires, spreading justice, equality and compassion with wisdom ('adl - justice, ihsan - benevolence, rahmah- compassion and hikmah - wisdom are concepts of goodness in the Qur'an which are repeatedly stressed).

As it is duty of believers to engage in spreading what is good, it is also their duty to engage in containing what is evil. Thus, a believer has to constantly strive to fight against oppression, injustice, iniquity and cruelty. All these result in spreading evil on earth. The world, as we all know, is full of injustices and oppression, and it will be a lifetime mission of a believer to contain them. This is real jihad.

A fight is not always with weapons. It could equally be through moral and intellectual means - through persuasion, wisdom, spreading the good word, and setting good examples. It is for this reason that the Prophet has said that the ink of a writer's pen is more sacred than the blood of a martyr. The word written with ink is lasts longer than a martyr's blood. The Qur'an says, "And fights in the way of Allah against those who fight against you but be not aggressive. Surely Allah loves not the aggressors" (2:190) one has to strictly observe these conditions in jihad.

The noted Urdu poet Iqbal has beautifully described the meaning of jihad in day-to-day life in one of his couplets as follows:

Yaqin muhkam 'amal payham muhabbat fatihi 'alam

Jihad-e- zindagani mein yeh hain mardon ki shamshiren

(For a man with strong inner conviction, constant efforts and universe-winning love are the real weapons in the jihad of life.)

The meaning of jihad is not complete without the Qur'anic injunction for believers (men as well as women) to enforce good, and contain evil, and this is the lifelong mission of all the believers. To achieve this objective, believers have to use their persuasive skills, wisdom and goodliness. One cannot enforce good with Sword. Goodness prevails only with goodness. What the Qur'an calls maw'izah hasanah (i.e. exhortation with goodness) and hikmah (wisdom) is more lasting than enforcing something forcibly.

The Prophet (PBUH) always tried all possibilities of negotiated settlement, and resorted to war in self-defence only if all efforts to find a negotiated settlement failed. The best example of this is what is known in the history of Islam as sulh-i-Hudaibiyah. He even accepted terms, which were not apparently favourable to Muslims to avoid human slaughter and in the interest of peace. The terms of peace appeared to be even humiliating to his senior companions.

We find mention of this in Sahih al-Bukhari. Abu Wa'il narrated, "We were in Siffin and Sahl ibn Hunayf stood up and said, 'O people! Blame yourselves! We were with the Prophet (PBUH) on the day of Hudaybiyyah, and if we had been called to fight, we should have fought.' But Umar ibn al-Khattab came and said, 'O Allah's Messenger! Aren't we in the right and our opponents in the wrong?' Allah's Messenger said, 'Yes'. Umar said, 'Then why should we accept hard terms in matters concerning our religion? Shall we return before Allah judges between us and them?' Allah's Messenger (PBUH) said, 'O ibn al-Khattab! I am the Messenger of Allah and Allah will never degrade me.'"

Sulh-Hudaibiyuyah is of fundamental significance in the interest of peace. Peace is the real objective, and war only a necessary evil in certain unavoidable situations. Also, it is a wrong assumption that it is duty of the Muslims to fight against all non-believers or kafirs. The Qur'an itself mentions treaties with unbelievers, and according to the Qur'an and Hadith, it is the duty of all Muslims to honour all treaties and alliances with non-believers. All such alliances must be respected by the Muslims as long as they are honoured by non-Muslims.

Thus we find again in Sahih al-Bukhari, "The pagans were of two kinds as regards their relationship with the Prophet (PBUH) and the believers. Some of them were those with whom the Prophet was at war, and used to fight against, and they used to fight him; the others were those with whom the Prophet (PBUH) made a treaty, and neither did the Prophet fight them, nor did they fight him.

Those who work for social justice are as good as mujahideen i.e. warriors in the way of Allah. Thus we find in Sahih al-Bukhari: The Prophet (PBU) said, "The one who looks after and works for a widow and for a poor person is like a warrior fighting for Allah's cause, or like a person who fasts during the day and prays all the night."

Thus any one striving for social justice and working to ameliorate the plight of the poor is like a warrior in the way of Allah. Thus, those who spend their own money or collect from others and spend for the poor in the way Allah is no less than a mujahid. According to the Qur'an, zakat money is to be spent on poor, widows, needy, paying off the debt of indebted and for liberation of slaves. These are all weaker sections of society. It is thus a great merit to help these poorer and weaker sections and to work for them is as meritorious as waging jihad in the way of Allah. One should wage war against poverty in all possible ways - by increasing production, by ringing about redistribution of economic resources and by not allowing wealth to be circulated only among the rich.

Even when first permission was given to fight in the Qur'anic verse 4:77, it was basically to defend the rights of weak from among the old men, women and children. In some extreme situations, it might mean fighting a war, but it could be a fight in various other ways, particularly in a democratic and modern society. It could be through democratic movements or parliamentary debates also. In those days, when the holy Qur'an was being revealed, such possibilities did not exist. Today, we will have to creatively re-interpret such Qur'anic provisions as above.

The 'Ulama and jurists in early Islam had divided the world into darul harb and darul Islam. The countries where Muslims could not enjoy the freedom of their faith, and were persecuted were declared by the Muslim jurists as darul harb. And it was thought necessary for Muslims to wage war (jihad) in such countries. However, it is important to note that the Hanafi jurists had also created a third category of darul aman i.e. those countries where Muslims, though in minority yet, could enjoy freedom of religion and were not persecuted because of their religious beliefs. India was always considered as darul aman by Islamic jurists, as Muslims here were not persecuted for their religious beliefs. India was always a pluralist society.

But in today's conditions when, democracy prevails, even if Muslims are persecuted in any country or any place, democratic remedies will have priority over waging war. Terrorism which involves shedding the blood of innocent people, and can never is elevated to the category of jihad in any sense of the Qur'anic term.

Also, a few individuals cannot get together and decide to wage jihad. The decision to wage jihad can be taken only by a properly constituted Islamic government ensuring that there is no other way left but to declare jihad. This can be done after due deliberation, and examining all possible consequences, including loss of human lives. In the modern democratic world such decisions can be arrived at only by a duly-elected government. And as far as the Qur'anic injunction on jihad is concerned, it should not in any case involve a selfish motive like grabbing the territory of others or consolidating any group's rule, but should be strictly for higher goals, like justice and fighting persecution.

It should also be noted that peace is far more funda-mental to Islam than war. War at best could be an instrument of establishing peace in some exceptional circumstances, or for defending against aggression. It is unfortunate that some youth come together, and decides that there is no way out but to use violence, and call it jihad. These youth ultimately shed a great deal of innocent blood, without achieving the ultimate objective. Such extremist violence results in more in-group fighting. Such extremist violence is not jihad.

In a modern world, real jihad is to use democracy and democratic institutions to realise the noble goals for which the Prophet of Islam (PBUH) struggled all his life.

THE MISUNDERSTOOD CONCEPT OF JIHAD

It cannot be over-emphasized that Islam upholds the values of reason, balance and responsibility in the conduct of its worldly affairs. There is nothing arbitrary about its legal provisions relating to matters of war, peace, international relationships and the rule of law. In this area there is considerable agreement between Islamic law and the legal systems currently practiced throughout the world. In addition to the real possibility that these legal systems were profoundly influenced by the legal heritage of Islam, this commonality can be explained by the fact that the protection and endorsement of basic human rights form the cornerstone of Islamic legislation.

The international community has come to agree, through the institution of the United Nations, on a body of human rights and interests which Islam has always endorsed. This ought not to surprise anyone if the basic realism, rationality and pragmatism of Islamic law are recognized.

The critics of Islam, however, insist that Islam and Muslims are openly hostile and intolerant towards communities other than their own. They refer to the Qur'anic verses that exhort the believers to fight the infidels, they point to the battles of early Islam and the eventual confrontation between the Crusaders and the Saracens or Moors, and now, the contemporary stereotype of the Arab "terrorist".

It must be noted that many Orientalists might object to this characterization of their views on the question. Indeed many of them subscribe to more nuanced positions. More recent scholarship has completely abandoned the emotionally-charged vocabulary of earlier Orientalism. It remains true, however, that Islam is still imagined as threatening, fanatical, violent and alien by significant sections of the world's media.

In formulating an answer to all of this, it is crucial to focus on a general definition of Islam, so as not to fall into any misunderstanding about Jihad and its place within the Din. The common expression that Islam is a "way of life" has become hackneyed to the point where we can well do without it. Islam is more accurately described as "establishing the kingdom of heaven on earth."

This latter statement must be carefully understood if we are to avoid the superficial moralizing or equally misleading literalism that characterizes much contemporary thinking about Islam. It is far from desirable to simply quote, as an apparent show of understanding, scriptural support for this or that personal opinion we may have about a particular subject. Neither is it enough to use Qur'anic or Prophetic texts without adequate knowledge of the human situation and cultural milieu in which they were revealed and first applied, as well as the precedence of some verses over others based on order of revelation or abrogation.

In other words, context and circumstance of Qur'anic revelation and Hadith are crucial in coming to terms with Jihad. It is an error to judge Islam and Muslims in the light of the kind of "Jihad" that has fallen victim to ideological tendencies. The critic also has to be wary of the interpretation of "Jihad" which is projected, and sometimes imposed, by the selective "religious reformism" so rampant today. They ignore central aspects of Islam's intellectual heritage, selectively repress important figures and disregard Islam's impeccable history of adherence to the standards of law and justice in affairs of state.

JIHAD IN HISTORY AND LAW

This being said let us now consider the nature of Jihad more fully as it appears in the history and law of Islam. Jihad in Arabic means "to strive for some objective". Thus, the common assumption, that Jihad is combat, is incorrect. In fact Jihad, in its technical meaning, has several branches, among which are the combative forms of Jihad.

Ibn Rushd, in his Muqaddimaat, divides Jihad into four kinds: "Jihad by the heart; Jihad by the tongue; Jihad by the hand and Jihad by the Sword." He defines "Jihad by the tongue" as "to commend good conduct and forbid the wrong, like the type of Jihad Allah (swt) ordered us to fulfilll against the hypocrites in His Words, "O Prophet! Strive hard against the unbelievers and the hypocrites" [9:73]. So the Prophet (s) strove against the unbelievers by Sword and against the hypocrites by tongue." Said Ramadan Buti, a contemporary Orthodox scholar from Syria states, in his seminal work on the subject Jihad in Islam "... even before he conducted Jihad by Sword against the unbelievers, there is no doubt the Prophet (s) invited these unbelievers peacefully, lodged protests against their beliefs and strove to remove their misgivings about Islam. When they refused any other solution, but rather declared a war against him and his message and initiated the fight, there was no alternative except to fight back."

One form of Jihad, usually overlooked in today's pursuit of newsworthy headlines, is the Jihad of presenting the message of Islam-da'wah. Thirteen years of the Prophet's (s) 23-year mission consisted purely of this type of Jihad. Contrary to popular belief, the word Jihad and related forms of its root word jahada are mentioned in many Makkan verses in a non-combative context.

Combative Jihad in the technical usage of Islamic law means "the declaration of war against belligerent and aggressive non-Muslim powers or against fellow Muslim transgressors". It is not a haphazard decision taken by anybody. The principles of Islamic jurisprudence state that the actions of the leader must be guided by the interests of the people and that the interests of the collectivity have, in some cases, precedence over the interests of the individual.

JIHAD AND ISLAMIC PROPAGATION

God states in the Qur'an, "Invite (all) to the Way of thy Lord with wisdom and beautiful preaching; and argue with them in ways that are best and most gracious: for thy Lord knoweth best, who have strayed from His Path, and who receive guidance." [16:125]

Calling people to Islam and making them acquainted with it in all its aspects through dialogue and kind persuasion is the first type of Jihad in Islam, in contrast to the imagined belief that Jihad is only of the combative form. This is referred to in the Qur'an where Allah (swt) says, "so obey not the disbelievers, but strive against them (by preaching) with the utmost endeavor with it (the Qur'an)" [25:52]. Here the word "strive" jaahidu, is used to mean struggle by means of the tongue – preaching and exhortation – and to persevere despite the obstinate resistance of some unbelievers to the beliefs and ideals of Islam.

Imam Nawawi in his book al-Minhaj, when defining Jihad and its different categories, said, "one of the collective duties of the community as a whole (fard kifaya) is to lodge a valid protest, to solve problems of religion, to have knowledge of Divine Law, to command what is right and forbid wrong conduct".

The explanation of Jihad in Imam al-Dardir's book Aqarab al-Masalik is that it is propagating the knowledge of the Divine Law commending right and forbidding wrong. He emphasized that it is not permitted to skip this category of Jihad and implement the combative form, saying, "the first [Islamic] duty is to call people to enter the fold of Islam, even if they had been preached to by the Prophet (s) beforehand." Similarly, Imam Bahouti commences the chapter on Jihad in his book Kashf al-Kinaa by showing the injunctions of collective religious duties (kifaya) that the Muslim Nation must achieve before embarking on combative Jihad, including preaching and education about the religion of Islam, dismissing all the uncertainties about this religion and making available all the skills and qualifications which people might need in their religious, secular, physical and financial interests because these constitute the regulations of both this life and the life to come. Hence, da`wah—performing the activities of propagating Islam and its related fields of knowledge—is the cornerstone of the 'building' of Jihad and its rules; and any attempt to build without this 'stone' would damage the meaning and reality of Jihad.

Removing all misconceptions and stereotypes in clarifying the image of Islam held by non-Muslims, building a trusting relationship and working with them in ways that accord with their way of thinking are all primary forms of Jihad. Similarly, establishing a strong community and nation which can fulfill all physical needs of its people, thereby creating for them conditions in which the message will be heard, rather than being lost in the strife and struggle of everyday life, are requirements and form a basic building block of the Jihadic concept. These foundations fulfill the Qur'anic injunction, "Let there arise out of you a band of people inviting to all that is good, enjoining what is right, and forbidding what is wrong: and these it is that shall be successful." Until this is accomplished the conditions of Jihad remain unfulfilled.

FORCED CONVERSION

So the foundation of Jihad is Islamic propagation (da'wah). The question often asked is whether Islam condones and teaches the forced and armed conversion of non-Muslims. This is the image sometimes projected by Western scholars and as any Muslim scholar will tell you, is seriously flawed. The Qur'an clearly states "There is no compulsion in religion, the path of guidance stands out clear from error" [2:256] and [60:8]. In this verse, the word "rushd" or "path of guidance" refers to the entire domain of human life, not just to the rites and theology of Islam.

There is no debate about the fact that pre-Islamic Arabia was a misguided society dominated by tribalism and a blind obedience to custom. In contrast, the clarity of Islam and its emphasis on reason and rational proofs excluded any need to impose it by force. This verse is a clear indication that the Qur'an is strictly opposed to the use of compulsion in religious faith. Similarly, Allah addressed Sayiddina Muhammad (s) saying, "Remind them, for you are only one who reminds." [88:21] Allah addresses the believers, urging them to obey the injunctions of Islam, "Obey Allah, and obey the Messenger, and beware (of evil): if you do turn back, then know that it is Our Messenger's duty to proclaim (the message) in the clearest manner." [5:92] However, this verse makes it clear that the Messenger's duty is only to proclaim and preach the message; it remains to each individual to accept and to follow.

CONDITIONS FOR COMBATIVE JIHAD

The ruler, the Imam, is completely answerable to the people and their legal apparatus, the most important representatives of whom are the scholars. The position of the law is that only at such a time when it can be reasonably proven that;

There are aggressive designs against Islam; and,

There are concerted efforts to eject Muslims from their legally acquired property;s

Those military campaigns are being launched to eradicate them.

At such a time the ruler can declare and execute the provisions of Jihad. It is a condition that there be a leader of the Muslims, an Imam, to declare combative Jihad. In al-Mughni,

Ibn Qudama states "declaring Jihad is the respon-sibility of the Imam and is his independent legal judgment." Al-Dardir says, "proclaiming Jihad comes through the Imam's assignment of a leader". Abu Bakr Al-Jazaa'iri states that the pillars of Jihad are: "A pure intention and that it is performed behind a Muslim Imam and beneath his flag and with his permission. ...it is not permissible for them to fight without an Imam."

Similarly the ruler, the political leader of the whole country, has the power to ratify peace treaties if they are consistent with the interests of the Muslims. Conscription has to be confined to young men of sound health on condition that they have parental permission to engage in combat. The exception is where the enemy has already entered the borders of a Muslim state in which case Jihad becomes unconditionally incumbent on every able man.

ISLAMIC TERMS OF TATIFYING PEACE

Allah said, "Enter into peace completely and do not follow the steps of Satan." [2:208] The Prophet (s) said, after establishing the Islamic state in Madina, that the way of the Muslims is one. No single group can autonomously declare war or fight, nor can any one group make peace by itself, but the entire Muslim nation must make peace. A peace treaty can be made by the nations' leader and all subjects of the nation are bound by that decision, regardless of whether the leader was appointed or elected. The final decision is up to the ruler after his consultation with others.

If a state has no leader then it must select one, or all the neighboring states and nations must come together and agree on a treaty with any foreign country. This applies as much to peace as it does to war. No individual or group may come forth and declare a Jihad: such will be a false Jihad. All Muslim nations and their leaders must come together for a decision of war or peace and that is the only accepted process.

Naturally every community has the right to self-defense and in the case of Islam, where religion is the primary dimension of human existence, war in defense of the nation becomes a religious act. A lack of understanding of this quality of Islam, its non-secularism; has also contributed considerably to the fear that when Islam talks about war it means going to war to convert. This might be true in other cultures, but Islam must be allowed to speak for itself.

Al-Dardir says of this, "Jihad becomes a duty when the enemy takes [Muslims] by surprise". Said Ramadan al-Buti shows that fighting in this case is an obligation of the community as a whole. This is based on the Prophet's (s) saying "He who is killed in defence of his belongings, or in self-defence, or for his religion, is a martyr".

This verse mentions a fundamental principle of Islam regarding Muslim/Non-Muslim relationships. Muslims are enjoined to act kindly and justly towards members of other faiths except in two circumstances; firstly, if they dispossess Muslims of their legitimate land-rights, and; secondly, if they engage in hostilities towards Muslims or show clear intent to do so (al-hirabah) because of their religion with a clear intention to destroy the Islamic nation as a whole. In the second eventuality, it is the duty of the Muslim ruler to declare the Jihad as a defensive action to repel such attacks.

It is evident from the Qur'an and other sources that the armed struggle against the polytheists was legislated in the context of specific circumstances after the Prophet (s) had migrated from Makkah to Madina. There he secured a pact with the Jewish and Arab tribes of the city, who accepted him as the leader of their community. In the milieu of this newly-founded base of operations, under the governance of Divine legislation and the leadership of the Prophet (s), Islam attained the status of a nation with its co-requisite territory and the accompanying need to protect its self-interests. At that time the divine command was revealed permitting Jihad, but this occurred only after: Persistent refusal of the Makkan leadership (the Prophet being in Madina at the time) to allow the peaceful propagation of Islam in Makkah. This is in fact the most basic reason for armed Jihad.

Continuous unabated persecution of Muslims remaining at Makkah after the Prophet's (s) emigration to Madina triggered an armed insurrection against Qurayshite interests in the Hijaz.

Makkans themselves starts off military campaigns against the Muslims at Madinah with the sole objective of eradicating Islam. Key security pledges being abrogated unilaterally by a number of tribes allied to the Prophet (s), forcing him into a vulnerable position.

These conditions for Jihad involving armed struggle were then clearly specified in the Qur'an:

"And fight in the way of Allah those who fight against you, and do not transgress [limits] for Allah likes not the transgressors" [2:190] and "Will you not fight a people who have violated their oaths and intended to expel the Messenger while they did attack you first...?"

The picture that emerges here is that the command to fight was given in relation to specific conditions. Thus the declaration of war is not an arbitrary act at all. A further implication here, as the Hanafi School in fact argues, is that war was declared by the Prophet (s) as the head of the Islamic nation, and as such no one else can legitimately declare Jihad except a ruler who is head of an Islamic state. The duty lies squarely with the religious/political leadership to determine whether the conditions for Jihad exist and to then give the appropriate judgement.

In later times, the Muslims engaged in warfare to establish the "Pax Islamica" or Islamic Order. The legal and political order must flow from the divine imperative (Qur'an, Sunnah, etc.). It alone guarantees the rights of every individual by keeping in check all the dark psychic tendencies of man and so preventing him from indulging in anti-social behaviors, from political aggression, right down to the commonest criminal act. It is for this that the Qur'an calls on the believers to go forth in defense of those whose rights and liberty have been trampled by the unbridled tyranny of oppressors and conquering armies, or who are prevented from freely hearing the word of Allah espoused to them by preachers and educators. Allah says, "How should ye not fight for the cause of Allah and of the feeble among men and of the women and the children who are crying: Our Lord! Bring us forth from out this town of which the people are oppressors! Oh, give us from Thy presence some protecting friend! Oh, give us from Thy presence some defender!"

No reliable evidence exists that Muslims ever intended or attempted to impose the specific rites and beliefs of Islam. The histories of Spain, India and the Balkans are concrete proof of this.

The idea, often postulated in the media, that Islam is hostile to non-Muslims simply because they are non-Muslims, is a major a misconception. Beyond the conditions described above there exists no valid reason to hold any hostility towards them for the Qur'an states: "Allah does not forbid you from those who do not remove you from your homes (by force) and who do not fight you because of your religion that you act kindly and justly towards them..." [60:8] The reference in this verse is to the non-Muslims in general.

JIHAD BETWEEN MUSLIMS

Properly speaking Jihad, in the case of internal dissension, only occurs when these two conditions—a just Imam fighting unjustifiable insurrection—are met and the Muslims fight in support of the Imam against the offending parties. In Islam allegiance and obedience to a just authority is obligatory. It must be noted also that rebellions against authority and especially political authority simply for the sake of rebellion have no place in the concept of Jihad. In this age of relativism, the spirit of rebellion seems to have penetrated every layer of society. However, Islam and its principles cannot be made subservient to these cultural trends.

In some of the contemporary "Islamic" groups, Jihad has been adapted to a virtually Marxist or Socialist concept of class revolt aimed at overthrowing the authority of the state. In the often fervently materialistic milieu of contem-porary political and revolutionary ideologies, Islam is inevitably reduced to nothing more than a social philosophy. This reductionism simply amounts to an abysmal misunderstanding of the essential function of Islam, which is to turn the "face" of the human receptacle away from the world of disharmony and illusion to the tranquility and silence of Divine awareness and vision. Inward Jihad, as we alluded to at the beginning of this essay, has a key role to play in this respect.

REBELLIION AGAINST RULERS

The scholar Ibn Nujaym said "it is not permitted for there to be more than one state leader (Imam) in a time period. There may be many judges, even in one state, but the leader is one." Al-Bahjouri said "It is an obligation to obey the leader, even if he is not fair or trustworthy or even if he committed sins or mistakes." Abu Hanifa's school says that the head of the state, the Imam, cannot be expelled for being a corrupt person (fasiq). Hudhaifa bin al-Yaman (r) narrated a hadith in which he said, "The Prophet (s) said, 'there will be after me leaders who do not follow my guidance and do not follow my Sunna, and there will be among them men whose hearts are like those of Satan in the body of a human being.' And I asked the Prophet (s), 'What I should do at that time if I reach it?' He said, 'listen and obey the ruler, even if he lashed your back and took your money, listen and obey.'"

In another narration, Auf bin Malik (r) said, "O Prophet of Allah, do you recommend that we fight them?" He said, "No, don't fight them as long as they do not prevent you from your prayers. And if you see from them something that you dislike, dislike their acts, do not dislike them. And do not take your hand out from obedience to them." Bukhari and Muslim narrated from Abdullah ibn al-Abbas (r), "if someone dislikes his ruler, he must be patient, because if he comes against the ruler in a rebellious or destructive manner by only a handspan and dies, he dies in a state of pre-Islamic ignorance (jahiliyyah) and sin."

These source texts are clear evidence that whoever lives under a particular government must obey the ruler and live peacefully. They are prohibited from taking up arms against him. Uprising or violence by any group against the ruler is completely rejected in Islam, and was prohibited by the

Prophet(s) and will be a cause of death on the way of ignorance (jahiliyya). Thus Islam considers rebellion against the ruler a great iniquity. These hadith affirm that one must be patient with one's ruler, even if he commits oppression. These hadith refer to the leader of a nation, not the leader of a small group. Therefore groups that take up violent struggle against their regimes are prohibited in Islam and are by default illegal and blameworthy.

In fact the true path to correction of the mistakes of a ruler is according to the hadith "a most excellent Jihad is when one speaks a word of truth in the presence of a tyrannical ruler." Note here the hadith does not mention fighting the ruler, but rather praises the one who corrects the ruler by speech. Armed and violent opposition to a state regime can never be recognized as Jihad in the way of Allah, despite the claims of many groups. Unfortunately we see today countless individuals and groups who label their rulers and their governments apostates or unbelievers, thereby giving themselves the excuse to declare "jihad" against them, asserting that this is because they do not rule by what was revealed to the Prophets. Even worse, they go further by terrorizing and killing government officers, members of the armed forces and public servants, simply because they are easy targets. These groups use a "militant Islamic" ideology to justify such felonious action, declaring the ruler, the government, and its officers to be criminals standing in the way of "true Islam", who must be eliminated. Thus, those who are innocent of any crime, but who are earning a living and raising their families, such as officers and officials of ministries and departments, county and city officials and police, become targets of these extremist ideologues. Such groups do not hesitate to kill them in surprise attacks, terrorizing the entire nation by blasting here and there and harming the innocent.

If the ruler commits wrong, it is not permitted to label him an apostate, nor to indoctrinate people to use militancy to oppose him. In the time of the Prophets after the conquest of Makkah, a Companion named Hatib ibn Abi Balta, assisted some of the enemy by supporting them extensively and passing them secret information. It may be that no one today supports a tyrannical ruler as Hatib supported the unbelievers at that time. When questioned as to his motives, Hatib replied, "O Allah's Prophet! Don't hasten to give your judgment about me. I was a man closely connected with the Quraish, but I did not belong to this tribe, while the other emigrants with you, had their relatives in Mecca who would protect their dependents and property. So, I wanted to compensate for my lacking blood relation to them by doing them a favor so that they might protect my dependents. I did this neither because of disbelief nor apostasy nor out of preferring disbelief (kufr) to Islam." Allah's Prophet (s), said, "Hatib has told you the truth."

We see here that the Prophets, though fully aware of Hatib's actions, never considered him to be outside the fold of Islam, nor did he inflict any punishment on him. Regarding Hatib and his support of the unbelievers Allah revealed the following verse: "O you who believe! Do not take my enemy and your enemy for friends: would you offer them love while they deny what has come to you of the truth, driving out the Messenger and yourselves because you believe in Allah, your Lord?" [60:1] Though the verse reprimands Hatib, showing him in the wrong, nonetheless Allah (swt) did not take him out of the state of faith yet continued to address him with the honorable title "O you who believe", despite his assisting the enemies of Islam.

This constitutes proof that even if someone assists a regime that does not support Islam, one cannot harm that person as the Prophet (s) did not inflict any punishment on Hatib. One wonders then how today so many groups freely label those working for the government as renegades and apostates, and issue fierce edicts to kill them? Their work with the government might be for their livelihood, or for building a bridge of trust for the Islamist community to ensure a better future relationship or a better understanding of Islam. Such actions are baseless in Islam and are founded on an extremist ideology, far removed from the middle path which always constitutes this blessed religion of Allah.

THE INNER JIHAD

Islam is not a rhetorical religion; it is based on unity, love and rational action. Soon after the Prophet's (may the peace and blessings of Allah be upon him) death, Islam radiated outwardly from its earthly center, the Ka'aba, implacable symbol of the faith. Jihad was the dynamic of this expansion. Outwardly it embodied the power of Islam against error and falsehood, while inwardly it represented the means of spiritual awakening and of transcending the self. Referring to this, the Prophet (may the peace and blessings of Allah be upon him) said while returning from battle: "We are now returning from the lesser Jihad to the greater Jihad, the Jihad against the self." The Prophets is reported to have said during the Farewell Pilgrimage, "... The Fighter in the Way of Allah is he who makes jihad against himself (jahada nafsah) for the sake of obeying Allah."

The means of the combative Jihad, the Sword, was adopted and internalized by Islam as the charismatic symbol of sacred warfare. It symbolizes the qualities of strength and vigilance, indispensable for the spiritual wayfarer in his quest for illumination and the beatific vision. This symbolism deeply inspired Muslim artists and craftsmen. In calligraphy, for example, one finds the Sword-motif embossed in gold and silver as the initial letter of the testimony of faith, the Shahada. Historical evidence and current practice indicate that this symbol often forms a central feature of cultural events of the Muslim world, such as folk-dancers sporting gleaming blades as they chant and move to rhythmic Sufic recitation.

Allah says in the Holy Qur'an, "Those who have striven for Our sake, We guide them to Our ways" [29:96] In this verse, God uses a derivative of the linguistic root of the word" Jihad" to describe those who are deserving of guidance, and has made guidance dependent on Jihad against the false desires of the soul. Therefore, the most perfect of people are those who struggle the most against the selfish promptings of the ego for God's sake. The most obligatory Jihad is that against the base side of the ego, desires, the devil, and the lower world.

The great Sufi Al-Junayd said: "Those who have striven against their desires and repented for God's sake shall be guided to the ways of sincerity. One cannot struggle against his enemy outwardly (i.e. with the Sword) except he who struggles against these enemies inwardly. Then whoever is given victory over them will be victorious over his enemy, and whoever is defeated by them, his enemy defeats him."

DHIKR: THE REMEMBRANCE OF GOD

The Prophet peace be upon him said: "Shall I tell you something that is the best of all deeds, constitutes the best act of piety in the eyes of your Lord, elevates your rank in the hereafter, and carries more virtue than the spending of gold and silver in the service of Allah, or taking part in Jihad and slaying or being slain in the path of Allah?" They said: "Yes!" He said: "Remembrance of Allah."

Thus one finds the principles of the spiritual Jihad are based on eliminating the ugly, selfish and ferocious characteristics of the ego through spiritual training and mastery of dhikr, the Remembrance of God. This remem-brance takes many forms: each school of Sufism focuses on a different form of ritual dhikr to enable the seeker to approach the Divine Presence, varying from individual silent recitation and chanting to vocal group sessions. It is this spiritual struggle that raises humankind and instills in him the sense of relationship with His Creator, and the proper perspective in relating to all creation, always calling for love between humanity and striving in Allah's Way for better understanding between various communities of all faiths. Through this spiritual Jihad the effect of the selfish ego on the soul of the seeker will be removed, uplifting his state from depression, anxiety and loneliness to one of joy, satisfaction and companionship with the most high.

8

The Origins of Terrorism

AMNESIA

Attention deficit disorder seems to flourish under conditions of late modernity. The past becomes itself more quickly. Memories, individual as well as collective, tend to be recycled and consulted only by the old. For everyone else, there are only current affairs, reaching back a few months at most. Orwell, of course, predicted this, in his dystopic prophecy that may have been only premature; but today it seems to be cemented by postmodernism (Deleuze), and also by physicists, who are now proclaiming an almost Ash'arite scepticism about claims for the real duration of particles.

This is a condition that has an ancestry in the stirrings of the modernity which it represents. Hume anticipated it in his stunning insistence on the non-continuity of the human self: we are 'nothing but a collection of perceptions which succeed each other with inconceivable rapidity and are in perpetual flux and movement;' or so he thought. Modern fiction may still explore or reaffirm identities (Peter Carey) and thus define human dignity as the honourable disposition of at least some aspects of an accumulated heritage. But this is giving way to the atomistic, playful, postmodern storytelling of, say, Elliot Perlman, which defines dignity - where it does so at all - in terms of freedom from all stories, even while lamenting the superficial tenor of the result. It is against the backdrop of this culture that the scientists, now far beyond Ataturk's 'Science is the Truest Guide in Life', raise the stakes with their occasionalism, and, for the neurologists, the increasing denial of the autonomy of the human will - a new predestinarianism that makes us always the consequence of genes and the present, not the remembered past.

Our public conversations, then, seem to be the children of a marriage of convenience between two principles, neither of them religious or even particularly humanistic. The elitist mystical trope of the moment being all that is, significantly misappropriated by some New Age discourses, has become the condition of us all, albeit with the absence of God. Journalism thus becomes the privileged discourse to whose canons the public intellectual must conform, if he or she is to become a credible guide. More striking still is the observed fact that amidst our current crisis of wisdom it also seems to provide the language in which the public discussion of faith is carried on. Thus Catholicism becomes the humiliated cardinal of Boston, not St Augustine. Its morality is taken to be that which visibly clashes with the caprice of characters in Home and Away, not a severe but ultimately liberating cultivation of the virtues rooted in centuries of experience and example. Judaism, in its turn, becomes the latest land-grab of a settler rabbi, not a millennial enterprise of faith and promise. Of course, our new occasionalism does invoke the past. But it does so with reference either to scriptures, stripped of their normative exegetical armature, or to those events which remain in the consciousness of a citizenry raised on enlightenment battles with obscurantism. So again, we recall Galileo, not Eckhart; we recall the interesting hatreds of the Inquisition, not the charity of St Vincent de Paul. Otherwise, our culture is religiously amnesiac. Winston Churchill, near the end of his life, began to read the Bible. 'This book is very well-written,' he said. 'Why was it not brought to my attention before?'

It is in this frankly primitive condition that we seek to discuss religious acts which, against all the predictions of our grandparents, claim to interrupt the progress of history towards a world in which there will be no continuity at all.

To our perplexity, history, despite Fukuyama, does not seem to have ended. Humans do not always act for the economic or erotic now; Tamino still seeks his Sarastro. A residue of real human diversity persists. For the human soul is not yet, as Coleridge wrote,

This failed ultimacy, this sense that we, the Papageni, have to dust down the armour of an earlier generation of moral absolutes, when history was still running, when the victory of the corporations and of Hollywood was not yet assured, accounts for the maladroit condition of the world's current argument about terrorism. The most active in seizing the moment, as they elbow impatiently past the fin de siécle multiculturalists and postmodernists, are the oddly-named American neoconservatives, who invoke Leo Strauss and roll up their sleeves to defend Washington against Oriental warriors who would defy the dialectics of history and seek to postpone the apotheosis of Anglo-Saxon consumer society, which they see as the climax of a billion years of evolution. But despite such ideologised aversions to the longue durée, secularism seems to have little to offer that is not short-termist and reactive, and determined to reduce the globe to a set of variations on itself.

Traditionalists, who should be more helpful, seem paralysed. Much of the fury and hurt that currently abounds in the Christian and the Muslim worlds reveals a sense that the timetable which God has approved for history has been perverted. Christendom is not a virgin in this respect; in fact, it was first, with scholastic and Byzantine broadsides against Christian sin as invitation to Saracenic chastisement (Bernard, Gregory Palamas). Then it was the turn of Islam, when, from the seventeenth century on the illusion of the Muslims as materially and militarily God's chosen people was dealt a series of shocking blows. Now it is, once again, the turn of Christendom (if the term be still allowed), which is currently wondering why history has not yet experienced closure, why a former rival should still be showing signs o life, either as the result of a misdiagnosis, or as a zombie-like revenant bearing only a superficial resemblance to his medieval seriousness. Certainly, the American president and his frequently evangelical team see themselves in these terms. Architects of a society which, Disney-like, appropriates the past only to emphasise the glory of the present, these zealots appeal to a prophecy-religion in which the Book of Revelation is the key to history. For them, too, the promised closure is imminent, and its frustration by the other an outrage.

President Reagan, while less captivated by end-time visions than his successors, could offer these thoughts to Jewish lobbyists:

> You know, I turn back to your ancient prophets in the Old Testament and the signs foretelling Armageddon and I find myself wondering if we're the generation that is going to see that come about. I don't know if you've noted any of these prophecies lately, but, believe me, they certainly describe the times we're going through.

The protagonists of the current conflict, then, are unusual in their confidence that history has not ended, although millennialism seems to hover in the background on both sides, helped along by the frequently Palestinian scenery. The triumph of the West, or the resurgence of an Islam interpreted by bestselling Pentecostal authors as a chastis-ement and a demonic challenge, signals the end of a growing worry about the religious meaninglessness of late modernity. Tragically, however, neither protagonist seems validly linked to the remnants of established religion, or shows any sign of awareness of how to connect with history. Fundamentalist disjuncture is placing us in a kind of metahistorical parenthesis, an end-time excitement in which, as for St Paul, old rules are irrelevant, and Christ and Antichrist are the only significant gladiators on the stage. Fundamentalists, as well as mystics, can insist that the moment is all that is real.

SUNNA CONTRA GENTILE

In such a world of pseudo-religious reaction against the postmodern erosion of identity, it follows that if you are not 'with us,' you are with the devil. Or, when this has to be reformulated for the benefit of the blue-collar godless, you are a 'cheese-eating surrender monkey'. Where religion exists to supply an identity, the world is Augustinian, if not quite Manichean. The West's ancient trope of itself as a free space, perhaps a white space, holding out against Persian or Semitic intruders, is being coupled powerfully, but hardly for the first time, with Pauline and patristic understandings of the New Israel as unique vessel of truth and salvation, threatened in the discharge of its redemptive project by the Oriental, Semitic, Ishmaelitic other. In the West, at least, the religious resources for this dualism are abundant and easily abused. Take Daniel Goldhagen, for instance, who in his most recent book suggests that the xenophobia of the Christian Bible is qualitatively greater than that of any other scripture. New Bibles, he urges, must be printed with many corrections to what he describes as this founding text of a lethal Western self-centredness. Semites of several kinds would be well-advised to beware a culture raised on such a foundation.

It is remarkable that both sides, in constructing thems-elves against a wicked, fundamentalist rival, mobilise the ancient trope of antisemitism. The Self needs its dark other, preferably nearby or within. That other has standard features: in the case of Christian antisemitism it is that it stands for Letter rather than Spirit, for blind obedience rather than freedom, for a discreet but intense transnational solidarity in place of Fatherland and Church. It is sexually aberrant (hence the Nazi polemic against Freud). It hides its women (who should, instead, join the SS, or practice nacktkultur). It imposes archaic and unscientific taboos: diet, purity, circumcision. Such are the categories in which an almost dualistic West historically defines its relationship to its nearest and most irritating other.

Antisemitism is, in Richard Harries' words, a 'light sleeper'. But part of its strength is that it is not asleep at all; and never has been. As Christendom seeks its identity, the Dark Other today is now more usually Ishmael. Torched mosques, terrified asylum-seekers, bullied schoolchildren, and, we may not unreasonably add, a journalistic discourse of the type that is now being labelled 'Islamophobic', are less new than they seem. They represent a vicarious antisemitism. 'Islamic law is immutable' is a chorus in the new Horst Wessel song. 'Circumcision is barbaric.' 'Their divorce laws are medieval and anti-woman.' 'They keep to themselves and don't integrate.' Such is the battle-cry of the resurgent Western right: Pim Fortuin, Jean-Marie Le Pen, Jorg Haider, Filip de Winter. It has become startlingly popular, though always volatile at the polls. Thus is the old antisemitic metabolism of Europe and its American progeny being reinvigorated by the encounter with Ishmael. Again, history has started up again, and again our amnesiac culture ignores the vast cogwheels, deep beneath the surface, which move it.

On the other side, now, crossing the Mediterranean, or the Timor Sea, we generally find not a bloc of sincere fundamentalist regimes, but an archipelago of dictatorships, Oriental despots after the letter, which are in almost every case answerable not to their own electorates - for they recognise none - but to a distant desk in the State Department. These are the neo-mamluks, ex-soldiers and condottieri of a system that penalises ethics. Ranged against them we observe the puritans, iconoclasts with El Greco eyes, whose claim it are to detest the modernity of the regimes. Such puritans, led by the memory of Sayyid Qutb, have no illusions about the nature of secular rule. They see clearly that the regimes are more modern than those of the West, because more frank in their conviction that science plus commerce does not equal ethics. Where the Western journalistic eye sees retardation, the Islamist sees modernity. Hitler and Stalin were more modern than Churchill and Roosevelt, more scientific, more programmatic, and more distant from the past. The future is theirs, and it is neither Christ's millennial reign nor the triumph of small-town America. It is Alphaville.

The Islamist, then, is not the caricature of the envious, uncomprehending Third Worlder. Typically he has spent much of his life in the West, and is capable of offering an empirical analysis, or at least a diagnosis. Sayyid Qutb, in his writing on what he calls 'the deformed birth of the American man,' sees Americans as advanced infants; advanced because of their technology, but puerile in their ignorance of earlier stages of human development. There is something of Teilhard de Chardin in his account, which inverts Tocqueville to identify an American idiot-savant mania for possession. Technology made America possible, and ultimately, America need claim nothing else. Linked to Christian fundamentalism, it is an enemy of every other story; and unlike the East, it will not remain in its place. It must send out General Custer to subdue all remnants of earlier phases of human conscious-ness rooted in nature, spirituality or art. Its client regimes are therefore its natural, not opportunistic, adjuncts in its programme to subdue the world. They are not a transitional phase; they are the end-game.

Antisemitism forms part of this vision too, certainly. But since, as Goldhagen confirms, this is an essentially Christian phenomenon, to be healed by correcting the views of the Evangelists, in an Islamic context which lacks a letter-spirit dichotomy it seems a hazier resource for identity construction. Qutb was influenced by the Vichy theorist Alexis Carrel (1873-1944), through his odd, vitalist tract L'Homme, cet inconnu, which remains an ultimate, though unacknowledged, source text for much modern Islamism. No medieval Muslim thinker of any note wrote a book against Judaism, although homilies against Christianity were quite common. If medieval Islam had a dark Other, it was more likely to be Zoroastrianism than Judaism, which, in Samuel Goitein's phrase by which he summed up his magisterial work A Mediterranean Society, enjoyed a close and 'symbiotic' relationship with Islam. But today's Qutbian Islamist purges midrashic material from Koranic commen-tary, and studies the Tsarist forgery The Protocols of the Learned Elders of Zion, and, even, Mein Kampf. Nothing can be discovered, it seems, in the Islamic libraries, so that this importation into an ostensively nativist and xenophobic milieu becomes inescapable - the fundamentalist's familiar appeal to necessity.

As he surveys the wreckage of Istanbul synagogues and Masonic lodges, the journalist, as ibn al-waqt, is oblivious to the happier past of Semitic conviviality in the Ottoman Sephardic lands. And perhaps he is right, perhaps, under our conditions, the past is another religion. But the paradox has become so burning, and so murderous, that we cannot let it pass unremarked. The Islamic world, instructed to host Israel, was historically the least inhospitable site for the Diaspora. The currently almost ubiquitous myth of a desperate sibling rivalry between Isaac and Ishmael is nonsensical to historians.

Here, at the dark heart of Islam's extremist fringe, we find what may be the beginnings of a solution. No nativist reaction can long survive proof of its own exogenous nature. And no less than its Christian analogues, Islamic ghuluww, at least in its currently terroristic forms, betrays a European etiology. It borrows its spiritual, as well as its material, armament from Western modernity. This, we may guess, marks it out for anachronism in a context where intransigence is xenophobic.

This is an unpopular diagnosis; but one which is gaining ground. It cannot be without significance that outside observers, when not blinded by a xenophobic need to view terrorism as Islamically authentic, have sometimes intuited this well. Here, for instance, is the verdict of John Gray, in his book *Al-Qaeda and What it Means to be Modern*:

> No cliche is more stupefying than that which describes Al-Qaida as a throwback to medieval times. It is a by-product of globalisation. Its most distinctive feature - projecting a privatised form of organised violence worldwide - was impossible in the past. Equally, the belief that a new world can be hastened by spectacular acts of destruction is nowhere found in medieval times. Al-Qaida's closest precursors are the revolutionary anarchists of late nineteenth-century Europe.

And Slavoj Zizek, a still more significant observer, is convinced that what we are witnessing is not 'Jihad versus MacWorld' – the standard leftist formulation - but rather MacWorld versus MacJihad.

This implies that if ghuluww has a future, it will be because modernity has a future, not because it has roots in Islamic tradition. That tradition, indeed, it rules out of order, as it dismisses the juridical, theological and mystical intricacies of medieval Islam as so much dead wood. The solution, then, which the world is seeking, and which it is the primary responsibility of the Islamic world, not the West to provide must be a counter-reformation, driven by our best and most cosmopolitan heritage of spirit and law.

A point of departure, here, and a useful retort to essentialist reductions of Islam to Islamism, is the fact that orthodoxy still flies the flag in almost all seminaries. The reformers are, at least institutionally, in the Rhonnda chapels, not the cathedrals. Perhaps the most striking fact about regulation Sunni Islam over the past fifty years has been its insistence that religion's general response to modernity must not take the form of an armed struggle. There have been local exceptions to this rule, as in the reactive wars against Serbian irredentism in Bosnia, and Soviet intrusion into Afghanistan. But a doctrine of generic jihad against the West has been conspicuous by its absence.

It is not immediately clear how we gloss this. In the nineteenth century Sunni Islam frequently elected to resist European colonial rule by force, giving rise to the figure of the Mad Mullah who formed part of the imperial imagination, in the fiction of John Buchan, or Tolstoy's Hajji Murad. In the twentieth century, however, the traditional pragmatism of Sunnism seemed to generate an ulema ethos that was certainly not quietist, but had nothing in common with Qutbian Islamism either. Hence the Deobandi movement in India, and its Tablighi offshoot, supported the Congress party, and generally opposed Partition. Arab religious leaders sometimes resorted to force, as with the Naqshbandi shaykh Izz al-Din al-Qassam in mandate Palestine; but the independence movements were overwhelmingly directed by secular modernists. The ancient universities, al-Qarawiyyin, al-Zaytuna, al-Azhar and the rest, regarded the modern period as a mandate for doctrinal retrenchment and the piecemeal ijtihad-based reassessment of aspects of Islamic law. In other words, mainstream Islam's response to the startling novelty of a modernity that was forced on its societies at the point of an imperial or postcolonial bayonet was self-scrutinising and cautious, not militant.

Traditional wisdom and the texts, of course, were the reason for this. Sunnism, as inscribed by the great Seljuk theorists, had put its trust in prudence, pragmatism, and a strategy of negotiation with the sultan. So in British India, the Hanafi consensus decided that the Raj formed part of dar al-islam. In Russia, Shihab al-Din Marjani took the same view with regard the empire of the Tsars. But for Qutb, all this was paradigmatic of the error of classical Sunni thought. Islam was to be prophetic, and hence a liberation theology, challenging structures as well as souls, not by preaching and praying alone, but by agitation and revolution. Given his education and sitz im leben in the golden age of anti-colonialism, probably nothing could have extricated Qutb from his critique of what he saw as Sunni indifferentism, rooted, he suspected, in Ash'ari deontology and a presumed Sufi fatalism. The prophetic is not meant to be accommodating; it fails, or it succeeds triumphantly. The normative political thinkers, Mawardi, Nizam al-Mulk, Ghazali, Katib Çelebi, and their modern advocates, had to be jettisoned. Technological empires had made the world anew, and, if it was to cope with an increasingly bizarre and offensive Other, Islamic thought had to be reformed in the direction of an increasingly unconditional insurrectionism.

Qutb's resurrection of Ibn Taymiya, via Rashid Rida, became paradigmatic. In the fourteenth century this angry Damascene had attacked ulema who acquiesced in the rule of the nominally Muslim Mongols. Loyalty could be to a righteous imam alone. Rida and others had taken pains to dissociate this from the Kharijite slogan 'No rule other than God's', for an unpleasant odour hung about the name of Kharijism. But de facto, the hard wing of Hanbalite Islam seemed vulnerable to a Kharijite reading. Prototypical al-Qaida supporters wrote to condemn the Syrian neo-Hanbali scholar Nasir al-Din al-Albani, when he released a series of taped sermons entitled Min Manhaj al-Khawarij, 'From the Method of the Kharijites', in the early 1990s. Often the word used by less radical puritans in Saudi Arabia for those engaged in terrorism is, precisely, 'Kharijite'.

What everyone agrees, however, is that al-Qaida is far, far removed from medieval Sunnism. For some, it is Kharijite;

for others, an illicit Westernisation of Islam. As Carl Brown puts it, 'it cannot be stressed too often just how much Qutb's hardline interpretation departs from the main current of Islamic political thought throughout the centuries.' For Brown, Qutbism is kharijism redux; but we would add, with Gray, that it is a Westernised kharijism. Like all identity movements, it ends with only a very arguable kind of authenticity.

The convergence between a malfunctioning Hanbalism and modern revolutionary vanguardism may owe its strength not to a shared potential for an instantiated xenophobia, although this will attract many party cadres; instead, I suspect, it relates to deeper structures of relationality with the world and its worldliness. The new Islamic zealotry is angry with the Islamic past, as Ibn Taymiya was. For Ibn Taymiya, the ulema had not adequately polarised light and dark. In the case of the mystics, they had disastrously confused them. There is something of the Augustine in Ibn Taymiya: a concrete understanding of a God who is radically apart from creation, or, in patristic terms, alienated from it, and a consequently high view of scripture that challenges Ash'arite and Maturidi confidences in the direct intelligibility of God in the world, and revives essentially dualistic readings of the Fall narrative. It may be that Ibn Taymiya's roots in Harran, scene of neo-Gnostic and astral speculations, parallel Augustine's Manichean background. But there is certainly a furious, single-minded zeal in both men that expresses itself in a deep pessimism about the human mind and conscience, and hence the worth of intellectuals, poets, logicians and mystics. In such a cosmology, which deploys the absolute polarity abhorred by Deleuze's Pli (his love of nomadic arts, with their 'blocs of sensations' is Islamically suggestive) gentilizing becomes first, not second nature.

Seljuk accommodationism, by contrast, had been driven by an ultimately Ghazalian moralism that feared the spiritual entailments of this crypto-dualism. Nizam al-Mulk, paradigm of high Sunni realpolitik, does not enforce a norm, but enforces the toleration of many norms. He finds that like all scripture, the Koran is super-replete, overflowing with meaning, and no exegete may taste all its flavours; this destabilising miracle may express itself in schism, historically the less favoured Islamic option, or in adab al-ikhtilaf, the forced courtesy of the scholar-jurist well aware of the ultimately unfixable quality of much of holy writ. The Sunni achievement, which was a moral as well as a pragmatic achievement, was to incorporate a wide spectrum of theological and juristic dispute into the universe of allowable internal difference. For zealotry, as Ghazali puts it, is a hijab, a veil? It is a form of, in the Rabbis' language, loving the Torah more than God. A besetting odium theologicum which can only be healed through self-scrutiny and a due humility before the often baffling intricacy of God's word and world.

It was on the basis of this hospitable caution that non-Qutbian Sunnism engaged with modernity. Reading the fatwas of great twentieth-century jurists such as Yusuf al-Dajawi, Abd al-Halim Mahmud, and Subhi Mahmassani, one is reminded of the Arabic proverb cited on motorway signs in Saudi Arabia: fi'l-ta'anni as-salama - there is safety in reducing speed. Far from committing a pacifist betrayal, the normative Sunni institutions were behaving in an entirely classical way. Sunni piety appears as conciliatory, cautious, and disciplined, seeking to identify the positive as well as the negative features of the new global culture. Thus it is not the orthodox, but the merchants of identity religion, the Sunna Contra Gentiles, who insist on totalitarian and exclusionary readings of the Law and the state.

If this is our curious situation, if al-Qaida is indeed a product and mirror not of the Sunni story, but of the worst of the Enlightenment's possibilities, if it is, as it were, the Frankenstein of Frankistan (as Zionism is a golem), how effective can be America's currently chosen antidote? This takes the form of killing, imprisoning and torturing the leadership, and many of the rank and files, using the methods which have been reported by British and other detainees released from Guantanamo Bay, and by Red Cross officials disturbed by news from Bagram air base in Kabul. Again, our occasionalism has allowed us to forget the history of revolutionary movements, which suggests that such measures are self-defeating, sowing the dragon's teeth of martyrdom, and announcing to the world the depth of the torturer's fear. A civilisation confident of victory would not resort to such desperate means. For after violence and internment, there is no last resort. Both moral advantage and deterrent threat have already been used up.

Traditional Sunnis intuit that al-Qaida is a Western invention, but one which cannot be defeated in a battleground where the logic is Western. This was one of the messages that emerged from the 2003 summit meeting of eight hundred Muslim scholars at Putrajaya. Al-Qaida is inauthentic: it rejects the classical canons of Islamic law and theology, and issues fatwas that are neither formally nor in their habit of mind deducible from medieval exegesis. But it is not enough for the entire leadership of the religion to denounce al-Qaida, as it did at Putrajaya, and then to hope and pray that the same strange logic of modernity that bred this insurgency can spirit it away again. The West inseminates, but does not so easily abort. Faced with this, the Sunni leadership needs to be more alert to its responsibilities. Even the radical Westernisation of Islamic piety remains the responsibility of Muslim ulema, not, ultimately, of the Western matrix that inspired it. And it has to be said that the Sunni leadership has not done enough. Denunciations alone will not dent the puritan's armour, and may strengthen it; this the Counter-Reformation learned by experience.

JUS IN BELLO

The war against neo-Kharijite ideology can only be won by Sunni normalcy. Washington's rhetoric of 'religion-building' disguises either a Texan missionary instinct or the triumphant relativism of the secular academy. Franklin Graham and the Ashcroft Inquisition will fail, as Christianity always does against Semitic monotheism, while liberalism, at once its rival and its hypocritical bedfellow, cannot be relied on to supply ethics under conditions of stress. For the Occidental energy all too often responds to such conditions either by apathy (remember the wartime Parisian intelli-gentsia), or by suspending the ethical teleologically, the classic revolutionary gambit since the days of the Paris commune, if not the English civil war.

The zealots of both sides insist that the validating of 'soft targets' is a representative Islamic act. How might they respond to evidence that it is, in fact, a representative secular-Western one? The evidence, as it turns out, is compelling, being a matter of historical record. Despite its claims in times of obese complacency to abhor the killing of the innocent, the secular West reverts with indecent haste to Cicero's maxim, Silent enim leges inter arma - laws are silent during war. And it is in this Occidental culture, and not in mainline Islam, that we should seek the matrix of radical Islamism. Let us survey the record.

W.G. Sebald has been a recent and helpful contributor here. He writes lyrically of the vengeance visited by the RAF on Germany's cities in the early 1940s, focussing on the thirty thousand who died in Operation Gomorrah against the city of Hamburg. The object of such campaigns was military only in a very indirect way, for Churchill's purpose in what he called 'terror bombing' (where it was not straightforward vengefulness) was to sap the morale of Germany's civilian population. As Sebald shows, Parliament restructured the whole British economy to support the area bombing campaign, for one reason alone: it was the only way in which Britain could successfully strike back.

In 1930, the British population had generally shared the view of one politician that to bomb civilians was 'revolting and un-English.' But with its back against the wall, the population changed its mind with impressive speed. In 1942, Bomber Command's Directive No. 22 identified the 'morale of the enemy civil population' as the chief target. By the end of the war, a million tons of high explosive had rained down on German cities, and half a million civilians were dead. By that time a majority of Britons explicitly supported the bombing of civilian targets. As the MP for Norwich put it: 'I am all for the bombing of working-class areas of German cities. I am Cromwellian - I believe in "slaying in the name of the Lord",' while after Operation Gomorrah, a popular headline crowed that 'Hamburg has been Hamburgered.' A third of the war economy was directed to serve this onslaught, with the development of new weapons of mass destruction, such as incendiary bombs, designed specifically to maximise devastation to private homes. Yet after Dresden, which the postwar official history hailed as the 'crowning achievement' of the bombing campaign, Churchill was forced to reconsider:

> It seems to me that the moment has come when the question of bombing of German cities simply for the sake of increasing the terror, though under other pretexts, should be reviewed. Otherwise, we shall come into control of an utterly ruined land.

This was no sort of repentance. To his last breath Churchill defended the terror campaign which he had insti-gated and which underpinned so much of his popularity. Mass destruction from the air of a target whose details were often obscured by clouds or the absence of moonlight was not, for this icon of English defiance, a moral problem.

A largely secular person of the stamp of our wartime Prime Minister was clearly following a fairly standard Enlightenment philosophy which had replaced the wars of kings with the wars of peoples. Clausewitz, the chief architect of post-medieval military thought, was certain that 'war is an act of force which theoretically can have no limits,' a view that the most influential military theorists of the twentieth century extended to the use of airpower to terrorize civilians (Liddell Hart, Douhet, Harris). One might have hoped that this illustration of the moral calibre of secularity was found appalling by the Christian conscience of the day. But the stance taken by the leaders of British Christianity was already deeply influenced by modernism. The Archbishop of Canterbury William Temple, followed by his brother bishop of York, consistently refused to join the anti-terror minority within the Anglican Church. As a historian records, 'only a handful of the clergy objected outright to area bombing;' George Bell, the outspoken Bishop of Chichester, was a lonely exception in upholding earlier ideals of a just war which had regarded women and children as sacrosanct.

After the war, the victors reset the moral template to its rhetorical default position, and their earlier fatwas in favour of terror bombing were relegated to an outer, uncomfortable edge of the national memory. Once again, England and America (which had carried on its own targeting of civilians in Japan) reverted to the traditional notion of civilian immunity, with its pre-Enlightenment roots. So five years later, the British press felt able to excoriate Menachem Begin as a terrorist, simply because, as he puts it in his memoirs: 'our enemies called us terrorists [...] but we used physical force only because we were faced by physical force.' And today, who can claim that Al-Qaida's logic is different? The 777 has become the poor man's nuclear weapon, his own Manhattan Project. Again, he has turned traitor to the East by embracing the utilitarian military ethic of his supposed adversary. He, even more than the regimes, shows the cost of Westernisation.

SAMSON TERRORISTS

The targeting of civilians is more Western than otherwise; contemplating the Ground Zero of a hundred German cities, this can hardly be denied. Yet it will be claimed that suicidal terrorism is something new, and definitively un-Western. Here, we are told by xenophobes on both sides, the Islamic suicide squads, the Black Widows, the death-dealing pilots, are an indigenously Islamic product.[33] And yet here again, when we detach ourselves from the emotive chauvinism of the Islamists and their Judeo-Christian misinterpreters, we soon find that the roots of such practices in the Islamic imagination are as recent as they are shallow. The genealogy of suicide bombing clearly stretches back from Palestine, through Shi'a guerillas in southern Lebanon, to the Hindu-nativist zealots of the Tamil Tigers, and to the holy warriors of Shinto Japan, who initiated the tradition of donning a bandanna and making a final testament on camera before climbing into the instrument of destruction. The kamikaze was literally the 'Wind of Heaven', a term evocative of the divine intervention which destroyed the Mongol fleet as it crossed the Yellow Sea.

Hindu and Buddhist tributaries of Middle-Eastern suicide bombing are conspicuous, and it is significant that the Islamists, driven as ever by nativist passion, recoil from them in fits of denial. (How happily, in the sermons, hunud rhymes with yahud!) Yet some scenic images may be instructive for those who take the philosophy of isnad seriously. After describing the Christian martyr Peregrinus, who set fire to himself in public, Sir James Frazier records:

> Buddhist monks in China sometimes seek to attain Nirvana by the same method, the flame of their religious zeal being fanned by a belief that the merit of their death redounds to the good of the whole community, while the praises which are showered upon them in their lives, and the prospect of the honours and worship which await them after death, serve as additional incentives to suicide.

But it was in South India that holy suicide seems to have been most endemic:

> In Malabar and the neighbouring regions, many sacrifice themselves to the idols. When they are sick or involved in misfortune, they vow themselves to the idol in case they are delivered. Then, when they have recovered, they fatten themselves for one or two years; and when another festival comes around, they cover themselves with flowers, crown themselves with white garlands, and go singing and playing before the idol, when it is carried through the land. There, after they have shown off a good deal, they take a Sword with two handles, like those used in currying leather, put it to the back of their necks, and cutting strongly with both hands sever their heads from their bodies before the idol.

The atmaghataka, the suicidal Hindu, was a familiar sight of the pre-modern Indian landscape, where 'religious suicides were highly recommended and in most cases glorified.' Suicide often functioned as the culmination of a pilgrimage: 'the enormous Tirtha literature (literature on pilgrimage) curiously enough describes in detail suicide by intending persons at different places of pilgrimage and the varying importance and virtues attached to them.' Ibn Battuta and al-Biruni, among other Muslim visitors, had been particularly shocked by Hindu customs of sacred suicide, particularly bride-burning and self-drowning. Altogether, in such a culture the development of suicidal methods as part of war is hardly surprising; they are deeply rooted in local non-monotheistic values.

Today's Tamil extremists extend this tradition in significant ways. Each Tamil Tiger wears a cyanide capsule around his neck, to be swallowed in case of capture. The explosive belt, used to assassinate hated politicians as well as Sinhalese marines and ordinary civilians, predates its Arab borrowing: the first Tamil suicide-martyrs in modern times appear in the 1970s. The Tiger's Hindu roots thus nourish the current Palestinian practice; as one observer notes: 'the Black Tigers, as the suicide cadres are known, have been emulated by the likes of Hamas.' But there is also a strong Western precedent, in pagan antiquity, in early Judaism, and in Christianity.

Suicide had been a respectable option for many ancients. Achilles chooses battle against the Trojans, knowing that the gods have promised that this will lead to his death. Ajax takes his own life, in the confidence that this will not affect his honour. Chrysippus, Zeno, and Socrates all opt for suicide rather than execution or dishonour. Marcus Aurelius praises it to the skies. It was only the neo-Platonists and late Platonists (who not coincidentally became the most congenial Hellenes for Islam) who systematically opposed it.

The Biblical text nowhere condemns suicide. (Judas is condemned for betrayal, not for taking his own life; although Augustine will claim otherwise.) On the contrary, it offers several examples of individuals who chose death. Saul (the koranic Talut) falls on his own Sword rather than be humiliated in Philistine captivity (I Samuel 31). Jonah (Yunus) asks the frightened mariners to cast him into the sea (Jonah 1.12), and begs 'Take my life from me,' (4.3) for 'it is better for me to die than to live' (4.8-9). Job (Ayyub) prays: 'O that I might have my request, and that God would grant my desire; that it would please God to crush me' (Job 6:8-13), and even 'I loath my life' (7:15). Later, during the Maccabean revolts, the hero Razis falls on his Sword to avoid falling into the hands of the wicked (2 Maccabees 14:42, 45-6). A notion of vicarious atonement has developed, so that the militant's suicide which enrages the enemy brings a blessing to the people (4 Maccabees 17:21-2).

The early rabbis typically accept self-immolation in situations of military desperation, to avoid humiliation and to impress the enemy. The deaths of Saul and Samson were regarded as exemplary. And in 'the Jewish Middle Ages, enthusiasm for martyrdom (at least in Ashkenaz - northern Europe) became so great that it proved a positive danger to Jewish existence.'[46] Religious voices raised in support of 20th century Zionism could link this tradition to their own militancy.[47] Hence Avram Kook, the first Ashkenazy Chief Rabbi of mandate Palestine (in Walter Wurzburger's words) permitted individuals to volunteer for suicide missions when carried out in the interest of the collective Jewish community. In other words, an act that would be illicit if performed to help individuals would be legitimate if intended for the benefit of the community.

In the nascent Christian movement, Jesus came to be presented as a suicide, albeit one who knew that he would be resurrected. Some historians are convinced that Jesus, having armed his band with Swords (Luke 22:36), formed part of the larger Zealot movement against Roman oppression, while others adhere to the orthodox view that his deliberate death was to be a cosmic sacrifice for human sin; but in either case, the dominant voice in the New Testament presents him as going to Jerusalem in the awareness that this would bring about his certain death (see Mark 10:32-4). Hence the insistent courting of martyrdom by many early Christians praised by Tertullian (here in the words of a modern scholar):

> In 185 the proconsul of Asia, Arrius Antoninus, was approached by a group of Christians demanding to be executed. The proconsul obliged some of them and then sent the rest away, saying that if they wanted to kill themselves there was plenty of rope available or cliffs they could jump off.

And for Chrysostom, blasting the infidels, the Christians were better than the ancients, since Socrates had had little choice, while Christians volunteered for martyrdom. In fact, most orthodox Christian martyrs appear to have been volunteers, many of them appearing from nowhere to clamour for the death penalty, or emerging from the crowds to join the flames consuming one of their brethren. It was only with Augustine that this self-immolating behaviour came to an end, as involuntary martyrdom was established as the only acceptable Christian norm in the West.

Orthodoxy, however, remained closer to the primitive tradition. As Frazier records (of sixteenth to nineteenth-century Russia): 'whole communities hailed with enthusiasm the gospel of death and hastened to put its precepts into practice.' Although at first the volunteers were dropped into doorless rooms in which they starved to death 'for Christ', fire became the most popular method.

Priests, monks, and laymen scoured the villages and hamlets preaching salvation by the flames, some of them decked in the spoils of their victims; for the motives of the preachers were often of the basest sort. They did not spare even the children, but seduced them by promises of the gay clothes, the apples, the nuts, the honey they would enjoy in heaven. [...] Men, women and children rushed into the flames. Sometimes hundreds, and even thousands, thus perished together.

Combining the practice of suicidal martyrdom-seeking with the pursuit of warfare, resulted, for Europeans as well as for Tamils, in what would today be called suicidal warfare. This had the advantage of generating tremendous publicity for the cause in worlds such as the Indic and the Greco-Roman which, like today's, had a penchant for the bizarre.[And for this, the most spectacular precedent was in the Bible. Brian Wicker, a modern Catholic interpreter, remarks that 'to us, Samson just appears like a cross between Beowulf and Batman,' while Bernhard Anderson in his book The Living World of the Old Testament, neutralises the Samson story by viewing him as the object of divine punishment.[Yet he is presented by the narrator of Judges 13 to 16 as an unambiguous hero, and traditionally the churches regarded his self-destruction and his massacre of three thousand Philistine men, women, and children, as a valid act of martyrdom. Augustine and Aquinas both pose the question: why is self-murder not here a sin, and answer: because God had commanded him, and the normal ethical rule was thus suspended.

This suicide-warrior rises to the top of Western literature in Samson Agonistes. Milton is here smarting from the horror and shame of the Restoration. Once again, England is under the idolatrous law of king and bishops, a kind of jahiliyya, and Cromwell's city of glass has been shattered. His poem, then, is autobiographical: Samson is a true hero, humiliated, blinded by an unjust king, kept captive in the world of the dark other.

But perhaps the most recent, and also the most fascinating, mobilisation of the Samson 'ideal' in Western literature is the novel Samson by the Zionist ideologue Vladimir Jabotinsky. 'Homeland, whatever the price!' is the captured Israelite's slogan. Like the Islamist, the Zionist hero stresses the impossibility of conviviality:

> The second thing I have learned in the last few days is the wisdom of having boundary-stones [...] Neighbours can agree so long as each remains home, but trouble comes as soon as they begin to pay each other visits. The gods have made men different and commanded them to respect the ditch in the fields. It is a sin for men to mix what the Gods have separated.

Like a good Islamist, the Zionist Samson combines this xenophobia with a passion to acquire the Other's technology. When asked if he had a message for his own people, he cries:

> They must get iron. They must give everything they have for iron - their silver and wheat, oil and wine and flocks, even their wives and daughters. All for iron! There is nothing in the world more valuable than iron. Will you tell them that?

Like the Islamist, too, Jabotinsky's suicide-hero is envious of the unbeliever's skills at organisation:

> One day, he was present at a festival at the temple of Gaza. Outside in the square a multitude of young men and girls were gathered for the festive dances [...] a beardless priest led the dances. He stood on the topmost step of the temple, holding an ivory baton in his hand. When the music began the

vast concourse stood immobile [...] The beardless priest turned pale and seemed to submerge his eyes in those of the dancers, which were fixed responsively on his. He grew paler and paler; all the repressed fervor of the crowd seemed to concentrate within his breast till it threatened to choke him. Samson felt the blood stream to his heart; he himself would have choked if the suspense had lasted a few moments longer. Suddenly, with a rapid, almost inconspicuous movement, the priest raised his baton, and all the white figures in the square sank down on the left knee and threw the right arm towards heaven – a single movement, a single, abrupt, murmurous harmony. The tens of thousands of onlookers gave utterance to a moaning sigh. Samson staggered; there was blood on his lips, so tightly had he pressed them together [...] Samson left the place profoundly thoughtful. He could not have given words to his thought, but he had a feeling that here, in this spectacle of thousands obeying a single will, he had caught a glimpse of the great secret of politically minded peoples.

Lest this be thought an aberrant, marginal use of the suicide-hero, let us recall the words of another Zionist thinker, Stephen Rosenfeld: 'All our generation was brought up on that book.'

Samson provides an important Biblical archetype for the national hero who is a semi-outcast among his own people, but who saves them nonetheless. In the dying months of Nazi Germany, selbstopfereinsatz missions were flown by Luftwaffe pilots against Soviet bridgeheads on the Oder. In 1950, Cecil B. DeMille used Jabotinsky's novel as the basis for his film Samson and Delilah. And a still more recent example is the film Armageddon, in which a group of socially marginalised Americans sacrifice their lives by detonating their spacecraft inside a comet that is on a collision course with Earth. In doing so they are defying tradition and even lawful orders, but they earn thereby the eternal gratitude of their people. As Robert Jewett and John Lawrence have shown, this image of the American hero as the ordinary man impatient of traditional authority who risks or destroys himself to save the world (John Brown, Charles Bronson, Sylvester Stallone, Captain America,

Superman, Spiderman, and Captain Picard in the final episode of Star Trek), is the great monomyth of today's West. In some Eastern parts, the popularity of magically vanishing Bin Laden figures, who emerge from undistinguished lives to break conventional laws in order to save the world, offers another suggestion of how deeply Westernised Arab culture has become.

Let no-one claim, then, that suicide bombing is alien to the West. It is a recurrent possibility of Europe's heritage. What needs emphasizing, against the snapshot thinking of the journalists, is the absence of a parallel strand in Islamic thinking. For Islam, suicide is always forbidden; some regard it as worse than murder. Many Biblical stories are retold by Islam, but the idea of suicidal militancy is entirely absent from the scriptures. Saul's suicide is not present in the Koran, nor do we find it in Tabari's great Annals (which wish simply to record that he died in battle). The Koranic Jonah does not ask to be pitched overboard, and Job does not pray for death. Similarly, the suicidal istishhad of Samson is absent from the Koran and Hadith, no doubt in line with their insistence on the absolute wickedness of suicide. The same Islamic idealism that cannot accept David's seduction of Bathsheba, or Lot's incest, has here airbrushed out Samson's killing of the innocent and his self-destruction.

Again, the point is clear: the scriptural and antique sensibilities which provided some cultural space for suicidal warfare in Western civilisation appear to have very thin foundations in Islam. Flying into a skyscraper to save the world is closer to the line which links Samson to Captain America, with a detour through the Book of Revelation, than to any Muslim conception of futuwwa.

Here are Buruma and Margalit, in their important study of Westernised anti-Westernism:

Bin Laden's use of the word 'insane' is more akin to the Nazis' constant use of fanatisch. Human sacrifice is not an established Muslim tradition. Holy war always was justified in defence of the Islamic state, and believers who died in battle were promised heavenly delights, but glorification of death for its own sake was not part of this, especially in the Sunni tradition. [...] And the idea that freelance terrorists would enter paradise as martyrs by murdering unarmed civilians is a modern invention, one that would have horrified Muslims in the past. Islam is not a death cult.

Let us now move on to consider other hints of the Western roots of radical Islamism. One symptom may be detected in a shared fondness for conspiracy theories. The messianic importance of the hidden deliverer is emphasised by the machinations of the forces of darkness which are ranged against him. The mu'amara, or Plot, is everywhere, as Robert Fisk, that dauntless lamentor of Mid-East fantasies, regularly observes. A sadly typical example is given by Abdelwahab Meddeb:

Again, this is historically unusual for Muslims. Healthy communities far from Western influence find it incredible. The current prevalence of a kind of Islamic McCarthyism, often hysterical in its attempts to reduce a complex and enraging modernity to a monomaniac opposition, is simply another indication of how far the Islamists have travelled from the tradition. Religion makes us more attentive to reality, while secularity bereft of real disciplines of self-knowledge and self-disdain, permits a dream-self. 'They think that every shout is against themselves,' says the Koran of the hypocrites (63:4), while praising the believers for their clear-sighted faith that only God is simple, and it is only He that should be feared. The correct mindset is specified in scripture:

Those to whom the people said: 'The people have gathered against you, therefore fear them!' But it increased them in faith, and they said: 'Allah is enough for us, an excellent Guardian is he!'

So they returned with grace and favour from Allah, and no harm touched them. They followed the good-pleasure of Allah, and Allah is of great bounty.

It is only the devil who would make [men] fear his allies. Fear them not; fear me, if you are believers. (3:173-5)

The context is the aftermath of Uhud, when waverers warned of the strength of the combined enemies around Medina. Paranoia thus becomes the marker of imperfect faith and undue respect for the asbab. But despair is kufr: Islam's Samson could never say:

> Hopeless are all my evils, all remediless;
>
> This one prayer yet remains, might I be heard,
>
> No long petition, speedy death,
>
> The close of all my miseries, and the balm

Moreover, it requires an apparently unbearable humility for the Islamist conspiracy theorist to recognise that until very recently Muslims have seldom been perceived by the United States as a noteworthy enemy. For most of its history, America has opposed and feared and stereotyped Englishmen, Rebels, Red Indians, Spaniards, Huns, Reds or Gooks. The current preoccupation with Muslims is shallow in the US memory, if we discount the brief and long-forgotten enthusiasms of the Decatur episode.

Again, as with the conspiracy theories which urgently needed to see 9/11 as the work of Mossad, and the utilitarian justification of the vanguard's suspension of the ethical, the radical Islamists are an expression of the very Westernising alienation they profess to defy. In a sense, the West hates them because they are more modern than it, and thus remind it of the unbearable risks it has taken by following the road of Enlightenment. It is as Meddeb reminds us: 'Who are those who died while spreading death in New York, Washington and Pennsylvania? [...] They are the sons of our times, the pure products of the Americanisation of the world.'

Self-immolation in Gaza to bring down the unbelieving temple and this is tragedy in Wagnerian mode. It is suicide, selbstmord, not really prefatory to redemption, but to publicity and therapy. It was Nietzsche, not any Islamic sage, who wrote: 'the thought of suicide is a great source of comfort: with it a calm passage is to be made across many a bad night. After being 'eyeless in Gaza, at the mill with slaves,' Samson experiences 'calm of mind, all passion spent'[- the English idiom begins with Milton's ending, linking, as do some readings of the Samson legend, eros and thanatos, desire and death.

But it is Nietzsche who introduces the modern superhero. If 'the splendrous blond beast, avidly rampant for plunder and victory' cannot take the revenge which heals his heart, he will end his unworthy existence in a magnificent, Hitlerian funeral pyre. Samson thus becomes an anticipation of modernity.

Religion, if it has the right to exist at all, must consider this a spurious healing. Neither vainglory nor despair can have a place in the metabolism of a religion based on the idea of God's unique mastery of history, the polar opposite of dualistic paganism, or of the romantic Enlightenment dream which found its tragic moods congenial. The scriptures denounce hamiyya, the feverish identity-politics of the pagan Arabs; the post-orthodox Islamist admits it to his heart. 'Roots of Muslim Rage' is the title of Bernard Lewis' most notorious piece on Islamism. His pathology of the roots is far astray; but the rage is undeniable. How are we to understand such rage in the heart of a religion built on submission to the Divine will, hulwihi wa-murrihi, the bitter and the sweet of it? Which insisted that 'it is not the wrestler who is strong; it is the man who masters himself when angry'? Why did the Blessed Prophet pray for 'a certainty by which You render slight in our eyes the calamities of this world'?

The roots are, as it turns out, instrumental reason, natural causality, and the enthroning of Aristotle over Plato or Newton over St. Denys. Without the certainty of an omni-potent God (and is not Islam here better at restraining passion than all other faiths?) the experience of adversity leaves us prey to wild emotion. It was this same jahili craving for revenge that led Churchill astray, as one historian suggests: 'In this superheated and bloody time emotion may have masqueraded as political thinking in a rationalizing Prime Minister's mind.'

Religion is never more tested than when our emotions are ablaze. At such a time, the timeless grandeur of the Law and its ethics stand at our mercy. 'Let the qadi not judge when he is angry,' as it is said. But here is the reality of Gaza:

'Hamas operations are not directed and have never been directed against children,' says Hamas political leader Ismail Abu Shanaab. 'It is directed at military targets.' When pushed, however, he goes further. 'To be frank with you, there are a lot of the moralities which got broken in this war,' he says. 'They are letting the Israelis kill Palestinians and they want the Palestinians to be moderate, to be moral. We cannot control the game because it has no rules, it has no limits.'

Revenge, rage, the teleological suspension of the ethical. It is Churchillian, but also aromatic with a not-yet-dispersed Marxism. Here, for instance, is Mawdudi, a tributary of the Hamas vision:

'Muslim' is the name of the international revolutionary party which Islam organizes to implement its revolutionary program and Jihad is that revolutionary struggle which the Islamic party carries out to achieve its objectives.

As Abdullah Schleifer goes on to remark:

Mawdoodi took as his enduring model a progression of dynamic relationships - the movement, the party, revolutionary struggle, the revolution - defined by one of the major desacralizing forces in contemporary times, in pursuit of a concept of state that draws its substance from non-Islamic sources, and all with that same innocence of the modern Muslim importing his 'value-free' technology.

The antinomian quality of this furious insurrectionist method confirms Gray's suggestion that Islamism is simply another modern weapon against religion. For theists, the ethical can never be suspended; on the contrary, it is needed most when most under strain. Yet the militant transgressions of radicals form only part of a much wider picture of covert but deep surrender to Enlightenment thought.

Islamism, that soi-disant hammer of the Franks, is ironically modern in very many ways. It is modern in its eagerness for science and its hatred of 'superstition.' It is modern in its rejection of all higher spirituality (Qutb recommends, instead, 'al-fana' fi'l-'aqida'). It is modern in its rejection of the principle of tradition, and, despite itself, cannot but impose the insecurities of Western-trained minds (and are they not all engineers and doctors?) on scripture. Intertextuality and the community of sages are barred.

The theopolitics of classical Islam, where both scholarship and the state are invigorated by mutual tension (the Men of the Pen and the Men of the Sword), is replaced by the finally Western model of the ideological totalitarian state, with a self-appointed clerisy (albeit composed of technocrats) requiring absolute control over policy and the Shari'a. The modular diversities of pre-modern Muslim societies, where villages, tribes, and millat minorities regulated themselves, give way to the Islamist appropriation of the machinery of centralised post-colonial etatism. Social subsets which flourished for centuries under, say, Ottomanism, already eroded by centralising colonial regimes, are finally liquidated by a vision that is purely Western, albeit camouflaged by loud religious language. As Maryam Jameelah puts it, in a courageous article in which she publicly announces her disillusionment with the Islamist model:

> The tragic paradox of the life and thought of Maulana Sayyid Abul Ala Mawdoodi was his subconscious acceptance of the very same Western ideas he dedicated his entire life to struggling against.

In such a system, those who should be serving God end up obeying the men of the state who are His all too fallible interpreters. They worship in fear of the police, not in fear of God. Dissidence becomes a simultaneous treason and blasphemy. The failure of this totalitarian model of the 'Islamic State', this 'carceral Islamism' which makes a Muslim land a prison rather than a landscape of options and regional variety, is today everywhere apparent, and is a sign, perhaps, that God will not allow victory to such a perversion. For the Muslims will not long be allowed to bow before any other than God.

DIES IRAE

Is this attack on tradition modernity with a future? Zealotry itself is not normally refuted, it has to subside. Often that subsidence is enabled by schism: Cromwell could not be replicated because of the powerfully fissiparous quality of Dissent. Calvin's Geneva hardly outlived him. Hutterites, Levellers, Anabaptists, and the other fragments of the Protestant detonation could perpetuate themselves, but their energy source seemed to have a half-life. Islamic extremism, what has historically been called ghuluww, excess, and has occasionally, though not often, troubled the religion's equilibrium, usually knows a similar deflation through internal factionalism and the disappointment which seeps into all annunciatory movements when the world does not either improve or come to an end. In the case of Muslim puritanism, we see, currently, infighting, as in Algeria, and on the streets of Riyadh. Apathy may not be long postponed.

This seems likely, to the extent that Islamism is the product of indigenous decay, a second Reformation. But will its porosity to Enlightenment thought prolong or accelerate this decay? (How ironic that Islam's Reformation should come after its Enlightenment!) Here predictions about Islamism may not be so different from predictions about a certain kind of exhibitionist postmodernism. Take Foucault, for instance. On his death, he had been praised by Le Monde as 'the most important event of thought in our century.' He was an iconic Western iconoclast, but more honest about the consequences of modernity than most liberal seekers after virtue. He had been strongly pro-Khomeini, and had also praised the Baader-Meinhof terrorists. Like many Islamists, he was a lapsed Marxist, concerned with making a statement, with angering the middle-class West, with disruption. A second Bakunin, he was concerned not with advancing a detailed and realistic agenda, but with a passionate desire to shock. And like his hero Nietzsche, he died of a venereal disease, his immensely careless sexual habits indicating the powerful allure of suicide for the sake of making a statement. We need to ask: is this too close for comfort to radical Islamism, with its penchant for épater les blancs by whatever means? For how long can the West portray the Islamists as its own polar opposite? Will it be harder to forget the zealots than to forget Foucault?

This is less hopeful: Foucault has not been forgotten. The ambient vacuum which permitted a philosophy of the absurd in France and in the Middle East shows no signs of abatement. Capitalist shortsightedness wedded to postmodern philosophy may offer the only real life-support system that the Muslim reformation can hope for. Thus the defeat of the Muslim aberration may depend on nothing less than the defeat of the current global system, and its replacement with an order grounded in the ethical brilliance of the monotheisms. This diagnosis places us far beyond both Qutb's chauvinism and the narcissism of the neocons. The same classical Islamic strength through cosmopolitanism that helped our ancient order to endure as a non-totalitarian expression of certainty must be remobilised to affirm the Other's heart, in order to reconnect the global system with religious reality. That is, a successful 'war on terror' cannot be detached from a humanly consensual war on environ-mental loss, on unfair trade, on identity feminism, and on genetic manipulation. If it is so detached, it will be lost.

Blake portrays the spirit of the industrial age as Urizen, blind ignorance, fettered in laws of causality unveiled by Newton, and sunk in feral emotionalism. Religion is indispensable to the nurturing of a true humanism because it fights this, and insists that humanity has a telos, and that the soul is therefore sacrosanct.

To succeed, then we must be able to realise that self-judgement, that greatest and most irreplaceable gift of the Abrahamic religions, is more than an evolutionary confidence trick. Consider Jürgen Habermas' latest book, which reflects on human nature as challenged by genetic science. Postmodernism seems to problematise self-judgement; and its associated ethical practice seems to reduce Aristotle's greatness of soul, which he, against later monotheist reaction, considered a virtue, to superbia, greatest of the seven deadly sins. But

Habermas reminds us that confronted by genetic science, we are required, after a long hiatus, to judge ourselves. For science seeks our permission to rebuild our bodies to reduce the suffering of future generations; yet in the process it must ask us to define what we presently are. Liberal ethics, which resist both such definitions, and any exercise in using human beings for our own purposes, however idealistic, are thereby interrogated. Habermas is quite clear that the West's conception of virtue is a Christian ghost, rooted in a Kantianism that has been the basis of liberal notions of individual autonomy. Yet he seems convinced that this ghost still lives, and can be maintained perpetually, and may even serve as the stable basis of ever more ambitious projects for universal codes of human rights, in the arena of bioethics, as elsewhere. This will include, presumably, the war on Carrelian Islamism.

John Gray, iconoclastically again, is unsure that this is as coherent as it is helpful. Gray, whose understanding of Al-Qaida as an Enlightenment project we noted earlier would rather we, revisited Schopenhauer's deconstruction of Kant. Frightened ethicists have deceived themselves that there is no Christianity in this Christian ghost. Yet true Kantianism would reject the categoric imperative as a false projection upon the Noumenon. Our desperate desire to find a new moral anchorage after the sinking of Christian scholasticism blinds us to what is for Gray the unanswerable insight that without God, we are beyond good and evil. Schopenhauer saw, as Gray put it, 'that the enlightenment was only a secular version of Christianity's central mistake.' There is no soul, only the individual will, and we have no reason to suppose that we are any more free in our decision-making than the animals from which religion taught us that we were so categorically distinct. Our consciousness is just one more part of the world. Heidegger turns out to be worse: he insists that he excludes Christian paradigms, but internalises them implicitly in his consideration of the human plight, suffering, guilt, and the paradox of being. And while Schopenhauer maintained a pure and private pessimism, Heidegger sought to intuit Being in his tribe. 'The Führer himself and alone,' he exclaimed, 'is the present and future

German reality and its law.' Hitler's xenophobia allowed the philosopher to repair his wounds, and reconnect with being. Qutbian fundamentalism is not far away.

It is impossible to exaggerate the debt Giddens' 'runaway world' owes to Christianity, for showing so much vitality even after Nietzsche proclaimed the death of its God. But for the Gospels, the Western empire would not have benefited from Kant's conjuring trick or Rawls' benign adversion to 'good people'. Yet the fact of its precariousness remains; and the risk of a tribal resolution are enormous. Science harnessed to Geist dragged up Hitler; and something similar has beset Islam. Solidarity, mythologically voiced, technologically imposed, is to be the cure for our desperate alienation. Remember the words of the Furies in Aeschylus:

> For many ills one attitude is the cure
>
> When it agrees on what to hate

The danger, then, is that liberalism will prove too weak to prevent one form of Enlightenment chauvinism - carceral Islamism - from triggering a sudden revival of another such form - Hitlerian essentialism. The prosperity of the far-right across the liberal West shows how far this march has already come. Post-modernity is methodologically incapable of resisting this; and monotheism must step into the breach. A monotheism, however, which bears all the arms it has acquired and sharpened during its travels: its intellectual appropriation of Athens, its hospitality to the autochthonously non-Semitic, its insistence on diversity, all enabled and preserved by the centrality of spiritual purgation. The civil war within Enlightenment modernity that Gray identifies as the essence of the 'war on terror' is suicidal. Only a ressourcement in the anchored past can deliver us.

Bibliography

Abraham, A. J. *Islamic Fundamentalism and the Doctrine of Jihad*. Lima, OH: Wyndham Hall Press, 2002.

AbuKhalil, As'ad. *Bin Laden, Islam, and America's New 'War on Terrorism'*. Open Media Pamphlet Series. New York: Seven Stories Press, 2002.

Aho, James. *Politics of Righteousness: Idaho Christian Patriotism*. Seattle, WA: University of Washington Press, 1995.

Alexander, Yonah. *European Terrorism Today & Tomorrow*. Brassey's Terrorism Library. Washington, DC: Brassey's, 1992.

Alexander, Yonah. *Middle East Terrorism: Selected Group Profiles*. Washington, DC: Jewish Institute for National Security Affairs, 1994.

Al-Khattar, Aref M. *Religion and Terrorism: An Interfaith Perspective*. Westport, CT: Praeger, 2003.

Anderson, Chris. *The Billy Boy: The Life and Death of LVF Leader Billy Wright*. Edinburgh: Mainstream, 2002.

Anderson, Sean. *Terrorism: Assassins to Zealots*. Lanham, MD: Scarecrow Press, 2003.

Anti-Defamation League, *Extremism on the Right: A Handbook*. New York: Anti-Defamation League, 1988.

Appleby, R. Scott. *Ambivalence of the Sacred: Religion, Violence, and Reconciliation*. Lanham, MD: Rowman & Littlefield Publishers, 2000.

Bar, Shmuel. *Warrant for Terror: Fatwas of Radical Islam and the Duty of Jihad*. Hoover Studies in Politics, Economics, and Society. Lanham, MD: Rowman & Littlefield, 2006.

Bartholomeusz, Tessa J. *Buddhist Fundamentalism and Minority Identities in Sri Lanka*. New York: State University of New York Press, 1998.

Barton, Greg. *Indonesia's Struggle: Jemaah Islamiyah and the Soul of Islam*. Sydney, Australia: University of New South Wales Press, 2004.

Cateura, Linda Brandi. *Voices of American Muslims: 23 Profiles*. New York: Hippocrene Books, 2005.

Catholic Institute for International Relations, *Guatemala, Never Again*. Maryknoll, NY: Orbis Books, 1999.

Davies, Barry. *Terrorism: Inside a World Phenomenon*. London: Virgin Books, 2003.

Devji, Faisal. *Landscapes of the Jihad: Militancy, Morality, Modernity*. Ithaca, NY: Cornell University Press, 2005.

Emerson, Steven. *Worldwide Jihad Movement: Militant Islam's Target the West*. Jerusalem, Israel: Institute of the World Jewish Congress, 1995.

Esposito, John L. *Islam: The Straight Path*. 3rd edition. New York: Oxford University Press, 1998.

Esposito, John L. *The Islamic Threat: Myth or Reality?*. New York: Oxford University Press, 1992.

Esposito, John L. *The Oxford Dictionary of Islam*. New York: Oxford University Press, 2003.

Esposito, John L. *Unholy War: Terror in the Name of Islam*. New York: Oxford University Press, 2002.

Etzioni, Amitai. *How Patriotic is the Patriot Act? Freedom Versus Security in the Age of Terrorism*. New York: Routledge, 2004.

Fandy, Mamoun. *Saudi Arabia and the Politics of Dissent*. New York: Palgrave, 2001.

Farah, Douglas. *Blood From Stones: The Secret Financial Network of Terror*. New York: Broadway Books, 2004.

Gardell, Mattias. *Gods of the Blood: The Pagan Revival and White Separatism*. Durham, NC: Duke University Press, 2003.

Gerges, Fawaz A. *The Far Enemy: Why Jihad Went Global.* New York: Cambridge University Press, 2005.

Habeck, Mary R. *Knowing the Enemy: Jihadist Ideology and the War on Terror.* New Haven, NY: Yale University Press, 2006.

Hiro, Dilip. *War Without End: The Rise of Islamist Terrorism and Global Response.* New York: Routledge, 2002.

Howard, Russell D. *Defeating Terrorism: Shaping the New Security Environment.* Guilford, CT: McGraw-Hill, 2004.

Huband, Mark. *Warriors of the Prophet: the Struggle for Islam.* Boulder, CO: Westview Press, 1999.

Hudson, Rex A. *Who Becomes a Terrorist and Why: The 1999 Government Report on Profiling Terrorists.* Guilford, CT: Lyon Press, 2002.

Jaber, Hala. *Hezbollah: Born with a Vengeance.* New York: Columbia University Press, 1997.

Jacquard, Roland. *In the Name of Osama bin Laden: Global Terrorism & the bin Laden Brotherhood.* Durham, NC: Duke University Press, 2002.

Jaimoukha, Amjad M. *The Chechens: A Handbook.* New York: Routledge Curzon, 2005.

Karawan, Ibrahim. *Islamic Impasse.* New York: Oxford University Press, 1997.

MacArthur, John. *Terrorism, Jihad, and the Bible: A Response to the Terrorist Attacks.* Nashville, TN: W Publishing Group, 2001.

Miniter, Richard. *Losing Bin Laden: How Bill Clinton's Failures Unleashed Global Terror.* Washington, DC: Regnery, 2003.

Mishal, Shaul. *The Palestinian Hamas: Vision, Violence, and Coexistence.* New York: Columbia University Press, 2000.

Napoleoni, Loretta. *Modern Jihad: Tracing the Dollars Behind the Terror Networks.* Sterling, VA: Pluto Press, 2003.

Noorani, A. G. *Islam & Jihad: Prejudice versus Reality.* New York: Zed Books, 2002.

Nusse, Andrea. *Muslim Palestine: The Ideology of Hamas.* Amsterdam: Harwood Academic Publishers, 1998.

O'Ballance, Edgar. *Islamic Fundamentalist Terrorism, 1979-95: The Iranian Connection.* Washington Square, NY: New York University Press, 1997.

O'Ballance, Edgar. *Islamic Fundamentalist Terrorism: 1979-95.* Basingstoke: Macmillan, 1997.

Ojeda, Auriana. *Islamic Fundamentalism.* San Diego, CA: Greenhaven Press, 2003.

O'Kane, Rosemary. *Revolutionary Reign of Terror: the Role of Violence in Political Change.* Brookfield, VT: Elgar, 1991.

Rana, Muhammad Amir. *A to Z of Jehadi Organizations in Pakistan.* Lahore: Mashal Books, 2004.

Randal, Jonathan C. *Osama: The Making of a Terrorist.* New York: Knopf, 2004.

Rapoport, David C. *The Rationalization of Terrorism.* Frederick, MD: University Publications of America, 1982.

Scheuer, Michael. *Through Our Enemies Eyes: Osama bin Laden, Radical Islam, and the Future of America.* Rev. ed., 2nd ed.. Washington, DC: Potomac Books, 2006.

Taheri, Amir. *Holy Terror: Inside the World of Islamic Terrorism.* Bethesda, MD: Adler & Adler, 1987.

Venske, Ben. *The al-Qaeda Threat: An Analytical Guide to al-Qaeda's Tactics & Targets.* Alexandria, VA: Tempest Publishing, 2003.

Waardenburg, Jacques. *Muslims and Others: Relations in Context.* New York: Walter de Gruyter, 2003.

Wiktorowicz, Quintan. *Global Jihad: Understanding September 11.* Falls Church, VA: 2002.

Zacharias, Ravi K. *Light in the Shadow of Jihad.* Sisters, OR: Multnomah Publishers, 2002.

Index

J

K

L

M

N

P

R

S